PSYCHOLOGY AND THE NEAR-DEATH EXPERIENCE

PSYCHOLOGY AND THE NEAR-DEATH EXPERIENCE

SEARCHING FOR GOD

by

ROY L. HILL, Psy.D

www.whitecrowbooks.com

Psychology and the Near-Death Experience

Searching for God

Published and printed in the United States of America and the United Kingdom
by White Crow Books; an imprint of White Crow Productions Ltd.

For information, contact White Crow Books
at 3 Hova Villas, Hove, BN3 3DH United Kingdom,
or e-mail to info@whitecrowbooks.com.

Cover Designed by Butterflyeffect
Interior design by Velin@Perseus-Design.com

Paperback ISBN 978-1-910121-42-9
eBook   ISBN 978-1-910121-43-6

Non Fiction / Body, Mind & Spirit / Death & Dying

www.whitecrowbooks.com

For Kyle

COVER DESCRIPTION

The cover picture captures the essence of a spiritual dream I experienced. Each person follows a path mission, depicted by the red carpet leading toward the portal door back home. None travel life alone, even when the journey feels lonely. Rather, spiritual beings, such as deceased relatives, applaud and guide us up and down the corridor of life. Finally stepping beyond the portal door, we rejoin the golden Light, moving eternally in love.

ACKNOWLEDGEMENTS

I consider writing *Psychology and the Near-Death Experience* a blessing from the Architect of creation. Indeed, I view God as the ultimate Source for this book. Truly, I initiated much but created little. I very much appreciate the courageous people who submitted their experiences on the NDERF and ADCRF websites. You are ambassadors of hope. I also appreciate the people willing to be interviewed. These courageous people include Teresa, Candy, Ray, Marie, Robert K., David, Mary, and "Big" Joe. I also thank Beth Rubel for painting the message displayed on the book cover.

Writing was a monumental task made easier by guidance from wise mentors. Important contributors included Herbert, Michelle, Jody Long, Helen and others. I would like to thank Rachel Hill, Loli-Gon-zales-Hill, Jody Long, and Carol Hill for helping cull the manuscript. I specifically thank Jody Long for her encouragement throughout the book writing process; she was a pillar of support from the beginning to the end. I appreciate Jon Beecher for this mission opportunity. I would also like to specifically thank my wife, Loli, for patiently supporting the long process.

CONTENTS

FOREWORD

BY JODY LONG

One of the more remarkable synchronicities when dealing with people and a spiritual website (www.nderf.org) is the people who are seeking to reconnect with and learn about themselves and God. Roy initially came to me with questions of a seeker. After several e-mails of questions and answers, he started to develop some intriguing concepts. These ideas were so good that he wanted to share them with others. He asked me if I wanted to collaborate on a book. At first, this sounded good, but early on, I changed my mind. One thing I learned very early was that Roy has some strong guidance from the other side. It felt like to me that this was Roy's spiritual journey and that he needed to do this one himself. So, I stepped back and took on more of a guidance role rather than an active participant in writing.

Basing a book on psychology is solid evidence. But is basing part of the book on the near-death experience evidential? Both prongs of evidence need to be solid in order for the conclusions to hold validity. Some of the best evidence for the veracity of NDE can be found in *Evidence of the Afterlife, the Science of Near-Death Experience* by Jeffrey Long with Paul Perry. Roy has also discussed the evidentiality of NDEs, so I won't go much into this here. However, there are a few points that I will stress.

Generally, in order for an explanation to be plausible, the evidence needs to address all of the components of observation. Skeptic arguments do not address all that is observed in the NDEs, ergo they are not evidence that the NDE is based in the body.

NDE seems to be the brass ring because it has become an ideological battleground over, does consciousness exist outside of the body, or are the fantastic tales of NDErs only hallucinations or gyrations of a dying brain? Many scientists have found that if they mention that their research shows that NDE is based in the brain, then they will be published no matter how tenuous the connection might be. But there are so many "flash in the pan explanations," that I call them the "theory de jour" of NDE skeptic arguments. The fact is that none of these explanations like dying brain, rem intrusion, angular gyros, brain chemistry, hallucinations, or delusions explains the NDE. In fact, Pim van Lommel's research published in the prestigious medical journal, the Lancet, in 2001 found that NDE was medically inexplicable. To date, that conclusion still holds true.

It is unfortunate that the NDE phenomena has been placed in the category of "paranormal," tending to make it less evidential than what we can see and experience through our five physical senses here on earth. In actuality, the NDE is a highly natural and normal phenomenon that some humans experience when they die and are resuscitated. Depending on whose figures you use, 5-15% of people who die and come back to life will have an experience. It does not depend on body chemistry, drugs, or emotions. There is no way to predict who will have an NDE or who will not have an NDE.

While scientists may ping-pong about the evidentiality of NDE, in a book based on psychology, it moves the focus of the book on to the spirit and the mind. The Thomas theorem is a theory of sociology that states, "If men define situations as real, they are real in their consequences." Most people who have an NDE or who read about the NDE consider them real. Moreover, the love, compassion, hope, and other messages contained in the NDE are real in their consequences. Many people are completely transformed when they meet God or Jesus. Instead of being a two-dimensional being talked about in Church, the NDE makes God, Jesus, and love more real than we would ever experience on earth. When NDErs come back to earth, their values and choices on earth are based on their experience. Many NDErs change their diet, friends, spouses, and jobs. Choices made will more often be those that show loving concern for self and others, less focus on material goods, and a desire to compassionately help others.

Back to the initial question, is it scientific to base conclusions on the NDE? Given what I know about NDE, I would say unequivocally "Yes!" Where the mix gets really interesting is the fact that the NDE is spiritual. For instance, if the NDE is real and the NDEr meets God, Jesus, angels, and deceased relatives, then it necessarily follows that we are immortal beings. This, in conjunction with what we learn from the after death communication website (www.adcrf.org), allows us to understand that no matter what state of consciousness we are in, we can interact with each other – in this plane or the next. If we communicate with those on the other side, through prayer or other means, we get answers and guidance here on earth. Roy's progression of discovery in writing this book is only partly about reconciling science with spirituality. The other part is learning to trust his spiritual guidance.

Roy's unique background as a correctional psychologist helps him bring a necessary expertise that has been largely missing in books on near-death experience such as the mental, emotional, and transformative aspect that an NDE has on people. Among topics of interest are themes of redemption, purpose, forgiveness, love, hope, healing and transformation. He is a man grounded in science with expertise in the psyche. Yet, he is also a very spiritual man with sound roots in Christianity. This book is his spiritual journey to reconcile the two disparate viewpoints into a cohesive, loving, and compassionate work. And as he is able to bring love, peace, and compassion between the two parts within himself, so does it help bring these qualities into the world.

PROLOGUE

A PERSONAL REVELATION

The book you are about to read has foundation in personal revelation. There is a great distinction, I have discovered, between learning facts from a book and learning by experience. This lesson piqued during my clinical training in graduate school. I quickly determined that learning about therapy in a textbook was different than actually *doing* psychotherapy. Whereas psychology textbooks cover technical procedures, the act of psychotherapy involves the interplay of emotions, personality forces, and personal histories. In my clinical experience, all these relationship dynamics become charged during every session. What was more real to me, reading instructions about how to do therapy or undertaking the process of therapy? The answer is the latter. While undergraduate "book knowledge" provided me with a conceptual understanding to practice my profession, the actual experience of doing therapy was defined by the experience of authentic being. In this manner, therapy became transformed from an abstract, mysterious endeavor, into a tangible, knowable experience.

A whopping 95% of people who report a near-death experience claim that their experience was "definitely real," whereas most of the remaining 5% answered "probably real".[1] In fact, most responders deemed the near-death experience to be more real than their earthly existence. The person who experiences a near-death experience (NDEr) does not need scientific proof to know that life after death is real. The vast majority know, beyond a shadow of a doubt, that their experience was not a hallucination because their entire being witnessed, first hand, a new reality. Like my experience undertaking therapy, the NDE personally transformed the spiritual realm from an abstract, mysterious consideration into a tangible, knowable reality.

I view NDE reports to be wondrous beyond human imagination. Although I have not personally experienced an NDE, I have had a profound encounter with the spiritual realm that has made a great impact on my life. In fact, I would say that my experience created a completely new spiritual orientation in my life, perhaps even a revolution of meaning. I will share my story here:

I have worked as a clinical psychologist for nineteen years in several prisons. One of my duties has been to monitor and manage mentally ill inmates. There was an inmate on my caseload who suffered from periodic depression accompanied by hallucinations. The auditory hallucinations, in this case, were generally experienced as unwanted "voices" telling the inmate to kill himself. The voices became more pronounced when the inmate's depression became worse, generally resulting in the initiation of suicide watch and medications. One day, about twelve years ago, I learned that this inmate's sister had died as a result of an automobile accident. Knowing this inmate's propensity for a significant and rapid decline, I evaluated him immediately. Sure enough, the inmate endorsed symptoms of severe depression, suicidal ideation, and voices telling him to kill himself. I immediately placed the inmate on suicide watch. One day passed without change. On the second day, the inmate stated that his depression and suicidal ideation had disappeared. He stated that he was ready to be taken off suicide watch.

There are two clinical questions to ask when someone rapidly improves: "Why now?" and "What has changed?" Rapid recovery sometimes lacks credibility, leading to questions about ulterior motive. Yet, the inmate's answer surprised me. He stated that his deceased sister was freely talking to him. Specifically, the sister informed the brother that she now existed in a better place and that he should not be grieving for her on suicide watch. She told him that his life had purpose. She also told the inmate that she was allowed to help him out of love. I hesitated and thought about the delicate situation I faced. I was the master of this man's immediate future. If I made an error on the side of caution,

I would unnecessarily be taking away his freedom. If I made an error on the side of haste, then the inmate might attempt suicide. Normally, I make clinical decisions on the side of caution. However, I also knew that auditory hallucinations, especially from those victims who are depressed, are generally cryptic and negative. I had yet to meet any psychotic person who experienced comforting or helpful voices. Yet, here was a man hearing the comforting voice of his recently deceased sister. There was a part of me, too, that entertained the possibility that God might be working through a deceased sister to minister. I made the call to take the inmate off suicide watch on the condition that he would be monitored and that I would see him early the next morning.

The inmate arrived to his appointment as scheduled. I assessed immediate suicide risk factors. There didn't seem to be any immediate concerns based on his self-report. The inmate's presentation, or mental status, also seemed clear. I asked the inmate if his deceased sister was still talking to him. He answered, "Yes."

Then I asked, "What is she telling you?"

He answered, "She is telling me that you do not believe me. And so that you shall believe, she has a message for you." At that point, the small hairs on my arm stood straight up.

With some trepidation, I gingerly asked, "What is her message?"

He answered, "Quarter."

I felt completely lost by the inmate's answer. "What do you mean, quarter?" I asked. "Do you mean quarter of something, like a measurement, or quarter as in the coin?"

The inmate looked at me, shrugged, and said, "I don't know. I'll ask her." So, he sat quietly in his chair and glanced askew for about fifteen seconds. Was I supposed to believe that he was really communicating with the dead? Our discussion may have looked comical to an outsider. It would have looked that way to me, if not for the seriousness I felt toward the situation at hand. The inmate looked at me and said, "She says, quarter as in the coin."

"What does that mean?" I returned.

He answered, "I don't know. She won't tell me."

The inmate left shortly thereafter and returned to his housing unit. About fifteen minutes later, another inmate came to see me on a scheduled appointment. This inmate was a Muslim. On this day he endeavored to teach me, with poorly masked delight, about the hypocrisy of the United States government. During this tedious conversation, he drove his point home with this challenge, "Do you know what is written on a quarter?!"

I immediately answered without thinking, "In God We Trust."

The inmate pointed a finger at me and said with authority, "That's right!"

I immediately felt blood rush down from my head. I don't think I half listened to anything else during the session. I immediately knew the ramifications of the question. The temporal occurrence of the "quarter" revelation could not be a coincidence - no one had asked me that question before. These two inmates did not "run" together. It was unlikely they were colluding to play a joke on the psychologist (not something the inmates typically do anyway). Besides, the question was too outlandishly obscure for them to think up on their own. I rescheduled the inmate to be seen for the next morning.

The inmate came to his scheduled appointment. I asked him if his sister revealed any other information. He said, "Yes. She said that your wife is pregnant, you will have a son, and he will be born on Christmas day." Indeed, my wife was pregnant. Other staff knew about the pregnancy, so did the inmate overhear inappropriate staff conversations? This scenario was possible, but highly unlikely. Moreover, he also had a 50-50 percent chance of correctly guessing the sex of my child. Thus, the truth of his prophesy would rest on my son being born on Christmas day.

Christmas day came and went without a birth; my son was born on January 7th. For the next eleven years I was troubled about the inconsistency between the amazing "quarter" story and inaccurate prophesy. I came to believe that the dead sister talked to her brother; the quarter message seemed beyond coincidence. The more I thought about why the dead sister had challenged my faith, the more I questioned my questioning. It was not enough that I had enough faith to take the inmate off suicide watch. My belief was partial and subject to verification. Through her challenge directed by God, I learned that partial faith wasn't really faith at all. Now I was looking at this set of experiences, eleven years later, with partial faith. Maybe I was meant to learn faith by acting in complete faith.

But what did God want me to do? My son was clearly not born on Christmas day. What was I to do with that clear and undeniable fact? I was inspired by a possible answer dwelling deep inside myself. I decided to have enough faith to Google Christmas and January 7th. Amazingly, a number of "hits" came up on the search engine. It turns out that much of Christendom today uses the old Roman Julian calendar. That wasn't always so. There was a time when Christendom used the Gregorian calendar, otherwise known as the Christian calendar. In fact, over a half billion Orthodox members still celebrate Christmas on January 7th to this very day.

Reflecting on this unusual experience twelve years later, what does it mean? I believe that the sister's prophesy was meant to test my faith. Although it took years to pass, my faith metamorphosed from a quasi-state of hope to knowing that God exists. There is a great liberation knowing that my essence has eternal purpose within a divine master plan. For me, subconscious fear was replaced with a stronger state of peace stemming from a greater awareness of soul. I have even used this state of peace as a compass to reinforce my plodding, but purpose-driven, journey towards growth. The emotional states of anxiety, fear, and hatred have less relevance now. In sum, my heart began to know and my mind started to feel.

I recently attended a funeral for a friend who died of brain cancer. I felt saddened for a few seconds after learning about his death. However, divine knowledge quickly reminded me that my friend had been liberated into a greater existence. Although I frequently miss my friend, I have not felt the weight of grief since I first learned of his death. In fact, I had never felt such an overwhelming peace come over me than during his funeral.

Many people who have experienced a near-death experience report similar life reactions, as will be explored throughout the book.

The renowned expert in death and dying, Dr. Elisobeth Kübler-Ross, writes, "Not one of my patients who has had an out-of body experience was ever again afraid to die. Not one of them, in all our cases."[2] Living with a new revolution of meaning, I also have little fear of death because death does not exist.

A common question that people who have near-death experiences ask is, "What changes am I supposed to make in my life?" I initially asked the same question after my after-death communication experience. Yet the traditional answers I found were frustratingly indefinable until I began to read near-death experience accounts. My interest has since been insatiable. So far I have learned much by reading over three thousand NDE accounts through the Near-Death Experience Research Foundation (NDERF) and a good number of books on the subject. I now recognize that I was meant to share these conclusions with others. So, I will provide the reader with a spoiler alert. I have learned that the crux of existence consists of the following: YOU have an important connection to the divine; YOU will never die; YOU have nothing to fear; YOU are greatly loved; YOU have an important mission to fulfill in your life; YOU should spend your limited life on earth learning to love others. It's all quite simple, really – and many other NDE writers repeat that message. But how profound the message! If everyone fully accepted this revolution of meaning, and lived their lives accordingly, then the world would greatly change for the better.

The near-death experience has recently gained popularity in the last few decades. A number of writers have broached the subject, including some people from scientific backgrounds. This current book is unique in that it approaches the topic from a new slant. Specifically, I discuss the topic from the viewpoint of a psychologist. Because I write from a psychological perspective, the reader may be confused regarding my purpose in writing this book. In order to avoid any misinterpretation, I want my intentions to be clear from the very start. This book is a spiritual work. It is not a psychology textbook on the near-death experience. The field of psychology typically grounds itself in the scientific method. If this were purely a psychology text, the content would be limited to phenomena that are definable and measurable. Given the spiritual nature of the topic, I deviate radically from the materialist objective. Nevertheless, I include many psychological constructs to clarify psychological phenomena associated with the near-death experience. Consequently, most of my references include psychological research or theoretical books written by established psychologists.

I also sprinkle a number of scientific and philosophical references in similar fashion. The materialist reader may find this hybrid approach objectionable. This book may be more fitting for people open to both science and new spiritual possibilities.

Spiritual change propelled me to write this book. Although I try to write objectively, I cannot hide that my own spiritual journey impacts my writing. Likewise, this book records the spiritual journey of many other people, especially those who have had a near-death experience. The collective spiritual journey will take the reader many places: scientific evidence for the near-death experience; psychological attributes of soul; divine mission for the human being; the psychological aspects of unconditional love; the role of spiritual beings; a new understanding of diversity; the impact of time on earth and in the spiritual realm. Several case chapters have also been included to illuminate and personalize these core ideas. We will begin the journey by stepping down a philosophical path, namely how: the near-death experience represents a revolution in meaning for all humanity.

CHAPTER ONE

THE REVOLUTION OF MEANING

It is human nature to seek meaning. People have always sought purpose in existence, even when that purpose seems elusive. They ask, "Is there purpose in my life, or is it all for nothing?" Or, they may inquire to the heavens, "Do I have some eternal purpose?" As knowledge accumulates, and as new ideas replace old, people create novel solutions to answer these fundamental questions. The answer depends on who you ask. Moreover, the answers have varied over the course of history depending on the culture and its place in history. In this manner, one can catalogue the evolution of myths, religions, and philosophies. Evolution of spirituality does not mean that religious belief systems are invalid. By the end of the book, the reader will understand that I argue quite the opposite. But would it not be helpful to have a universal belief system that everyone can agree on? That would be a true revolution of meaning. It would give people an anchor to live their lives with purpose. The purpose behind this book is to talk about a new revolution of meaning through the near-death experience. It differs from relative systems of faith. Foremost, the near-death experience is rooted in universal experience rather than human systems of belief. To understand why this is important, it may be helpful to take a short journey discussing the evolution of varied belief systems. First, this chapter will examine the spiritual development of myth and religion. Next, we will look at the "deep" perspective of existential philosophy. Lastly, the chapter will look at the revolutionary nature of the near-death experience.

The Progression of Myth and Religion

Humanity has a long and complex spiritual history. As mentioned, people create different solutions to fundamental spiritual questions as culture and knowledge advance forward in time. These different solutions really represent different meaning systems, or widely accepted world views about life and death. In pre-history, religious shamans provided meaning through special knowledge and the exercise of ritual. For instance, the hunter and gatherer living 50,000 years ago may have believed that animals and humans exchanged souls.[1] With the development of agriculture 9,000 years ago, special knowledge developed into more complex stories. The myth was created. Colorful characters were invented, like Thor and Zeus, giving ancients a very human way to conceptualize powers they did not understand. Many of these mythological stories displayed a pantheon of gods wielding great power over human survival and death. Sacrifices were made to appease the gods when life and death were at a razor's edge. It was believed that a soothed god would help ensure rain, bountiful crops, birthing, and safety from enemies. In this manner, ancient man invented a system of secret knowledge and ritual to control the chaotic forces of nature, and to some extent, death itself.

Religion has since developed far beyond mere sacrifice and magical ritual. Most religions today advocate the worship of a single, all-powerful God. They also teach moral behavior as defined through religious code. Brilliant theologians, of differing faiths, have advanced humanity's understanding of ultimate meaning over the centuries through personal reflection and inspiration. In other words, humankind's search for meaning has become increasingly complex, devotion-centered, and intimate with the divine.

Religion has provided ultimate purpose for humankind for thousands of years. Although consistently revered over time, religion has not monopolized the tough answers about human existence. Since the period of ancient Greeks, great secular philosophers have also tackled the "big" questions about existence. The secular approach has gained popularity over the last several hundred years, especially those who advocate existential philosophy. Existential philosophy challenges widely accepted religious and cultural beliefs by rejecting the widespread belief that humanity has any ultimate purpose. More specifically, it does not support the premise that humanity has any special, eternal role in the universe. We are here simply because we are. Irvin Yalom and Earnest Becker stand out as academic experts in this area of study. Let's examine how they describe the existential position.

The Finite, Purposeless Existence

Existentialists tackle many of life's "bottom-line" questions about existence in a predictably pessimistic manner. They would assert that human lives lack purpose in a meaningless universe. Not only does life lack purpose, but everyone is truly alone. Facing the prospect of meaninglessness and isolation can be frightening. Rollo May, in his description of existentialism, writes, "Existentialism is not a comprehensive philosophy or way of life, but an endeavor to grasp reality."[2] To an existentialist, searching for the truth requires staring into the cold, hard, blackness of reality, or "the abyss." Only the courageous stare at the truth, but in doing so, may find the freedom to live boldly before their fictional dreams are taken away by time.

If what existentialists propose is true, then the terrifying human condition may create dire consequences: anxiety, loneliness, depression, and other serious psychological problems. To maintain a functional rudder in life, the human psyche must defend itself. Irvin Yalom writes, "We can mount a self-protective campaign – that is, we can either avoid the thing we fear, seek allies against it, develop magical rituals to placate it, or plan a systematic campaign to detoxify it."[3]

Ernest Becker, an existential social psychologist, speaks further to man's efforts to either "avoid" or "detoxify" the truth. Becker believes that cultural activities, rituals, and nationalism help ward off fear and anxiety. Becker writes, "When we survey the lush variety of ways of life over the planet, we can truly marvel at man's natural genius for giving himself the kind of world he needs."[4] Sport may be a telling example of how humanity gifts itself with the world it needs. For some die-hard fans, sports players bring more than just entertainment. They become larger than life fictional heroes, allowing the fan to attach fictional meaning to an organized physical activity through personal affiliation. In this manner, the exclamation "my team won!" has special meaning beyond some stranger making an extra basket or running into the end zone.

Why would a nation grieve the death of seven space shuttle astronauts when thousands die of hunger every day without notice? Earnest Becker would respond that deceased astronauts provide fictional meaning by serving the country as national heroes. Their untimely demise threatens the national "self-protective campaign" to hide meaninglessness. By the act of public grieving, an adoring population endows meaning to an otherwise meaningless tragedy. For the existentialist, it is all smoke and mirrors. It is all made up.

With death, everyone is faced with a very ugly proposition. Specifically, humankind is just another animal; each person will ultimately be crushed into nothingness by time and the laws of nature. Becker challenges:

> Try repeating 'man is an animal' a few times, just to notice how unconvincing it sounds. There seems to be no way to get this idea into our heads, except by long rumination over the facts of evolution or perhaps by exposure to a primitive tribe or being raised on a farm.[4]

From the existential position, humans are just a product of the natural world. Facing that reality lowers us to the level of a groundhog or fish. Through death, everything becomes equally meaningless.

Human cultural systems are only as good as their creators. Because human beings are imperfect, cultural meaning systems are bound to fail. Football teams lose and space shuttles blow up. Becker highlights this point by saying, "Man's freedom is a fabricated freedom, and he pays for it. He must at all times defend the utter fragility of his delicately constituted fiction, deny its artificiality."[4] For the psychologically sophisticated, the power of denial has its limits. Fiction cannot independently stand against the relentless, ruthless truth. Cultural meaning systems are threatened when the weak become marginalized by the powerful. People sometimes fail in their jobs. Relationships dissolve. Some people walk the streets hungry. Eventually we all become sick and we die. For whatever the reason, humanity's search for relevance often turns hollow and fictional meaning systems fail us. Fortunately, mankind has developed a crucial savior. That savior is religion.

Religion: The Savior of Man?

From the existentialist point of view, religion teaches that the faithful are very special. Not only are they very special, but the faithful will live forever at the right side of God. In a symbolic sense, people will live forever as cosmic heroes. Thanks to God's grace, it does not matter whether human nature, brutish and selfish, deserves cosmic recognition or everlasting life. Grace is an unwarranted gift. Becker writes:

> You take your special secret separateness and you make it ultimately meaningful by linking it to the mysterious service of creation, you draw a full circle on yourself, heal the rupture of your loneliness and isolation. By serving the highest power you serve the best power, not any second-rate one, by linking your destiny to that of creation you give it its proper fulfillment, its proper dignity.[4]

According to Becker, it is difficult to refute religion because the supernatural exists within the realm of the unseen. Evidence to the contrary is beside the point. Religion serves such a powerful purpose, a lifeline of hope, that the majority of people will never abandon the possibility of a secure, meaningful future in favor of facing their own insignificant non-existence. With religious faith, anxiety about death is placed deep in the mind under lock and key. Anyone who tries to dislodge religious belief and threatens to turn the key, becomes a very dangerous threat. Wars and jihads are waged against such threats.

Any attack against dogma can be met by a vigorous defense by the group. Inconsistent evidence or alternative beliefs can be explained, rationalized, or denied. The trick is to select the right religion and, in turn, exclude heretical beliefs from competing religions. Spiritual seekers need to pick from at least five competing "major" religions (Christianity, Islam, Judaism, Hinduism, Buddhism) and a large number of "smaller" religions, all insulated by their own, exclusive ideologies. Once selected, the religious seeker must select the right sect, or denomination, in order to perform the proper rituals and correctly interpret the religion's respective holy books. The religious selection process would be overwhelming if not for the societal and family culture indoctrinating children at an early age, thereby saving us from making such difficult choices.

Religions are not universally accepted. Despite their power over despair, organized religion may fall short and cast doubt with some of the faithful. Becker writes, "Religion, like any human aspiration, can also be automatic, reflexive, obsessive."[4] For this reason, some people become disenchanted with religion but still desire purpose in their lives. When society and religion both fall short, where do people turn? Unfortunately, the existentialists do not offer any pleasant alternatives.

Existentialists propose that we wrestle with isolation, meaningless, and death, even if it results in despair. This is not a solution really, as everything is still meaningless. Yet, existentialists would argue that the truth, no matter how pessimistic, is better than an invented cultural or religious system. Yalom references the existential philosopher Nagel, "If nothing matters, it should not matter that nothing matters. This should permit us to return to our absurd life laced with irony instead of with despair."[3] Is living an absurd life laced with irony the best we can hope for?

The Near-Death Experience

Not everyone is completely satisfied with either choice between unquestioning belief and existential despair. But what if there is a third choice that revolutionizes meaning? What if there is a way to receive spiritual knowledge that is observed first-hand by tens of thousands of people, documented with high reliability of subject matter, and shared by observers who are not seeking fame, political influence, or financial gain? The third way is the near-death experience. The near-death experience is a means to obtain knowledge directly without religious ritual, prophets, coercion, politics, or strict moral judgments. It further refutes the existentialist position; philosophy has little influence over first-hand knowledge.

At this juncture, it may be useful to provide a brief description of the near-death experience for the reader unfamiliar with the subject matter. In a broad sense, the term "near-death experience," or NDE, is self-explanatory. The NDE includes any experience reported by people who briefly died and were revived, usually by advanced life-saving medical technology. Although every NDE experience is unique, there are common elements that occur regardless of culture, age, or race. For instance, most people who have near-death experiences report a different type of universe composed of energy and interconnected consciousness. It is a realm where spiritual beings collectively work in accordance with relative time. Most importantly, the spiritual realm is filled with God consciousness and love. If this brief description whets the reader's appetite for more, be patient. Many more details about the spiritual realm will be shared throughout this book.

The skeptic may challenge that the near-death experience is just a new religion. It is vitally important to point out that the near-death experience is not a religion, nor is it meant to replace religion. Religions have always offered believers loving community support, avenues for spiritual expression, and comfort against the brutal human condition. Specifically, believers benefit from mutual support, music, prayer, meditation, fasting, community outreach, and so forth. Moreover, religions provide useful, profound, spiritual viewpoints that brilliant religious thinkers have expounded throughout the millennia. If the religious believer can be flexible in religious belief, and recognize that everyone's spiritual journey is unique, then the near-death experience can enhance one's unique spiritual journey within his or her religious framework of choice. It is not the aim of this book to challenge the readers' cherished religious beliefs. Rather, it is the aim of this book to stretch the readers' understanding of the divine, for the spiritual seeker to think about the large questions about existence in a new way.

The near-death experience may revolutionize spiritual thought, in part, because it is not bounded by corporation, political affiliation, nationalism, or culture. Consequently, the near-death experience may allow the believer to discriminate between spiritual integrity and religious corruption. By corruption, I refer to the dark coercive side of religion engineered by human power and greed, as most clearly evidenced by personal indiscretions, historical inquisitions, and war. The near-death experience may also allow the frustrated agnostic, railing against religious corruption, to believe in God and the hereafter. The near-death experience may also allow the scientific agnostic the means to believe in God without compromising reliance on the scientific method. For example, a debate over the age of the earth is unnecessary. Finally, the near-death experience may provide the existential atheist an alternative to despair.

I can imagine that many scientifically-minded readers are groaning with discomfort. The scientist might concede superficial differences between mainstream religion and the near-death experience. Yet, for them, the central problem remains. In a purely material universe, all spiritual beliefs are superstitious. To the science materialist, the near-death experience represents just another repackaged religion, although with a new bent. The central problem is not spiritual superstition, as I see it, but the limited conceptual understanding of the human brain. There appears to be a scientific hubris surrounding the human aptitude for discovery. Not everything in the universe is observable or measurable by present day science. In response, the materialist-centered scientist may challenge, "Are we just to take the near-death experience on faith?" The answer is "no". The near-death experience differs from religion in at least one important aspect. Indirect empirical evidence has been gathered in support of the near-death experience. In the next chapter, we will explore empirical evidence supporting the validity of the near-death experience.

CHAPTER TWO

EMPIRICAL SUPPORT FOR THE NEAR-DEATH EXPERIENCE

Many scientists view the near-death experience as just another superstitious idea packaged under a pseudo-scientific name. Popular media presents the NDE accounts as "paranormal," oddball reports lumped in with alien abductions, Bigfoot, and the Loch Ness Monster. Even reputable bookstores sell NDE books under the New Age heading. Here is the problem. The majority of scientists regard spiritual beliefs to be at odds with the material basis of science. Such variant world views reflect more than academic disagreements. A long, unpleasant history sours the debate. Many scientists have remained embittered after conflicts with evangelical Christians ranging from geologic age dating to evolution. In turn, evangelical Christians believe that scientists are undermining the Bible. The antagonism has only been heightened by pro-creationist politicians advocating the teaching theology as science within the public school system. Consequently, most scientists share in the sentiment that Christian fundamentalism represents an affront against the genuine quest to gain knowledge. Unfortunately, anger precludes useful dialogue between those that advocate a material world view and a spiritual world view.

As a psychologist and a scientist, I am skeptical of most paranormal experiences. I have typically viewed them as the subject of misinterpretation or hoaxes. Support for these paranormal experiences usually comes from sensationalized cable-television shows where the documented evidence appears manufactured, at best. Yet, near-death experiences fall into another category altogether. The power of the near-death experience derives from a large N (statistical total). At the time of writing, there are over 3,800 written first-hand reports on the Near-Death Experience Research Foundation website alone. One survey suggests that 5% of the American population has experienced an NDE (about 15 million people).[1] Although accurate figures are lacking, there are at least a hundred thousand NDE's experienced throughout the world and probably many more. Despite these huge numbers, reliability between first-hand observers is very high. As discussed throughout the remaining chapters, central tenets of the near-death experience repeat, and unusual reports usually reflect sensible experiences when understood in the context of the individual's life history. Consistently, research has shown that there are no significant differences between near-death experiences across nationality, culture, educational backgrounds, age, race, or religion.[1]

The importance of reliability cannot be understated. As my research methods professor used to say ad nauseam, it is impossible to demonstrate validity without establishing reliability first. Reliability is a problem when comparing world religious beliefs. Neil Peart, insightful lyricist and lay philosopher, writes, "Put ten believers from the major religions of the world in a circle, and their 'thought balloons' are going to read the same as mine: 'You believe in that?'"[2] Religious fundamentalists typically interpret discrepancies as reason to believe that their doctrine is correct whereas other doctrines are wrong. Clearly, such fundamentalist beliefs are a matter of faith, because there is no empirical evidence supporting one religion over another. The near-death experience, on the other hand, represents a more or less universal understanding of life after death. Moreover, the NDE is supported by empirical evidence.

The materialist scientist might take issue that the NDE is supported by meaningful empirical evidence. Indeed, NDE research cannot be compared with the "hard" sciences, like physics or chemistry. Mathematical proof, capable of predicting the NDE, may never be forthcoming.

NDE research can better be compared with research in the behavioral sciences. The behavioral sciences may be called a "soft" science because much of human behavior can only be measured indirectly. For example, cognitive research, or the psychological study of thinking, relies on the indirect measurement of thought through self-report and consequent behavior. Unfortunately, the only way a scientist can measure thoughts directly is through a mind-reading device. Until such an apparatus is invented, cognitive psychology will remain a "soft" science. Likewise, until science can observe and measure life after death, NDE research will also remain a "soft" science.

As a psychologist trained in the scientific method, I concede that near-death experience reports do not easily lend themselves to testable and reproducible research. Yet, some physicians, psychologists, and other professionals have boldly made the effort. There are entire books written on evidence for the near-death experience. For example, Dr. Jeffrey Long, a radiation cardiologist, wrote a bestselling book called *Evidence of the Afterlife: The Science of Near-Death Experiences*. In his book, Dr. Long outlines nine lines of evidence supporting the near-death experience. Let us take a moment to briefly review these nine areas:

1. There is lucidity, or clarity of thought, that near-death experience reporters (NDErs) experience while deceased. A brain devoid of cell activity, or neurotransmission, should not produce any thought at all. Some skeptics claim that near-death experiences involve fragments of memory encoded just before and after clinical death. However, medical research demonstrates that the memories surrounding a heart attack are disorganized and fragmented. NDErs, on the other hand, report that their thoughts are more organized and complete during the NDE than during their alert state prior to illness, accident, or resulting death.

2. About half of the NDErs report an out-of-body experience (OBE) just after death. Typically their consciousness floats above their body, often toward the top corner of a hospital room. Conversations are heard and resuscitation efforts are observed. The NDEr witnesses all the frantic events to save his or her life with mild curiosity or detachment. Reported conversations and surgical procedures can often be corroborated by others. Because NDErs provide measurable observations, the OBE is a great opportunity for researchers to empirically test the validity

of the near-death experience. Indeed, several independent researchers tested technical knowledge the NDEr may have gained following resuscitation efforts conducted by medical personnel. They compared the NDEr medical "know-how" with random people in the public. The results were profound. The NDErs understanding of resuscitation efforts was highly accurate whereas the random public's understanding was highly inaccurate. Not surprisingly, the general public's perception of emergency resuscitation mimicked medical interventions as shown by television actors.

3. There have been several NDE studies involving people who have been blind since birth. The perceptual understanding of a blind person's world is limited to hearing, touch, and taste. The blind cannot even imagine seeing objects in a world of perceptual darkness, because they have no experiential frame of reference of vision in the brain. In the rare cases of sight being restored by surgical intervention, there is often a long period of time in which the patient has difficulty making sense of their visual environment. Yet, when a blind person experiences an NDE, the individual always experiences a fantastic, full, visual experience while deceased. They enthusiastically share these visual experiences when resuscitated, even though they remain physically blind. They would not be able to accurately describe physical phenomena without their near-death experience being real.

4. Neural activity becomes erratic and then ceases seconds after death. When a person is brain dead, they should not be conscious - assuming that consciousness comes from neural activity in the brain. Of 613 NDERF submissions surveyed, 74.4% reported a heightened level of consciousness and more awareness of their surroundings than prior to their near-death experience. The lucidity of consciousness rules out brain death. Moreover, the lucidity of consciousness probably rules out brief hallucinations caused by chaotic, last second neural firing.

5. Almost a quarter of NDErs experience a review of their life. Specifically, highlights of life were experienced like viewing a 3-D movie. By examining both positive and negative aspects of

life choices, the NDEr learns how their life choices impacted themselves and others. Skeptics claim that the life review is caused by electrical discharge in the brain just prior to death. One would expect the last electrical discharges to be chaotic, which should produce only incoherent experiences at best. NDERF research has demonstrated, however, that NDEr life review memories are organized, content appropriate, and realistic.

6. Many NDErs encounter beings in the afterlife, mostly relatives. Unlike the surreal quality of a hallucination or dream, reunions with relatives are meaningful and content appropriate. Consistent with reality, all relatives encountered were deceased prior to the NDE. One would expect a random assortment of people, living or deceased, to be perceived during a pre-death hallucination.

7. Cynics of the NDE blame the popular media for implanting the NDE experience into the mind of the population, especially through the suggestive influence of popular daytime television. Yet, there is no empirical evidence supporting that the masses are brainwashed. Conversely, there is strong evidence that the NDE is independent of cultural factors. First, two-thirds of NDErs state they did not have any prior knowledge of near-death experiences. Second, NDERF research states that very young children below the age of five experience identical elements of the near-death experiences as older children and adults. These young children have been minimally exposed to popular adult Western culture; there are very few, if any, three-year-old Oprah fans. It is doubtful that any of the young children below five have ever heard of a near-death experience. Additionally, developmental psychologists have long determined that very young children have a limited and different understanding of death itself. Yet, very young children report the same elements of the NDE as adults. Dr. Long writes, "I see that their thinking may be childlike during the NDE. However, I also see a deeper dimension of their NDE that goes beyond even the very detailed NDERF survey questions."[1]

8. Through NDERF, Jeffrey and Jody Long have completed the most comprehensive research study on cross-cultural differences of the near-death experience. They have found that there are no statistical differences of the near-death experience between

different religions and cultures. It should be noted that NDErs may interpret their experience differently when they return based on their personal understanding of religion or culture. But in terms of the near-death experience itself, every element of the NDE occurs at about the same frequency and order around the world.

9. The NDE serves as a watershed moment for those who have experienced the wonders of life after death. Most people are changed profoundly for several reasons: the NDErs often report stronger devotion to spirituality; they no longer fear death; they report greater love for both others and self; they appreciate genuine, loving relationships and often discard abusive, unloving relationships; many make lifestyle changes consistent with their spiritual changes; many enter service related professions. Skeptics, however, retort that life changes are a product of serious, life threatening related health problems, such as a heart attack, but their claim is made without supporting evidence. Two NDE research studies actually suggest the opposite. Both studies show that NDE heart attack victims exhibit significantly more profound life changes than non-NDE heart attacks victims. Moreover, the deeper and more complex the near-death experience, the deeper and more long lasting are the reported personal life changes.

At the beginning of his book, Dr. Long correctly explains that nine lines of evidence are better than one. In statistics, the power of research increases as more statistical variance is explained.[1] Put more simply, a research hypothesis is stronger when supported by different types of evidence because there is less of a probability that alternative explanations are true. Thus, empirical research that supports the NDE may further strengthen if results are replicated and/or new lines of evidence are supported by future research.

The materialist skeptic will likely reject all nine lines of evidence for life after death, or any other line of evidence for that matter. With unwavering faith in materialism, the skeptical scientist believes that human behavior can *only* be the result of biology. Evidence of the supernatural is no evidence at all. Personally, I find the argument ironic. Materialist skeptics are quick to dismiss NDE research and yet provide weak alternative explanations. Although seemingly scientific at first glance, most of the materialist research has been on the basis of indirect evidence, at best, and wild guesses, at worst. Pim van Lommel, a Dutch cardiologist, points out that most scientists view the near-death experience as a biological survival mechanism - a product of evolution. In other words, they suggest that the NDE somehow increases the survival rate of the individual and the species. What exactly happens to the body at time of death? According to Pim van Lommel, the biological scientific explanation reduces the NDE to a release of chemicals. He presents the medical explanation as follows: "The NDE is experienced as a result of anoxia (lack of oxygen) of the brain, possibly caused by the release of endomorphines (feel good brain chemicals), or NMDA receptor blockade (the blockage of certain brain chemicals)."[3] Although these biological terms sound very scientific, the underlying empirical support is lacking. First, no one has demonstrated a causal link between chemistry and the near-death experience. Second, it is difficult to understand how any evolutionary survival mechanism applies to a dying person. Being dead does not increase the survival rate of the individual or the species. There is no evolutionary purpose to comforting an organism during its last few moments of life. Perhaps more profound, brain-based explanations are not relevant to a non-functional, dead brain.

In 1988, Dr. van Lommel conducted a study of 344 heart attack survivors two weeks after they were pronounced clinically dead at the hospital. These accounts were verified by hospital medical records. Sixty-two of the test subjects reported a near-death experience during their heart attack, despite complete brain dysfunction secondary to anoxia.[4] Pim van Lommel describes the rapid deterioration and stopping of brain activity (a flat EEG) after a heart attack with the following medical language:

> Through many studies in human, as well as in animal models, cerebral function has been shown to be severely compromised during cardiac arrest and electric activity in both cerebral cortex and the deeper structures of the brain has been shown to be absent after a very short period of time... In the case of prolonged cardiac arrest of more than 37 seconds, the EEG activity may not return for many minutes to hours after the cardiac arrest has been restored.[4]

In other words, sixty-two people reported a comprehensive, organized awareness of their surroundings during death. They also experienced awareness of their own thoughts, emotions, perceptions, and memories. Amazingly, they experienced all these activities without any associated brain activity. Materialists assume that a physiological explanation for the near-death experience is in the wings of discovery. Pim van Lommel counters, "The current concept in medical science states that consciousness is the product of the brain. This concept, however, has never been scientifically proven."[3] The support for spiritual consciousness is strong. The crux of support can be put forward simply, no one can provide an acceptable physiological explanation of consciousness in a dead brain.

The skeptic could argue that all sixty-two near-death experiences, as well as all other NDE accounts, were fabricated. Yet, it is unlikely that tens of thousands of people would fake near-death experiences, especially given the high content consistency between reports. What would be the secondary gain? It is extremely rare that NDErs seek any financial reward for their shared experiences. Most NDErs are not motivated by attention, either. Rather, most NDErs are very reluctant to share their experience due to fear of ridicule. Indeed, many NDErs report negative reactions from family, friends, clergy, and doctors - ranging from quiet belief to accusations of devil worship. When they do share their experience, they usually do so without recognition. In regard to the NDERF website, all 3,800 entries were submitted anonymously.

Recent empirical evidence supports that near-death experiences are neither imagined nor faked. Several studies have demonstrated that imagined memories have fewer conscious features on average than real memories.[5] NDERF survey results indicate that 74.4 percent of NDErs report that they experienced more consciousness than normal during their NDE.[1] Consistent with the NDEr's perception of self-consciousness, recent research conducted by the University of Liege Medical School concluded that NDEr memories have significantly more conscious elements than the other groups tested. For those interested in the basic research design of this study, the other tested groups included an imagined memory group, a coma memory group, and a control group. Results demonstrated that NDE memories contained further clarity, more emotional depth, and increased references to the person than the imagined memory group or the coma memory group. Amazingly, NDE memories were even more vivid than real life memories measured from the control group.[6] With these results, the researchers concluded that the NDE memories do not appear to be imagined events. It should be noted that skeptics have not produced any evidence supporting their accusations of malingering. Specifically, they make scientific sounding conclusions without using science.

Adding to the credibility of near-death experience, NDE reports are supported by frank, thoughtful accounts by reputable people all over the world. People making NDE reports are not typically hucksters, media hounds, or criminals. Rather, tens of thousands of NDErs reflect a wide representation of society: housewives, physicians, blue collar workers, atheists, agnostics, Christians, Hindus, Native Americans, philosophers, military personnel, nurses, children, retired elderly, etc. Near-death experiences also gain credibility through the authority of professional supporters. Many well-respected physicians, psychologists, and other researchers have placed their full support behind the near-death experience. For example, Dr. Elisabeth Kübler-Ross, a renowned psychiatrist and the foremost expert in death and dying, wrote extensively on near-death experiences due to her frequent contact with dying patients throughout her long career. As Dr. Kübler-Ross's career changed focus, she half-jokingly wrote, "Many people say, 'Of course Doctor Ross has seen too many dying patients. Now she starts getting a bit funny.' "[7] Despite ridicule from her materialistic colleagues, Dr. Kübler-Ross could not ignore the ongoing evidence provided by her patients. Her work to promote love and faith on earth were more important than maintaining her professional reputation. Perhaps NDE research will vindicate her courage.

My own view of the near-death experience has changed with the presentation of evidence throughout the years. I was raised in a scientific household awash with discussions of physics and geology. When I first heard about near-death experiences, I was naturally skeptical. My belief in the near-death experience increased after reading the pioneering book by Dr. Raymond Moody, *Life after Life*, while studying in college at the University of Arizona.[8] I maintained some doubt, of course, because I was limited by a materialist, scientific world-view. The near-death experience might be explained by natural causes, I thought, a natural neurological function of the brain shutting down and dying. Perhaps it was a type of hallucination. Despite my skepticism, I was at least willing to consider a non-materialist view because the scientific explanations were even more unsatisfying. Mario Beauregard, a near-death advocate and neuroscientist teaching at the University of Montreal, noted that many scientific colleagues will never believe in the supernatural, no matter the evidence presented, because they equate all reality with the world they see, measure, or define through mathematical equation. Beauregard proposes a different vision for science. He finishes his book, *The Spiritual Brain*, by writing the following:

If we are to make significant breakthroughs with regard to our understanding of human mind and consciousness as well as the development of the spiritual potential of humanity, we need a new scientific frame of reference. Such a frame will recognize that dogmatic materialist scientism is not synonymous with science. A scientific frame of reference must bring together the inner and the outer, the subjective and the objective, the first-person perspective and the third-person perspective. Mystical experience from various spiritual traditions indicates that the nature of mind, consciousness, and reality, as well as the meaning of life can be apprehended through an intuitive, unitive, and experiential form of knowing.[9]

Beauregard appears to be saying that scientists should be open to different avenues of learning beyond the usual scientific method of materialist discovery. Materialist scientists need to recognize that intuitive approaches have value within the human experience. For instance, a scientist cannot measure all facets of consciousness or spiritual experience by using brain imaging machines. Beauregard suggests that the scientific and intuitive need to be integrated. Dr. Pim van Lommel puts it more succinctly. He states: "Science is asking questions with an open mind, and not being afraid to reconsider widely accepted but scientifically not proven concepts, like the concept that consciousness and memories are a product of the brain."[4]

Rollo May, a well-respected existential psychologist, offers a similar point of view. Interestingly, May attributes human existential motives behind the rigid adherence to scientism. May writes:

The odd belief prevails in our culture that a thing or experience is not real if we cannot make it mathematical, and somehow must be real if we can reduce it to numbers. But this means making an abstraction out of it - mathematics is the abstraction par excellence, which is indeed its glory and the reason for its great usefulness. Modern Western man thus finds himself in the strange situation, after reducing something to an abstraction, of having then to persuade himself it is real. This has much to do with the sense of isolation and loneliness which is endemic to the modern Western world.[10]

Rollo May was a proponent of being, a psychological concept that cannot be easily mathematically defined. In his quote, May points out that mathematics is not a perfect description of reality. Rather, mathematics is an abstraction of reality. Math is a tool mankind invented to help explain *how* nature works. However, it does not answer why nature works the way it does. Nor does it capture the conscious experience of reality.

Mathematics can also sometimes explain the unseen, such as spooky action observed in quantum mechanics. Quantum mechanics is a complicated subject and will be addressed in a basic way in another chapter. Suffice to say, spooky action involves the effects of conscious thought on matter at the sub-atomic level. The important point here is that science will need to accommodate the non-material action in quantum mechanics in order to achieve a greater understanding of the universe. If science must accommodate new knowledge from quantum mechanics, how can science not also accommodate the near-death experience? By ignoring the near-death experience on materialist grounds, science may be missing the most profound aspect of reality – the reality of our true existence.

Why do materialists strongly reject the near-death experience as spiritual? Why do they propose their own "scientific theories," even when they are unsupported by measurable evidence? Perhaps such strong reactions are elicited by the scientist's own emotional resistance, or repugnance, to the idea of spirituality. Specifically, they feel they must explain away the supernatural in order to be scientists. It can be difficult for a materialist to consider a non-materialistic point of view. After all, materialism is an axiom of science; anything else is superstition. Yet, Pim van Lommel, Mario Beauregard, Elisabeth Kübler-Ross and other scientists have taken a great leap to reject that axiom, because they followed the evidence provided by their patients. Their world-view matured because of a new revolution of meaning through the near-death experience.

My world-view also changed as a psychologist, be it slowly, with reflection as I matured. However, my doubt remained throughout the years because of my own materialistic roots. I am not so naïve to think that the world will readily accept the near-death experience as a new revolution in meaning. It will take time. Thomas Kuhn noted that scientific theories, individually or collectively, are either questioned or widely accepted by the scientific community. Widely accepted theories, or a collection of theories, are called paradigms. Kuhn notes that paradigms shift in a stepwise fashion over time. Change only gains momentum when a new theory topples the old paradigm with overwhelming evidence.[11] Change is slowed, however, by resistance from the "old guard" scientific community. Adherents of the old paradigm cling to their professional work like a mother clings to her child. Kuhn perceptively notes that shifts in paradigms can lead to an altered world-view. He writes:

> Paradigm changes do cause scientists to see the world of their research-engagement differently. In so far as their only recourse to that world is through what they see and do, we may want to say that after a revolution scientists are responding to a different world.[11]

The near-death experience may represent a paradigm shift gaining momentum, as evidenced by the growing number of research articles and books in the area. Perhaps it is possible that the near-death experience will someday radically change humanity's view of itself, God, and life after death. With this revolution in meaning, perhaps people will also learn to respond to their world differently.

CHAPTER THREE

WE ARE NOT ONLY HUMAN

S oul perception is made up of more than the five senses. People who experience a near-death experience almost universally report a remarkable metamorphosis when they die. Human life can be likened to living as a plodding caterpillar, terrestrial bound, whereas death can be likened to a butterfly hatching from a cocoon, taking flight in colorful splendor. After taking their final breath, NDErs often describe floating above their lifeless bodies with remarkable detachment. Why should they care about their mortal body when they realize their own eternal splendor? NDErs experience a continuity of consciousness that flows seamlessly from their earthly existence. As spirit becomes liberated from the constraints of space and time, personal essence expands without physical restraint. Knowledge and experience flood into the soul like a broken reservoir. Unlike the butterfly, however, a cocoon is unnecessary for human metamorphosis. Transformation is immediate. For the NDEr, true essence leaves the body at death and returns when it resumes earthly life. NDErs unequivocally understand that the brain is only a processor and does not equate to their real essence of being. Rather, they attest that the eternal soul is their true essence. In this chapter, we will investigate the nature of the soul. First, we will set out to define the soul and secondly we will discuss how spiritually-minded people can recognize and tap into the soul. Finally, we will explore how knowledge of the soul can contribute to spiritual wisdom.

The Existence of the Soul

Only a minority of people have had the benefit of a near-death experience. For the rest, the soul represents an imprecise belief. No one has conclusively proven that they have seen a soul much less measured its properties at the most rudimentary level. Webster's New Collegiate Dictionary defines the soul to be: "1) the immaterial essence, animating principle, or actuating cause of an individual life; 2) the spiritual principle embodied in human beings, all rational spiritual beings, or the universe; 3) person's total self; 4) spiritual or moral force."[1] Webster's multipart definition of the soul touches on the root of terrestrial life, spiritual existence, morality, and essence of the universe. Such an encompassing, inconclusive definition does not lend to the investigative understanding of the soul. Put more succinctly, the soul is a seemingly unknowable entity. Most scientists dismiss the idea of the soul on this basis. They might ask, "Describe me a soul?" Unfortunately, religion also defines the soul in vague mystical terms, which only supports the materialist position. The field of psychology, pushing toward acceptance in the broader scientific community, has likewise remained silent on the concept of the soul. There is one brilliant exception. The famous psychiatrist Carl Jung did not discount the soul during his psychoanalytic investigation into the psyche.

Carl Jung remains a towering figure in the field of psychology. One of the original founders of psychoanalysis, Jung's prestige ranks second only to Sigmund Freud.[2] Despite the historical recognition, Carl Jung occupies a small afterthought in modern-day psychology due to his mystical, Eastern based psychological constructs. Until recently, I generally discounted Jung as rambling and mystical. I now give his work a second look, especially given the consistency between his theory and the near-death experience.

Jung placed a great emphasis on the soul throughout his ample theoretical analysis. For instance, he wondered how the soul was accepted across cultures when it could not be seen. Jung dismissed that the common belief in the soul was mere coincidence. In response, he developed a psychological construct to explain the universality of the soul, namely the principle of archetype. An archetype is a collectively inherited unconscious symbolic image or thought present in everyone's psyche. Humans pass down these thoughts and images from generation to generation regardless of culture; their meaning often hidden in symbol, dream, and myth. Accordingly, an archetype can be repeatedly expressed throughout history, even in cultures that have no knowledge of each other. For example, a North American tribal myth may have the same form and theme as an ancient Greek myth. The archetype most relevant to the discussion in this chapter is the self-archetype, or the universal unconscious expression of the self.

Jung defines the self as the totality of human psychological phenomena that includes what can be experienced, what cannot be experienced, and what is not-yet experienced.[3] Psychology has a number of similar constructs of self. But only Jung associated the self with the soul. He writes:

> This self was evidently never thought of as an entity identical with the ego (conscious thinking and personal identity), and for this reason it was described as a "hidden nature" dwelling in inanimate matter, as a spirit, daemon, or fiery spark...it is clear that these ideas can have nothing to do with the empirical ego (testable conscious thinking), but are concerned with a "divine nature" quite distinct from it.[3]

In this paragraph, Jung proposes that the totality of self stems from the spirit made of inanimate matter. He clearly states that this real "self" does not derive from the brain.

Imagine if you could say "good morning" to both your body and soul. The notion seems foolish, at first glance. After all, you sense that you are one stream of consciousness, one identity, and one mind. Although most people experience themselves as individuals, the assumption of spirit/brain duality has been largely accepted since antiquity. In fact, most religions accept that soul and brain relate in a state of coexistence. Judaism and Christianity both recognize coexistence and a certain degree of separateness between both the brain and the soul; although the lines of distinction are not always clear. While these religions value the purity of spirit, they devalue the cravings of the body and other sins of the flesh. Hinduism boldly steps further. Hindu theology asserts that the soul manifests the same substance as truth, as manifest in the spiritual realm. Everything we see and touch in the physical world is illusionary.

Jung couldn't agree more with ancient concepts of duality. He writes, "Thus, it [soul] comes from man, and you are its raw mineral; in you it is found and from you it is extracted...and it remains inseparably in you."[3] In other words, Jung believed that the human body serves as a physical host for the soul, at least until the body dies. Jung would argue that the near universal acceptance of duality, as part of the self-archetype, supports his belief. Thus, various religious systems accept the soul/body duality, even though we live with the illusionary perception of individuality. According to Jung, we collectively know, deep inside, we are souls through our interconnectedness with God.

The Interconnection between Spirit and God

It may seem incomprehensible that soul and body, two separate entities, are experienced as one. Ironically, the process may be better understood by presenting a biological, material-based analogy. Namely, there exists a biological blending in the brain. The brain operates by using two somewhat repetitive hemispheres, the left and right, for adaptation and survival purposes. Put simply, you are thinking with two brains as you read this paragraph. Yet, humans experience only one consciousness, even though both hemispheres are working simultaneously in an integrated manner through a connecting neural bridge. Perhaps body and soul blend in a similar manner.

Two entities coexist in every person as spirit and brain. But it is only the universal spirit, or soul, that is interconnected with God. Many NDErs report they leave and re-enter the body through the head, sort of like being sucked up by a vacuum cleaner. Eben Alexander, a Harvard trained neurosurgeon, noted from his NDE that the brain worked as a "filter" or "reducing valve" for the soul.[4] In other words, the physical body hinders rather than enhances the soul. This makes intuitive sense. After all, the human brain becomes subject to the physical laws of aging and disintegration and dies after a brief existence. The soul, however, withstands the epochs of time. From the eternal perspective, the brain has little ultimate value compared to the soul.

Perhaps the greatest value of the soul has to do with its connection with God. Carl Jung theorized that the self-archetype, as part of the collective unconscious, exists as an integral part of the universal fabric of everything. Put more simply, he believed that every soul exists as an integrated element of the Whole. He wrote, "The collective unconscious, and we describe it as objective because it is identical in all individuals and is therefore one. But out of the universal one, there is produced in every individual a subjective conscious."[3]

Not only does Jung suggest that we make up the Whole of God, but that individuality derives from the Whole. Thus, soul has individual expression and, at the same time, integration with God consciousness. Jung elaborates: "The unity of the stone (meaning the experience of God in one's soul) is the equivalent of individualism, by which we are made one; we would say that the stone is a projection of the unified self."[3]

Jung's writing, although difficult to decipher, seems to say that the individual soul is projected from the Source. Because the Source includes the interconnected fabric of everything, it stands to reason that each individual soul serves as a singularity of God's creative conscious experience. Put more succinctly, we are not God, but our consciousness is a small part of God's consciousness. Although we actually exist as Source consciousness, we perceive separateness in our individual consciousness while living on earth as human beings. The misperception is necessary. Without it, we would not live with individual purpose and will.

Many NDE reports support that the soul is ethereal, emanates from the Source, and is interconnected with everything. Anita Moorjani captures the interconnectedness of the soul. During her NDE account, she uses a tapestry metaphor to explain interconnectedness. She writes, "Each one of us is like a single thread in a huge tapestry, woven in a complex and colorful pattern. We may only be one strand, yet we're all integral to the finished image."[5]

The weave is incomplete so far as individual strands are yet to be interwoven. The individual being is integral to God just as the individual strand is integral to the weave. Moorjani further explains:

> Understand that I'm referring to the part of me that was aware during the NDE that I'm not just my body – the part of me that felt I was one with every single thing. I was merging with pure consciousness as an infinite, magnificent being, feeling the clarity of why I'm in this body and life at this point in time. This is also the part of me that understood that the illusion of separation is created by identifying too strongly with the external.[5]

As human beings, we usually experience reality within the biological parameters of the human brain. Beyond the symbolic communication of language, we cannot share our thoughts, motives, emotions, perceptions, or sensational experiences. We appear to be alone, separated from each other, the broader reality, and God. But isolation is an external illusion because we choose to see a small part of existence. We only see the type of reality measured by scientists. NDErs typically resist returning to material existence because they no longer feel isolated. Rather, they experience pure love within the context of infinite consciousness interconnected with all of creation. Eben Alexander nails the limited human existence in his book, *Proof of Heaven*. From his NDE, he writes:

> We - each of us - are intricately, irremovably connected to the larger universe. It is our true home, and thinking that this physical world is all that matters is like shutting oneself up in a small closet and imagining that there is nothing else out beyond it.[4]

Given the immensity of the universe, it is easy to view ourselves as insignificant. People fail to recognize that they are an integral thread within a larger weave. Existentialists certainly view mankind as isolated and inconsequential. What is a human being but a miniscule speck within an infinite universe? Yet NDErs know otherwise. When examining their threads against the great weave, they realize that everything they have done and will do is important and interconnected. To understand better, let's look at an NDE account from the NDERF website:

> I then saw a picture in front of me. It was a pattern. I looked deep into this pattern, a tapestry. I could see the warp and the weft. This pattern was me. It felt ME. The man in the beard urged me to look closer and as I zoomed in to each stitch of color, I saw myself in a scene from my life. I was watching me in a past situation and each scenario showed me how my actions had affected other people. I began to see so many where I had been so selfish, greedy, unkind, calculating, and thoughtless that I began to feel thoroughly ashamed as it was an overwhelming sense of sadness for my behavior toward others. Then the kind man pulled me out of my misery and said, "Hey it's not all bad," and we visited other parts of the pattern and other incidents replayed like in a video. I watched scenes when I felt it was okay. I had been kind, helpful, loving, funny, all the nice things that made me feel it wasn't so bad. Then he showed me the other side and there were lots of loose strands and it looked a bit untidy and I mentioned this and he said, "That's because it's not finished yet." (VV, No NDERF Number)

Carl Jung, Anita Moorjani, Eben Alexander, VV, and many NDERF authors all emphasize the same profound understanding of interconnectedness. Everything we say, do, and think has cosmic importance because it affects everyone within the whole. Our true self, our soul, is connected to the magnificence of everything. Unfortunately, we are not always aware of our own magnificence.

The Conscious Mind

It seems ironic that our true essence, the soul, acts behind the curtain of the brain. After all, human thought is produced by the brain. Neuropsychologists can even pinpoint specific brain problems through psychological testing. For instance, they can localize brain injury, even the effects of dementia, by assessing significant deficits in intelligence, odd thinking patterns, and life functioning. This being the case, what could possibly lie behind the curtain? Consciousness lies behind the curtain of all human experience. Take vision, for instance. Visible light hits our retina, transforms into neural activity, and travels through the brain by electrical propagation. Vision is finally perceived through the integration of visual information in the lower-back part of the brain. Vision seems like a brain activity. Indeed, if severe damage is caused to the visual cortex, vision will be compromised every time. Although neuroscientists can measure how light is transformed into biochemistry and sent through various brain structures, they cannot describe the last transformation – the *experience* of vision. Think about the task of describing the color red to a color-blind person. It cannot be described because red is a purely experiential quality of consciousness. True, red cannot be perceived by the colorblind person due to the absence of red cones in the retina. So, how does the biochemical firing of cells translate into the vivid perception of red in our experience? Scientists cannot answer this question beyond making wild guesses. Even more to the point, how does the biochemical firing of cells translate into the experience of consciousness itself? Again, scientists cannot answer. To re-quote Pim van Lommel, "The current concept in medical science states that consciousness is the product of the brain. This concept, however, has never been proven."[6] Scientists do not have a good grasp on the mechanisms of consciousness. The most powerful computers can do amazing calculations, but they do not have consciousness. Even cognitive psychologists recognize the difference. Dr. Albert Bandura, a respected leader in the area of social learning states, "Computers are not exploratory or knowledge seeking. They do not deliberate about their past successes and failures or worry about, and plan for, the future."[7] A computer does not appreciate the color red, or even experience color. A computer does not self-deliberate on how to creatively incorporate the color red into an aesthetically pleasing painting. Computer calculations can be measured but consciousness is immeasurable. Consciousness remains a mystery to the materialistic purview of science because it is an inherent part of our spiritual nature.

If scientists dismiss spiritualism, how do psychological theorists explain human behavior? Sadly, theoretical opinions about the human psyche are not very flattering. Sigmund Freud taught that the human animal constantly seeks pleasure from the environment. Outside of seeking pleasure, the human animal is also driven by unconscious instinctual needs like hunger, aggression, and sex. B.F. Skinner, father of the behaviorist movement, understood the human as a kind of machine beholden to the reinforcements and punishments in the environment.[8] Recently, theoreticians from the cognitive movement claim that various types of thinking also shape behavior. Although cognitive theorists recognize the influential role of thinking and emotions, they also recognize that mental processes are also determined by the internal and external environment.

Although each psychological theory emphasizes different aspects of human behavior, they share one thing in common. They all profess that human behavior is determined by heredity and the environment. From this stance, the human brain is constantly barraged with instinctual animal urges, binding reinforcement contingencies, labile emotions, and error-ridden thoughts. Thus, the human brain must cope with a challenging and often contradictory world. What about consciousness? What about free will? What about spirituality? Too often these concepts are conveniently ignored. Given the seemingly mechanistic origins of human behavior, it is understandable that scientists focus on the animalistic nature of mankind. One can appreciate how issues relating to the soul can easily become an afterthought, not only to scientists, but to the casual observer. Unfortunately, this position may work to our detriment.

In her book, *Dying to Be Me*, Anita Moorjani shared how her death was caused by a fervent concentration on the external world at the expense of her own true self. In her case, external orientation manifested itself as a pervasive fear of being. She wrote:

"What was I afraid of? Just about everything, including failing, being disliked, letting people down, and not being good enough. I also feared illness, cancer in particular, as well as the treatment for cancer. I was afraid of living, and I was afraid of dying."[5]

Anita Moorjani made a full and immediate recovery from last stage cancer after her near-death experience. Her miracle of healing carries a message that we would do well to recognize our true nature of self and nurture our soul. After his NDE, Howard Storm wrote, "What separates us from God is our own sense of separateness. What unites us with God is awareness of our oneness with God."[9] To believe that we live in isolation in a purely material existence stunts our potential in fulfilling our spiritual mission to grow toward the divine.

As NDErs become more aware of the soul and oneness with God, they begin to realize that material values have little importance. God has little interest in human wealth, prestige, power, violence, or sex. The magazine aisle may be a good barometer of Western values and personal interest. After all, magazine publishers simply sell what the masses most want to buy. Perhaps ninety percent of the magazines fall into the following categories: gossip magazines (the building and tearing down of celebrities); men's magazines (the near display of nudity and sex); women's magazines (dieting, physical appearance, and sex); sports magazines (competition and dominance); muscle magazines (latent power and aggression); gun and hunting magazines (latent power and violence); pro-wrestling (blatant power and violence); car magazines (wealth and power); money magazines (wealth and power). It is not my intent to pass moral judgment on mainstream Western culture. My point is that humans are a product of biology; mass media sells packaged pleasures to stimulate our animal desires. Clearly, Western secular values are externally rooted. If we want to be consistent with God, our focus needs to be more inward on the soul and the Source of the soul. But how can one accomplish this? Some of the answers may come from secular psychology.

Connecting with Soul

A few cognitive theoreticians have devoted some attention to the study of consciousness. However, their analysis has been limited to what is observable and measurable. One area of study involves the concept of *metacognition. Metacognition* involves thinking about one's own thinking, which requires the interplay of brain-based language and consciousness. In other words, the brain uses consciousness as a mediator, to think about thinking. Albert Bandura concedes the notion of consciousness in the role of human thinking. He wrote, "To think about the adequacy of one's cognitive activities requires consciousness of them. Metacognitive functioning thus depends on accessibility of thinking and flexible use of one's thinking skills."[7] Before the term "metacognition" became in vogue, the great existentialist psychologist Rollo May used another term to convey the same concept, *Eigenwelt*, which means "eye of the world" in his native German. Rollo May writes the following about Eigenwelt:

> It is the mode of behavior in which a person sees himself as subject and object at once.
>
> The capacity to transcend the situation is an inseparable part of self-awareness, for it is obvious that the mere awareness of oneself as a being in the world implies the capacity to stand outside and look at oneself and the situation by an infinite variety of possibilities.[10]

Unlike Freud and Skinner, May seems to endow the human being with a certain measure of self-determination. May suggests that the human being exhibits creative consciousness capable of infinite possibilities, because consciousness acts as a mediator for the brain to evaluate itself. If consciousness is indeed the soul, as proposed, then it is the soul that redeems our base animal nature. Humans can go beyond their biological impulses and look at an "infinite variety of possibilities." Yet, metacognition is not the only means for a person to raise conscious awareness of being. Not only can the consciousness mediate humankind's thinking about thinking, but humankind's thinking can also monitor consciousness through the mediation of consciousness. Put more simply, we can be made more aware of our own awareness. Cognitive theorists call this ability *mindfulness*.

Mindfulness refers to complete awareness of the present moment while focusing on the flow of immediate experience. The seeker of mindfulness must put aside evaluation and judgment in order to achieve increased awareness. Mindfulness can be a challenging endeavor that requires diligent effort, as required in the ongoing practice of meditation. Consciousness, by default, exists in the here and now. Thus, the seeker of mindfulness must let go of past and future, as well as any emotions associated with stressful situations. For example, imagine that you are drinking a $5.00 cup of coffee while waiting for a delayed flight at an airport terminal. Your attention naturally turns to the external. Perhaps you attend to the ramifications of being late. You may worry about being too tired to go to work or missing the ball game when you get home. Consequently, you may feel a mixture of boredom, irritability, and mild anxiety. In the practice of mindfulness, however, you divert your attention to the flow of events around you. You savor the taste of freshly brewed coffee. You feel cool air flowing from the cooler vents. You hear a young father play with his little girl. Internally, you feel a lifting, so you also focus on feelings of peace. There appears to be a shift in consciousness with the act of mindfulness. In the act of "letting-go" on the bustle of life, the mindful-observer usually notices an increased awareness of sensory information. Perhaps more importantly, the mindful-observer also becomes more aware of personal being.

Mindfulness has psychological benefits as supported by cognitive research. Namely, individuals produce more positive emotions by quieting their inner dialogue and focusing on consciousness. In regard to mental health problems, mindfulness can be effective in reducing stress, depression, anxiety, and various associated disorders. Mindfulness may also have health benefits, as well.[11] Dialectical Behavior Therapy (DBT), a popular cognitive/behavioral psychotherapy, utilizes mindfulness. Specifically, DBT utilizes a variety of cognitive and behavioral techniques, including mindfulness, to help very troubled clients gain control over self-destructive thoughts and emotions. Marsha Linnehan, the founder of DBT, states that practicing mindfulness allows a person to become grounded in a *wise mind*. What is a wise mind? Linnehan writes, "Wise mind is that part of each person that can know and experience truth. It is where the person knows something to be true or valid. It is almost always quiet. It has a certain peace. It is where the person knows something in a centered way."[11]

As evidenced by this quote, even secular psychology recognizes a connection between consciousness and wisdom. Truth comes from the quiet, centered self. Where do we find mindfulness? From a spiritual perspective, it derives from that deep, peaceful center called the soul.

In the DBT tradition, therapists teach troubled clients mindfulness in order to manage or tune out an overload of sensory information. Although mindfulness has been demonstrated to help clinical populations, I believe everyone can benefit from the practice. Mindfulness teaches people to give the psyche rest from life overload. The practice allows people to focus on here and now rather than on future frets and past regrets. As discussed, it teaches people to know truth within the quiet. The idea of knowing truth within the quiet runs counter to 21st century culture. It seems that many people actually shun the quiet. They rather fill quiet gaps with television or other electronic distractions. Dr. Martin Seligman, one of the founders of positive psychology, wrote, "Mindfulness begins with the observation that mindlessness pervades much of human activity. We fail to notice huge swaths of experience. We act and interact automatically, without much thinking."[12]

What a misuse of existence to waste time mindlessly, to live life with little reflection. This is not God's intent for our lives.

As a psychologist, I have observed that people's thoughts are frequently wrapped up in wondering what others think about them. Dr. Dorothy Satten, a personal mentor from the psychodrama movement, used to tell me and other trainees, "Ninety-nine percent of what other people are saying or doing is about them. Best not waste time worrying that it's about you." I have found this to be terrific advice in working with patients, as well as a maxim for my own life. It is a tragedy people's thoughts and emotions are so wrapped up in false beliefs. Mindfulness turns awareness around 180 degrees, from the external to the internal. Mindfulness not only allows people to think with greater care and awareness, but it also allows people to think at a qualitatively different level, perhaps even at a spiritual level.

There are spiritual benefits to mindfulness in addition to psychological benefits. Interestingly, mindfulness has its deepest roots in Zen Buddhism. Within this religious framework, mindfulness serves three primary psychological and spiritual purposes. First, it reminds adherents to be consistent in their spiritual focus. Second, it helps them to understand events objectively by shutting out emotions and irrational thoughts. Third, mindfulness helps adherents to understand that physical reality is imperfect and temporary.[13] One does not have to be Buddhist to see the spiritual value in these teachings. If consciousness can be equated with the soul, then any effort to increase soul awareness will enhance spiritual growth. Perhaps being aware of the soul brings us closer to experiencing our true nature as magnificent spiritual beings connected to God and creation.

The skeptic may counter that soul awareness is illusionary, a product of every day normal thinking. Indeed, consciousness always includes a steady stream of unbroken thoughts generated by the brain. Due to constant brain interference, no one experiences pure consciousness in the physical world. The human brain is a necessary partner in any human conscious experience. But that does not negate the importance of mindfulness. Take the example of the marooned airport passenger;

when the passenger engaged in mindfulness, the brain took a "back seat" to the soul instead of the other way around.

Being Mindful of the Source

Carl Jung understood mindfulness as a spiritual concept. He wrote:

> The self is brought into actuality through the concentration of the many upon the center, and the self wants this concentration. It is the subject and the object in the process. Therefore it is the "lamp" to those who "perceive" it. Its light is invisible if it is not perceived; it might just as well not exist. It is as dependent on being perceived as the act of perception is on light...And just as a "door" opens to one who "knocks" on it, or a "way" opens out to the wayfarer who seeks it, so when you relate to your own center, you initiate a process of conscious development that leads to oneness and wholeness. You no longer see yourself as an isolated point on the periphery, but as the One in the center.[3]

This passage is long and a bit complicated, so let's dissect. Jung appears to be saying that greater awareness of consciousness creates greater awareness of soul. Increased awareness, in turn, connects a person with the Source. From the NDE experience, this oneness means integration with God's divine nature. Jung suggests that each spiritual wayfarer walks a path toward oneness and wholeness. But it is up to the individual to "knock" and "open the door" to greater awareness; it does not come automatically. Conscious development requires the observer to keep shining a light inward over the course of time. Conscious development, in other words, requires people to be intentionally mindful throughout life.

Although mindfulness opens doors to spiritual awareness, the human experience of the soul will always be incomplete. Spiritual awareness does not automatically translate into spiritual knowledge. Without a near-death experience, humans lack firsthand experience of the soul. Many NDErs report that people experience a profound amnesia about the soul while living on earth, along with most matters of spiritual existence. Amazingly, those who experience near death know their soul, their true self, at a level of fullness that a human being can never hope to obtain through mindfulness or any other earthly endeavor. It means that people live in relative darkness only to reach illumination when they die. Anita Moorjani uses an illuminating metaphor to highlight the discrepancy between earthly awareness and heavenly awareness. She writes:

> Imagine, if you will, a huge, dark warehouse. You live there with only one flashlight to see by. Everything you know about what's contained within this enormous space is what you've seen by the beam of one small flashlight...Next, imagine that one day, someone flicks on a switch. There for the first time, in a sudden burst of brilliance and sound and color, you can see the entire warehouse, and it's nothing like anything you'd ever imagined...The vastness, complexity, depth, and breadth of everything going on around you is almost overwhelming. You can't see all the way to the end of space, and you know there's more to it than what you can take in from this torrent that's tantalizing your senses and emotions. But you do get the strong feeling that you're actually part of something alive, infinite, and altogether fantastic, that you are part of a large and unfolding tapestry that goes beyond sight and sound.[5]

God limits our spiritual understanding on earth, by design, through amnesia and biological filtering. However, amnesia and biological filtering do not preclude us from boldly shining our flashlight into the mysterious depths of spiritual discovery. Humanity has been endowed with free will and spiritual curiosity. It is our task to seek growth of being by using whatever tools we have at our disposal, even if it is just a small flashlight. To accomplish our mission, both soul and mind must work together in singular, wise purpose.

The Wise Soul

The working relationship between mind and soul is a subject of mystery. On earth, humans experience the soul through conscious awareness. In the spiritual realm, NDErs report that all mental experiences are solely a function of the soul. It is less clear, however, whether the soul can reason, remember, and communicate while living in symbiosis with the human brain. There is strong evidence that most cognitive processes are functions of the biological, material brain. Neurological correlates can be demonstrated with most mental faculties, including language, judgment, visual spatial skills, processing speed, mathematical ability, mental abstraction, memory, and so forth. On earth, the brain acts as a filter for the soul. The brain pushes the soul into the background of consciousness. This does not mean, however, that consciousness does not have a central role in our everyday thinking. Albert Bandura notes that learning is largely dependent on consciousness. He writes, "Studies in which thought probes are conducted at each learning trial reveal no learning without awareness."[7] Soul, the true self, appears to take a back seat to brain in physical existence. Yet, the soul is always there, working closely with the mind. It is a necessary ingredient that makes the blended human being. Not only is learning dependent on consciousness, but so is moral growth.

Carl Jung proposed that the soul serves as a moral conscience to the mind, quietly nudging our selfish animal nature toward the Source. It quiets the beast by its own divine nature. He wrote:

> Since the relation of the ego (conscious thinking) to the self (soul) is like that of the son to the father, we can say that when the self (soul) calls on us to sacrifice ourselves, it is really carrying out the sacrificial act on itself. We know, more or less, what this act means to us, but what it means to the self is not so clear. As the self (soul) can only be comprehended by us in particular acts, but remains concealed from us as a whole because it is more comprehensive than we are, all we can do is draw conclusions from the little of the self that we can experience."[3]

The brain is limited by the physical limits of its neural capacity. Because the self, or soul, is so much more expansive than our physiology, it is also much wiser and more subtle than the physical brain. The wise mind may nudge us in the direction of sacrifice and love through quiet influence, be it a pang of guilt, a feeling of empathy, or inspiring thought that seemingly comes from nowhere. I have personally experienced disconcerting thoughts and images pop into my mind, leaving me wondering, "Where did that come from?" I have personally noted that these messages enter my mind during critical periods of challenge and growth. They actually seem inserted into my mind rather than being produced by my mind. Consequently, I have tried to listen to God with mindfulness and have acted accordingly within my limited human capacity to love. Not everyone hears these quiet messages, however. When people are constantly tuned into the external, it is unlikely that their minds are tuned to listen to the quiet deep of the wise soul.

The wise soul may assert personal messages in overt ways. Most of the time, however, it uses a more subtle approach by gifting the brain with divine inspiration. Ideas that we readily attribute to the brain may actually come from the spirit. Dr. Alexander notes that all "true-thought" is pre-physical – coming from a spiritual source before it is perceived by the brain. He writes:

> This is the thinking–behind–the–thinking responsible for all the genuinely consequential choices we make in the world. A thinking that is not dependent on linear deduction, but that moves fast as lightning, making connections on different levels, bringing them together. In the face of this free, inner intelligence, our ordinary thought is hopelessly slow and fumbling. It's this thinking that catches the football in the end zone, or that comes up with the inspired scientific insight, or writes the inspired song.[4]

Dr. Alexander appears to be referring to the concept of *insight*, the many "Aha!" moments people experience in life that are normally attributed to flash revelations of creativity. Neuroscientists clearly view insight as a biological brain function, which makes Alexander's comments all the more surprising given his medical training as a neurosurgeon at Harvard. If what Alexander says is true, then several questions come to mind. What percentage of our daily thought derives from the pre-physical? How much of this book, I wonder, might be inspired by divine inspiration? I am reminded of something my father once shared with me. My father is a preeminent leader in the area of plasma physics and optical harmonics. Whenever vexed with a difficult mathematical problem, answers would often be provided through his lucid dreaming. Often, the most difficult theoretical questions would be answered by a professor, such as Albert Einstein, explaining the solution with a blackboard. Could divine inspiration have been working though the collective unconscious of dream? Interestingly, Alexander is not the only NDEr providing support for divine inspiration. Howard Storm, reporting from his NDE, experienced a revelation that God had "inspired" every scientific discovery.[9] If one accepts this revelation to be true, science is not just a gift from man, but a gift to the soul from God.

If divine inspiration is channeled through the spirit, how does one take proper notice? In the spiritual realm we hear God directly. There is no misunderstanding of the message. On earth, the soul must communicate through the biological filters of the human brain. Specifically, we listen through mindfulness, as in the case of meditation, and we speak by prayer. Dr. Eben Alexander explains:

> So, I was communicating directly with God? Absolutely. Expressed that way, it sounds grandiose. But when it was happening, it didn't feel that way. Instead, I felt like I was doing what every soul is able to do when they leave their bodies, and what we can all do right now through various methods of prayer or deep meditation. Communication with God is the most extraordinary experience imaginable yet at the same time it's the most natural one of all, because God is present in us at all times."[4]

What a profound revelation! Many believe that they live alone in a cold, indifferent universe. In reality, everyone is always integrated with God whether they know it or not. Moreover, everyone has the ability to communicate with the divine through the soul. People can do this while living on earth today. This ability will only increase exponentially after we die.

Although we are all children of the divine, God designed our heavenly experience to be different than our earthly experience. The interdependent relationship between the spiritual soul and the human animal was created by divine design. God understands that humans are the product of a long biological development, a history rooted in violent survival instincts, the sexual procreation of the species, and the aggressive acquisition of resources. God knows that we are subject to maladaptive habits that have formed by conditioning. As unseemly as it appears, humans cannot honestly deny their brutish nature. A few have tried, unsuccessfully, by becoming religious hermits. But most of us choose to amble through flawed lives consistent with our baser nature. Consequently, I do not propose that mankind forsake the material. I do propose, however, that human beings can live happier and more spiritual fulfilled lives if they focus more on the internal and less on the external. There needs to be room for the soul in order for the spirit and mind to grow together. Personally, it is my quest to become more aware of self: be in concert with divine plan; live without the fear of death; learn to love other people more fully; be connected with all that is God. I believe this growth will continue as I shift my life balance from the external to the internal.

The present chapter explored various aspects of the soul while living on earth. The bottom line is that we are more than just human animals. Armed with that knowledge, each and every one of us has great spiritual growth potential by attending to the self, or the soul. As Dr. Kübler-Ross aptly points out, "You don't have to do anything except learn to get in touch, in silence, within yourself. Get in touch with your own inner self and learn not to be afraid."[14] But this is not the end of the story. After death, we metamorphose into grand spiritual beings connected with all existence. Prior to the documentation of NDE reports, nebulous definitions of the soul were limited to religious doctrine, individual spiritual belief, and the unconscious self-archetype. That has all changed now that humanity has entered a new era of spiritual discovery. *The search for the everlasting soul!* I can't think of any personal search as meaningful or exciting. In the next chapter, we will explore the defining characteristics of the soul as described by the near-death experience.

CHAPTER FOUR

THE SPLENDID SOUL

D o we have the keys to unlock our soul? Although we may be entrusted with some spiritual awareness, most keys are withheld
until death. As discussed in chapter three, every person can at
least experience a bit of soul through metacognition, mindfulness, and
inspiration. Yet our spiritual potential has an upper limit because our
bodies are grounded in the physical world. Thus, it is difficult to grasp
such a nebulous concept. Yet, some seekers try anyway. From Plato to
Thomas Aquinas, great philosophers and theologians have speculat-
ed about general characteristics of the soul. Although these ancient
works pique the imagination, their assumptions have limited use. Belief
based on speculation, no matter the level of brilliance, remains speculation. People returning from near death, however, are not engaging
in speculation. They are reporting consistent observations about the
nature of the soul because they are reporting from direct experience.
Put more simply, NDErs know the soul because they lived as the soul.
Arriving back to their bodies, they were entrusted with more keys to
their real essence.

Near-death experience reports qualitative changes in our understanding of spirituality. For the first time since the beginning of recorded time, humanity has specific information about the real essence
of the soul from travelers who return from death. Acquiring new data
is like appreciating the difference between a Rembrandt painting and

noticing freeway graffiti. From my perspective, this is not just a routine discovery, but a watershed event in human history. Fundamental questions about our true nature, the purpose of existence, and God, may now be answered.

Why has the near-death experience dramatically changed people's comprehension of the soul at this juncture in time? After all, there have been isolated accounts of near-death experiences across cultures throughout the millennia. Even the ancient Greek philosopher, Plato, described an NDE experienced by a warrior named Er, in his classic writing, *Plato's Republic*.[1] The quick answer is that humanity is finally taking the near-death experience seriously. It has only been within the last thirty years that near-death experience accounts have been documented and studied in a systematic way. Perhaps Raymond Moody's book, *Life after Life*, was the first popular, critical examination of the near-death experience in 1975.[2] The relative objectivity found in Dr. Moody's writing provided credibility to a budding field. As awareness increased, other investigators became likewise motivated to document and research NDE phenomena. But that is not the only explanation. The number of near-death experiences has also dramatically increased with advances in medical technology.

It was only during the 1960's that chest compression, combined with mouth-to-mouth breathing, has become widespread practice. Today, a substantial segment of the public has been trained in cardiopulmonary resuscitation (CPR). Automated external defibrillators (AEDs) are commonplace at the work site and more advanced defibrillator/compression machines are routinely used at hospitals. Amazingly, the very definition of death itself should be reconsidered. Brain cell death occurs naturally about four to five minutes after the heart and breathing stops. With recent advances in resuscitation technology, cells can be revived up to *four hours* after life functioning has ceased. Some hospitals are now using cold packs to enwrap recently deceased patients. The deceased may be revived by pumping a chilled saline solution through their veins providing a thin layer of oxygen to distressed cells.[3] As final death is pushed back further, scientists must delineate partial death by cardiac arrest from permanent death.[3]

It seems incredible that death has been pushed back from minutes to hours. There are important spiritual implications to these medical advancements. As more people become revived, an increasing number of people are reporting near-death experiences. Furthermore, I suspect that longer dips into death may also produce deeper near-death experiences.

With the abundance of NDEs, investigators are finally asking, "What does the soul mean?" NDE researchers have started to answer this question by interpreting objective evidence. However, research, although crucial, needs to be balanced by subjective analysis. First-hand NDE accounts provide rich, experiential understanding of the soul that cannot be captured by statistics. In this chapter, we will examine many specific qualities of the soul. First, we will explore the nature of a spiritual body followed by the experience of a universe-sized soul. Next, we will discuss the personality and emotional attributes of the soul. Let's first begin by looking at the spiritual realm as the soul's home.

Coming Home

The concept of home strikes a pleasant emotional chord for most people. These words prompt images of safety, comfort, nostalgia, and peace. Personally, the daily experience of home grounds me by diverting my attention from the uncertainties of life. I feel most relaxed reading in my bed, playing the piano, hugging my wife, or spending time with my son. Home serves not only a place of residence, but as a place of origin. The American culture is part of my natural habitat, for better or worse. For me, moving to a non-Western culture would feel unnatural. I am not alone in this perception. On average, it takes two generations for a family to assimilate to an unfamiliar culture[4] The human being can certainly adapt to unfamiliar habitats, but it usually takes time and effort.

The physical body is another type of home. Human tissues define the only bodily home I know. Hypothetically, I would probably feel lost and lonely if I suddenly was transformed into an alien living on another planet. Perhaps I would never adapt to such a radical change. Yet, most NDErs report feeling completely at home when they die, despite radical transformation from physical body to pure spirit. How can that be, when all they knew of existence was human life? The answer involves being 'home.' Specifically, the spiritual realm is our natural habitat, place of origin, and ultimate residence. While living on earth, we are just spiritual beings having a human experience.

The NDEr quickly realizes that he or she has returned home after having crossed over. There are no words to adequately explain this incredible experience from the human point of reference. Yet, NDErs describe this altered reality as real and natural. From the NDERF website, one NDEr wrote:

The feeling of being in His presence was something that felt like I was 'home' – in a sense that I have never known." (NDERF #2301).

In her book, *Dying to be Me*, Anita Moorjani communicates with her deceased father after death. She tells him, "Dad, it feels like I've come home! I'm so glad to be here. Life is so painful!"[5]

The moment after the body dies, consciousness exits the body in a seamless, natural transformation. The transformation is so seamless that the deceased may not immediately realize they have died. Most realize a radical change when they see themselves float above their body. Typically, they watch circumstances unfold below, often a chaotic scene marked by frantic resuscitation efforts conducted by medical personnel or pedestrians. Despite the chaos, few NDErs are alarmed by their own death and transition into spirit. Rather, they peer down with mild detachment. Some even report a sense of relief and liberation from pain, especially those wracked with advanced age or debilitating illness. Relatedly, one NDEr wrote:

> There was a strong suction coming from the top of my head (like a vacuum) and an absolute sense of relief. There was no longer a need to breathe, and no feeling of being drugged on the medication. (NDERF #2386)

Anita Moorjani, living years in pain from cancer of the lymphoma, celebrated release from bodily confinement when she transformed into spirit:

> Wow, this is incredible! I feel so free and light! What's going on? I've never felt this good! There are no more tubes, no more wheelchair. I can move around freely now without any help! And my breathing is no longer labored - how amazing this is!... I felt no emotional attachment to my seemingly lifeless body as it lay there on the hospital bed.[5]

One NDEr described her initial feelings associated with death in this manner:

> I was surprised at how comfortable I was, and how easy it was to die. It all happened within a couple of minutes. I said to myself, "Huh, I thought that one was supposed to last longer," and headed up in a light cloud. It felt so perfect. I felt like I was going home and I felt

comfortable and joyous with no doubts at all. It was like every cell of my body was happy and light. (NDERF #2834)

Based on these and other testimonials, the final act of dying is not scary in the least. How comforting is the knowledge that death is easy and natural. Death is not the arrival of a grim reaper, but rather a welcoming portal leading home. The NDEr's understanding of death provides hope for a brighter future and alleviates humanity of its deepest fear.

I have observed that some people fixate on death in an unhealthy way. Their fixation does not represent a process of positive liberation, but rather a psychological defense against fear. People often pretend to have power over things they cannot control. Perhaps death is the greatest uncontrolled power; humans will never have final jurisdiction over physical death. In an effort to control fear, sometimes people pretend to have power over life by taunting death and embracing the darkness. Look at the surrounding popular culture. How many people are drawn to horror movies, serial killer novels, or violent video games? How many people wear tee shirts imprinted with skulls? Existentialist psychologists, like Irvin Yalom and Ernest Becker, theorize that taunting death conceals unconscious anxiety about nothingness and meaninglessness. If so, this may not be the healthiest way to handle mortality. To fixate on death means to miss out on the positive gifts of life. To fixate on death disregards our eternal future. People who have near-death experiences teach us that we have nothing to fear about going home. They paint a beautiful portrait of eternal life filled with peace and purpose.

The Spiritual Body

The concept of a spiritual body is not new. In the Western tradition, many Christians reference the Bible for the existence of a spiritual body after death. For instance, the author Paul wrote, "If there is a natural body, there is also a spiritual body. So it is written: 'The first man Adam became a living being, the last Adam, a life-giving spirit'" (First Corinthians 15:44-45, New International Version). Paul's description is echoed by NDE reports. However, the Bible lacks the level of specificity that NDErs report when defining the spiritual body. To illustrate, NDErs often report that the spiritual body is made of an energy pattern existing beyond the physical senses. The spiritual body varies in appearance, ranging from bright white energy to vibrant colors of energy. One NDEr described the spiritual body this way:

> I looked down to see my body as to find out why they would not acknowledge me with a glance, when I realized I had no body to look at, no torso, legs or feet, I was looking straight down at the sand, I raised my arms to view them, and no arms were seen by me, but it did not alarm me in any way, I just felt energy, and I liked it. (NDERF #2368)

One NDEr reported that she examined her body while traveling in the tunnel:

> I didn't see my hands or feet, I just felt like I was a being of pulsating energy, sliding around. The feeling would be similar to being on a water slide, but sliding up instead of sliding down. (NDERF #3098)

Another NDEr saw herself outlined in nebulous form:

> I had something similar to my body but it was made of a transparent and milky substance. Like ghosts are described, with a slight glow. (NDERF #2521)

NDErs often describe meeting other spiritual beings. These spiritual beings usually appear as bright colored orbs of energy. From a distance, multitudes of spiritual beings appear like stars, even galaxies. The following NDEr wrote:

> These lights I took to be stars. That is to say that here we would ordinarily refer to them as stars. Their colors were more various than I have ever seen in an ordinary night-sky. But there, these 'stars' were something else. They were beings and they were utterly conscious. (NDERF #3253)

One NDEr noted a colored structure to spiritual beings:

> When I looked around I realized there were many beings around me. They appeared to be in a luminous fog with a gold core close to the top, a thin lucent pale greenish gold around the edges and had a wispy tail like bottom. As a group they all seemed to enjoy their existence very much. (NDERF #2139)

A body made from a pattern of energy represents a radical departure from the physical design of human flesh and blood. The entire field of neuropsychology is based on studying the physical brain. The brain is by far the most complex organ in the human body. In fact, there are over a hundred billion neurons in the brain.[6] Yet, the spiritual design allows for much greater thought and ability. The design of the soul remains mysterious, in part, because it is intricate beyond our human comprehension. Despite the radical change in design, transition into the spiritual state feels seamless because consciousness, intelligence, personality, and other primary attributes of the self remains intact. Using a crude computer analogy, there almost seems to be some sort of "download" from one mode of existence to another. Whatever the mechanism, we basically remain who we are after death. Let's read what some NDErs share about their continuous essence of self. The following NDEr reported:

> I retained the ability to think, just as I usually did, and I was actually still talking to myself." (NDERF #3098)

A spiritual guide helped another NDEr recognize her spiritual body after a moment of confusion. She wrote:

> Before me was a liquid pool of white, yet, it also appeared to be a mirror. I was completely mesmerized. Colors, brilliant colors were everywhere. I was an array of beautiful moving, shimmering, vibrating, colors. He came closer and said, "Do you understand now?" I realized I was pure energy, spirit, and part of a flowing consciousness; while still remaining 'Denise.' (NDERF #2658)

There are serious implications regarding the continuation of self into the spiritual realm. People cannot escape their earthly choices, whether they involve spiritual corruption, stagnation, or growth. As will be discussed in later chapters, continuity does not necessitate punishment from God. Rather, it means that each individual grows toward the divine at his or her own pace. Spiritual development, although variable, probably requires more than a brief lifetime. Many people maintain a preconceived belief in heavenly perfection. Although this may be generally consistent with the NDE experience, the human idea of perfection may be different than spiritual perfection. The typical human view of perfection perceives that there is only one best way of acting.

Specifically, there is only one course of action free of fault, sin, or imperfection. In such a system, there can be no variety, change, creativity, or development. If one thinks about heaven in this way, the perfect song, conversation, game would never alter. Every choice would repeat in a cycle of eternal tedium.

I doubt that all souls play the same, perfect, harp song over again in heaven. Likewise, God doesn't wave a magic wand to transform newly deceased people into perfect servants. The repetitive nature of perfection negates exploration, creativity, and self-determination. NDErs report that God is a creative force. Individual growth, based on self-determination, represents an extension of a larger creative plan. By expressing free will, souls choose to either grow or stagnate throughout time in both the material and spiritual realms. Souls respond differently when they first cross over. Some may respond favorably, especially those who embrace challenge, growth, and autonomy. Alternatively, others may initially experience some apprehension, particularly if they are failing to grow as intended on earth. In either case, people cannot escape the eternal imprint of their life choices. Everything we do becomes engraved into the tapestry of existence. Because every choice is self-determined over time, every individual is unique. Based on these first-hand NDE accounts, our uniqueness derives from our personal identity, experience, personality, and emotional style. Let's review each of these personal elements that we take with us into life after death.

Personal Identity

Personal identity is partly a classification system. People define themselves by what is most important to them. To illustrate, personal identity might include one's chosen profession, marital status, religion, personal beliefs, or hobbies. Identity usually derives from a combination of sources. For example, identity may be adopted from one's family, directed by culture, or be self-generated. These classifications are the standard by which people evaluate themselves, usually in categories of good or bad. In psychotherapy, a client's self-esteem may be bolstered by learning how to assess personal attributes more accurately. Depressed patients, for instance, often self-evaluate too harshly. Cognitive psychologists theorize that a harsh, negative style derives from the faulty processing of information. To illustrate, Aaron Beck[7] notes six types of thinking errors:

1. Drawing conclusions without evidence
2. Making decisions based on incomplete information
3. Drawing a general conclusion on singular incidents
4. Magnifying or minimizing the significance of a situation
5. Personalizing external events
6. To see the world in absolute black and white categories

Just about everyone can recognize faulty thinking in their life. Yet some people skew their thinking so profoundly that they no longer like themselves. Depressed people may become so overwhelmed by problems that they do not see the positive in others nor, more importantly, in themselves. By judging themselves in an irrational way, they lose sight of their worth and true spiritual identity; they do not comprehend that their inherent worth is interwoven within the divine tapestry. Developing an accurate, positive identity on earth becomes critically important because identity is carried into the spiritual realm. If a person refuses to honestly face themselves in life, they will have to do it in heaven. NDErs report that God, or other spiritual beings, challenge distorted thinking through a life review process. Every aspect of one's action is reviewed, not only from the conscious perspective of the reviewer, but from the perspective of everyone involved. One NDEr from the NDERF website describes the life review in this manner:

One of the first things I remember experiencing was the life review--which included everything that I'd experienced in my physical incarnation up to that point. It was like being at the cinema - watching a movie of my life and everything happening simultaneously. I think most NDErs will agree that the life review is one of the most difficult aspects of the NDE. Viewing your entire life before you - with every thought, word, action, etc., can be most unsettling indeed. Yet, what happened was the fact that no one passed judgement on me! I only felt the constant enveloping of divine love from the Being of Light that was always with me. What I came to realise then, is that we judge ourselves! There was no 'he-god' sitting on some throne, passing judgement on me. (NDERF #364)

The life review serves as the ultimate learning experience. Irrational beliefs are corrected by an irrefutable examination of the evidence. Sometimes the life content is expounded on by God, Jesus, or an important spiritual being. It is a system of complete honesty, so there is no place for denials, rationalizations, minimizing, inventing devastations, or other human acts of bending the truth. Although the life review is a type of confrontation, it is a gentle confrontation with a balanced focus on the negative and the positive. How much negative and positive aspects are shown will mirror the life that the person had lived. Moreover, the review is done in an atmosphere of safety and love. For the NDEr, the goal of the life review is to learn and grow. There is no external judgment or punishment. Only the NDEr will judge him or herself in order to learn to do better. Some may want to make major adjustments in redefining life goals. A change in personal identity may be in order. Others may want to make changes in their behavior that is more consistent with their life goals. Realigning behavior in concordance with personal identity may be in order.

The life review is a critical part of the near-death experience. Due to the impact on other topics, we will revisit the life review process later in the book. For now, it is important to recognize that our earthly existence is tied to a grand plan for personal development. However, the development of personal identity does not end at death. NDErs also report that our personal identity will continuously be refined, in a spiral of lessons, for eternity. The more we become aware of our true self, now or later, the faster a soul grows toward the divine. Piece by piece, the soul matures into a higher state of being, usually in qualitative step increases. It is a somewhat like a boyfriend taking on the big commitment of marriage. The identity of a husband requires greater maturity than the identity of a boyfriend. Likewise, the soul becomes more in sync with the divine identity in a stepwise fashion. During each step, the soul grows, not only in maturity, but also by redefining identity. It does so in a cumulative way based on the continuity of its own unique, history.

Personal Experience of the NDE

The interpretation and quality of the NDE is filtered by life involvement. Cognitive psychologists have developed a useful and related concept called *schema*. A schema is the mental structure of preconceived ideas learned through past experience.[7] These experiences may be influenced by friendships, family, religion, culture, and so forth. New ideas are filtered through a set framework of pre-existing beliefs. Thus, people often interpret or slant new information to fit their preconceptions. For instance, a person riding an elevator might become angry if a stranger strikes his or her leg with a stick. His or her automatic thoughts, filtered by their schema of being hit, might be, "I am in danger. I need to respond with anger." Suppose the individual turns and discovers that a blind man accidentally hit their leg with a walking cane. This would be an example of how information can be misinterpreted through faulty schema. Have you ever considered why people interpret a presidential debate so differently? Each person has a different set schema based on their own unique set of experiences in life. Schemas provide order to a chaotic world and allow people to make fast decisions with little thought. Unfortunately, accuracy is sacrificed for quick simplicity.

During near-death experiences, NDErs partly draw on their past life experiences to make sense of their new surroundings. However, that does not presume that NDErs are using faulty schema in the spiritual realm. Spiritual beings communicate and perceive with complete clarity; misunderstandings are quickly corrected. The problem arises *after* the spirit returns to its physical host back on earth. Specifically, NDErs must rely on the limited, physical brain to describe their experience in the spiritual realm. This can be a difficult and frustrating undertaking. Dr. Eben Alexander describes his frustration in explaining what he learned in the spiritual realm. He wrote about his frustration using the following metaphor:

> This doesn't mean, however that I can explain them to you. That's because – paradoxically – I am still in the process of understanding them myself... Conveying that knowledge now is rather like being a chimpanzee becoming a human for a single day to experience all of the wonders of human knowledge, and then returning to one's chimp friends and trying to tell them what it was like knowing several different Romance languages, the calculus, and the immense scale of the universe.[8]

It is my impression that the vast majority of NDErs are trying to convey their near-death experience as accurately as possible. Yet, NDErs return to mortal life without fully comprehending the complexity of the spiritual realm. Some report losing access to many of their memories. When interpreting NDE accounts, the reader should account for the limitations and structure of the human brain. This is why NDErs interpret their near-death experience somewhat subjectively, even though all the near-death experience elements are the same regardless of race, age, religion, or culture. For instance, both Anita Moorjani and Howard Storm understood that they were interconnected with the entire universe. Moorjani, a Hindu, interpreted this interconnection in terms of the Atman joining Brahman, or the real inner self becoming incorporated into the reality of One. Storm, a Christian, interpreted his interconnection as being an integral part of God's grand design. Both interpretations share the universal element of interconnectedness. But their interpretation of interconnectedness was influenced by different religious schemas. Namely, each interpreted reality was based on their unique learning and experiences from the physical world. That is not necessarily a 'bad thing.' It is my impression that most of these interpretations have strong merit; they are just different facets of a larger, complex truth. Perhaps Moorjani and Storm's interpretations can be likened to touching an elephant blindfolded. One says, "An elephant is a trunk" and the other says, "No, an elephant is an ear." Both are correct.

Personality

NDErs report that their personality remains intact in the spiritual realm. Personality can be defined as various repeating patterns of behavior, be it emotions, attitudes, or actions. Clearly, it is a very broad concept that captures much of our individuality. So broad, in fact, that personality overlaps with the concepts we just explored, such as identity and personal experience. Interestingly, there is a fair amount of research suggesting that behavior is more situation specific rather than trait specific.[9] Despite such conclusions, it seems evident that people tend to repeat individualized patterns of behavior that define their uniqueness. Think of a spouse or close family member responding differently than you do to situations, either to your liking or not.

On earth, the development of personality is influenced by both environmental and genetic factors. Genetics often dictates the upper and lower limits of personality, whereas environment fills in much of the rest. Perhaps the soul becomes integrated with human biology in order to develop personality. After all, God does not want duplicated robots in heaven. In order to develop a patterned response to aversion, the soul needs to experience pain. To develop a patterned response to grief, the soul needs to experience loss. To develop a patterned response to conflict, the soul needs to experience hurt. And so forth. Despite the soul's power, heaven is a structured place where good and evil do not mix. It is a great place to feel and express love. But it may not be a great place to develop one's individual personality through adversity and adaptive change. That is why souls are sent to the material realm in the first place; earth serves as a learning ground that shapes personal development and personality.

Humans exist as a part of God consciousness. Yet, we are still unique based on our qualities shaped over time and experience. Collectively, our personalities make a rich tapestry for the entire conscious universe. That is not to say, however, that we must maintain parts of our personality inconsistent with the Source. Just like personal identity, our personality developed on earth represents one piece of the puzzle that adds to our unique mosaic. There are parts of our personality that may be less consistent with the divine. It is our mission to refine these inconsistent aspects of personality.

Emotions

NDErs report that they carry all of their earthly emotions into heaven. I find this a little surprising since human emotions are mediated by a primitive region in the brain called the limbic system. Most animals, including reptiles, developed their limbic system to enhance the chance for survival in a violent world. For example, aggression helps the crocodile to kill the human for food just as fear helps the human escape the hungry crocodile. However, emotions serve a more complex role in humans. For instance, human emotions are influenced by symbolic thinking. Research conducted by Shachter and Singer[10] suggests that our thinking plays a role in how we feel. Specifically, they theorized that people experience general arousal when faced with undefinable situations. Emotions are often felt later, after a person interprets the situation. For example, you may feel quite startled after hearing a loud boom. How you feel about that boom will depend on whether you see a destructive explosion or a fireworks display. Unfortunately, our emotions can be in error when we label circumstances incorrectly, especially when we do not know all the facts. Psychologists call these types of thinking mistakes *misattributions*. Compounding the emotional deficiency on earth, the limbic system has difficulty regulating emotional intensity. As most know firsthand, reason becomes impaired when our emotions become too strong. Unfortunately, even the best intentioned person sometimes loses control and says something that hurts another.

In reading many near-death experience accounts, it seems that the more positive emotions take precedence over negative emotions, especially as NDErs transition further into the spiritual realm. There is little need, for instance, for primitive "fight or flight" emotions of fear and aggression, since nothing can harm the soul. There seems to be no need for anger either, with the possible exception of anger directed toward injustices on earth. Interestingly, a few NDErs have acknowledged expressions of anger during their NDE. However, I have not read any NDEr reports that they experienced hate during a positive NDE. NDErs report that the predominant emotions felt in life after death included bliss, joy, compassion, and love. Unlike most negative emotions, positive emotions are difficult to define because they are very complex and entwined with thinking. Can love be defined as a feeling? Or, is love actually a decision based on friendship, respect, and sacrifice? It is likely all of the above.

Individuals are emotional beings in both the material and spiritual realms. Although many human emotions emanate from relatively primitive brain structures, they apparently have great spiritual value. They seem to greatly enhance the quality of conscious existence. Personally, I think life would seem flavorless without experiencing deep feeling. Although emotional categories are basically the same, they are experienced very differently in heaven than on earth. On earth, emotions are a byproduct of brain physiology, yet are experienced by consciousness, or soul. Emotions enhance communication, whether in a simple conversation, or in life or death situations. However, the experience of emotional feeling on earth is limited to internal experience. Others may infer our emotions indirectly through a series of visual cues: facial expressions, tears, verbal outburst, etc. Yet, our emotions can only be felt by us. In the spiritual realm, emotions are shared by an interconnected awareness between spiritual beings. In other words, emotions are felt directly by our own experience and by other souls. Thus, the NDEr report feeling exactly what other spirits are feeling, and vice-versa. Differences between earthly and heavenly emotions are actually quite profound, as described here by Dr. Eben Alexander:

> Emotions are different up there. All the human emotions are present, but they're deeper, more spacious – they're not just inside but outside as well. Imagine that every time your mood changed here on earth the

weather changed instantly along with it. That your tears would bring on a torrential down-pour and your joy would make the clouds instantly disappear. That gives a hint of how much more vast and consequential changes of mood feel like up there, how strangely and powerfully what we think of as "inside" and "outside" don't really exist at all.[8]

Many people view emotions to be the very heart of our being. Dr. Alexander describes spiritual emotions as vast and powerful. If emotions on earth are like a mild seasoning, then emotions in heaven would be like eating a hot pepper. Experiencing and expressing emotions after death will certainly spice-up the spiritual life.

Interestingly, when NDErs encounter "seasoned" spirits that have long made full transition into death, they do not appear to express anger or any other negative emotions based on all of my readings. Some NDErs make the same conclusion from their first-hand experiences. The following NDEr wrote:

There was one major being of love and many other beings of love with actual personhood or souls. I could not see much but light and vague outlines. There was nothing but love, goodness, truth, and all things to do with love with NO ROOM for fear or evil or anything but this love. (NDERF #1993)

Another wrote more succinctly:

These souls, our souls, cannot experience certain things like pain, sorrow, hatred, and anger. (NDERF #1634)

Seasoned souls have fully transitioned to the spiritual realm. They are fully interconnected with the divine and have access to universal knowledge. They do not make mistakes in labeling emotions through misattribution like people do on earth. Thus, emotions expressed in heaven are appropriate to each and every situation and are consistent with divine purpose.

Perhaps another reason seasoned souls do not experience negative emotions is because they have obtained a higher spiritual level or frequency vibration. What does spiritual vibration mean? Unfortunately, spiritual vibration becomes a difficult concept to describe without having a common point of reference. Yet, NDErs consistently claim that they can sense another spirit's personality by perceiving their frequency and output of energy. Although this may seem odd at first, remember that spiritual beings are entirely composed of energy. One NDEr noticed a vibration, or muted hum, when she came across other spiritual beings. She wrote:

> The only way to describe it was the beat vibration of higher muted hum that resonated. I came to know that there are many different vibrations of afterlife. All are "good" just different depending on how you lived your earth life. (NDERF #2381)

Another made an association between higher and lower frequency qualities consistent with the Source. She wrote:

> I also came to an understanding that heaven isn't a place you are admitted to but it is a frequency that you attain. I understood that you take yourself with you everywhere you go. What must change in order to experience the higher frequencies of love, peace, joy, bliss and the tranquility I was a part of in that experience, is a person's own consciousness. (NDERF #2301)

Different energy frequencies, or vibrations, are fascinating in that they have little earthly precedent. However, it is interesting to speculate about isolated reports of colorful energy fields around other people. This energy field is called an *aura*. Perhaps seeing an aura may have connective relevance to the spiritual realm. In any case, NDErs report that all living beings function at different vibration levels. The higher frequencies seem to be associated with God-like qualities. Accordingly, one NDEr wrote an impressive account about the relationship between her vibration in heaven and on earth. The NDEr actually requested that God return her to earth because she wanted to raise her own vibration level through spiritual growth. She wrote:

> I received the understanding that I was the one who removed myself from the benefits and bliss of love by the anger I felt over some experiences I had growing up. I saw how important it is to project feelings of love instead of the energy I was projecting through my emotions and feelings about life. I saw how others either benefit from my energy or they are negatively affected by it... I only wanted to come back because I understood that my consciousness at the time didn't mesh with the unconditional love I was experiencing. Therefore I knew

that although it wasn't intended as punishment, I couldn't maintain that frequency that was allowing me to feel the bliss temporarily. I knew that somehow, I had to raise my vibration and become more loving in order to experience this indescribable love on a permanent basis. (NDERF #2301)

I find it most fascinating that she believed that her bliss could not be maintained indefinitely. Her report appears to be a rare NDE insight. If corroborated by others, it would add an important dimension to understanding the spiritual realm. Specifically, her experience would strongly support the premise that spiritual development is a continuous process across both the earthly and spiritual realms.

The Power of Knowledge

Death has always loomed as the ultimate unknown. Fear of non-existence plagues even the faithful. Therefore, any knowledge about the soul negates this natural fear. Describing and naming abstractions gives ideas shape and texture; it transforms a nebulous idea into something real. It is the difference between saying, "I heard about the existence of this most amazing flower" and personally describing the most amazing flower from petal to stem. This is the case with the soul. With the power of knowledge, the NDE understanding of the soul gives people hope and faith over non-existence. In this chapter, we have reviewed the fundamental nature of the soul. We have learned that the soul represents a new spiritual body made of energy. We have learned that each individual takes their core attributes into the spiritual realm, be it memories, identity, personality, and emotions. Armed with this knowledge, people can, in fact, actually look forward to death as a new mode of splendid existence rather than an event surrounded by sorrow, anxiety, and fear.

In the next chapter, we will continue discussing attributes of the soul. The topic will change by us exploring the soul's newfound capabilities in the spiritual realm; we will examine enhanced perception, perfect communication, and grand intelligence. Indeed, the splendid universe-sized soul exists as an amazing being of power and intelligence. Perhaps the most exciting part is that this splendid soul exists as both you and me.

CHAPTER FIVE

GOD'S OWN OPEN ROAD

God's open road travels in all directions. There are crossroads at every angle, leading to almost anywhere. In life after physical death, the soul can choose from infinite possibilities by using amazing spiritual abilities. Spiritual beings express magnificence because they are interconnected with the entire fabric of creation. It is understandable why many scoff at such a proposition. After all, it is difficult for humans, limited in intelligence and isolated from each other, to comprehend themselves within a context of united splendor. On earth, the body is a biological machine. It is easy to ascribe human attributes to the divine because the material world is all we know and remember. Look at Renaissance art. God is represented as an old, bearded, muscular, man. Angels have wings. The devil is represented as a skinny, red man, sporting a monkey tail and antelope horns. Yet, spiritual beings are nothing like material humans or animals living on earth. They are beings of energy interconnected with everything. In this chapter, we will explore what it is like to exist as spiritual beings. First, we will explore the complexity and ramifications of interconnectedness. Next, we will describe specific interconnected soul abilities, such as perception and communication. Lastly, we will explore the spiritual beings' access to universal knowledge.

Oneness of Being

Imagine that you are interconnected with everywhere, everything, and everyone. On a whim you could instantaneously see everything, know anything, or be anywhere. Not even the most powerful super-heroes or mythological gods had that kind of power. Yet, NDErs state that they displayed that kind of ability, limited only by the structure of divine rule. Anita Moorjani shares her experience of being a liberated soul. She writes:

> I continued to sense myself expanding further and further outward, drawing away from my physical surroundings. It was as though I were no longer restricted by the confines of space and time, and continued to spread myself out to occupy a greater expanse of consciousness. I felt a sense of freedom and liberation that I'd never experienced in my physical life before.[1]

Interconnectedness is a common theme shared by thousands of NDErs, especially those who have had deep, complex, near-death experiences. Many comprehend the minuteness of their brief, isolated, materialist existence on earth. Correspondingly, some NDErs become less bonded to earthly connections, especially material attachments, during their near-death experience. Decrease in attachment even carries over, to a lesser degree, to physical life after they return. Earthly aspirations are of no consequence to the eternal, interconnected soul. Temporal things that have meaning to humans - the coveted job promotion, the beach vacation, the NBA playoffs – are inconsequential. Perhaps this funeral rite sums it all up, "Ashes to ashes, dust to dust." Not only do these haunting words apply to our physical body, but to the entire physical world that so many cherish on earth. Having a big diamond ring, for instance, has no meaning to an interconnected being of energy. An NDEr wrote about her new perspective while in heaven:

> I realized that the entirety of my life had just been a game, like Monopoly (guess I just passed Go and collected $200.00!!), and "Pam" was the equivalent of one of the game's playing pieces, like the shoe or the car! All the troubles and joys, the accomplishments and limitations that made up the story of my life were revealed to be mere dust - an illusion. I realized that in truth, the 'I Am' was who I really was and ALWAYS had been and always would be. (NDERF #2356)

As NDErs go deeper into death, many learn that physical life on earth was not "a game", but an important growth experience. It is understandable, however, why this NDEr interpreted earthly life as a game or an illusion. Human life represents a meager, brief existence compared to that of a powerful, eternal soul. The difference is not just academic for the NDEr. They have directly experienced the discrepancy between the corporal illusion of meaning and the spiritual truth interconnected with all creation. By knowing the complexity of eternity, earthly prized possessions become trinkets, power plays seem petty, media gossip seems superficial, aggression appears mean, and control seems self-defeating. Adapting back to earth can be difficult, especially for those who had been steeped in self-centered, materialistic lives. I knew a coworker who had been resuscitated after dying from a heart attack. Prior to his heart attack, I recall him telling crude jokes, cussing, partying with buddies, looking to buy the next thing, and teasing his friends and coworkers. After his heart attack, the man presented as quiet and isolated. One day, he informally asked to have a word with me and another psychologist. He shared that he had a near-death experience and was having difficulty adjusting back to daily life. Namely, he could not find pleasure in the material world anymore and his wife could not understand why he wanted to die and leave her so that he could return to heaven.

It is difficult for the NDEr to share such transcendent views of existence, such as interconnectedness, with people who only understand existence from a material frame of reference. My coworker didn't try. For him, a boundless existence free from material anchors was largely inexplicable. Many other NDErs stumble to adequately capture the divine, even when using earthly metaphors. Following a probable near-death experience, the Apostle Paul shares his difficulty with sharing while writing to the church in Corinth:

> I know a man in Christ who fourteen years ago was caught up in the third heaven (beyond Earth's atmosphere where God exists). Whether it was in the body or out of the body I do not know – God knows. And I know that this man – whether in the body or apart from the body I do not know, but God knows – was caught up to paradise. He heard inexpressible things, things that man is not permitted to tell. I will boast about a man like that, but I will not boast about myself, except about my weaknesses. (2 Corinthians, 12:1-5)

It is likely that Paul was reporting a near-death experience from his first missionary journey in Lystra, Turkey. It was there, fourteen years earlier, that Paul was stoned to brief death by the resident Jews (Acts 14:19). Paul's use of the words "inexpressible things" probably relates to his own difficulty expressing the spiritual experience in the pre-scientific languages of his day. Paul's words, "forbidden to tell" likely relates to his realistic fear of rigid, orthodox religion that resulted in him being stoned in the first place.

There appears to be greater tolerance of different spiritual beliefs in the Western world today than two thousand years ago. The NDEr can share his or her experience from a wider world view, be it using Eastern philosophy, Western philosophy, religion, and science. Some have made the effort to capture challenging aspects of their near-death experiences, such as interconnectedness, without having a corresponding point of reference on earth. Dr. Alexander makes a good attempt. Regarding interconnectedness, he wrote:

> From my present perspective, I would suggest that you couldn't look at anything in that world at all, for the word at itself implies a separation that did not exist there. Everything was distinct, yet everything was also part of everything else, like the rich and intermingled design on a Persian carpet...or a butterfly.[2]

Although NDErs, like Alexander, can provide some understanding of the concept of interconnectedness through description and metaphor, their explanations can be enhanced by another modern avenue of knowledge, namely physics.

The Interconnection of Subatomic Particles

Nobel Prize winning physicist, Stephen Hawking, noted that everything in the universe, even light and gravity, are made up of particles at the most elemental level.[3]

Likewise, NDEr's indicate that the soul is made up of particle energy interconnected with existence. Without separation of matter, NDEr's state that we impact the universe directly and that the universe likewise impacts us. One NDEr wrote:

> It was very apparent that every single thought, word, and action affects everything around us and indeed the entire universe. (NDERF #2366)

How can humans possibly affect the entire universe and the entire universe affect us? Remarkably, many NDErs report that the entire universe is a conscious part of God. God is in everything and everything is in God. Although we maintain our individuality, people are also part of the entire conscious creation that makes up the totality of God. The universe is composed of energy organized into structure as manifested by God's own conscious thought. In other words, the universe is the expression of God's creative and conscious existence. God is not a white-bearded superman sitting on a golden throne in heaven, as some portray. In essence, God *is* the universe. God *is* the One and the Source. Because this point is so critical in understanding the nature of reality, I have included a sample of NDE reports, from different angles, describing the entire universe as the interconnected essence of God:

> The entire universe, in which I was now lying and beginning to observe, was completely and utterly aware. All of it is conscious. (NDERF #3253)

> I became ONE with ALL IN EXISTENCE, yet, I had a firm knowing that I was me. (NDERF #3291)

> I had that Knowing that there was the essence or spark of the Highest (as I'll refer to 'God') in EVERYTHING - in every atom, mineral, vegetable, animal, human, and beyond. I just knew that the Highest waited within everything to expand and create and grow and experience. (NDERF #2386)

> God is in the present moment, completely accessible, and it only requires a willingness to turn within to reveal Him as the very fabric of everything and every moment. (NDERF #2356)

> As for God - my experience of Oneness left me with the knowledge that all is God and God is in all things. To speak of "a" God or "a" Supreme Being is to imply a separateness that doesn't reflect my experience. (NDERF #2365)

People during Paul's era lacked the necessary scientific sophistication to understand the mathematical underpinnings of interconnectedness. Today, we can better grasp the concept of interconnectedness through theoretical physics, particularly quantum mechanics. The study of quantum mechanics involves studying the nature of subatomic particles, the tiniest building blocks that fill and construct the entire universe. The universe of the very small is completely different than the macroscopic universe that we perceive. Action at the subatomic level involves the interplay of a seemingly bizarre set of physical principles that include probability, entanglement, and the conscious influence on matter.

Mechanical forces can be mathematically described through the laws of classical physics. By understanding these laws, scientists can successfully land a probe on Mars 249 million kilometers away from earth.[4] The subatomic world is different. "Spooky action" is how Einstein described subatomic activity. The term "spooky" was coined due to the inexplicable manner in which atomic particles behave. Quantum research has consistently demonstrated that charged subatomic particles - electrons, neutrons, or protons - exist in a wave form until they are observed by a conscious being. Prior to observation, these particles do not have any physical attributes such as position, momentum, or direction of spin. Once the light wave is observed or measured, only then does the wave "collapse" into a particle. The particle can potentially collapse into an infinite number of locations. The final location of the collapse is based on probability.[5] Another quantum action, called the Zeno effect, indicates that these subatomic particles will never decay as long as they are observed.[5] In other words, conscious thought changes reality at the subatomic level.

Another astonishing aspect of quantum physics involves the concept of entanglement. When two electrons split from an atom, their spin has no definite direction until measured. When measured, their spin will always be opposite of each other. Quantum physicists then say that the two particles are "entwined." Opposite spin is an event that instantaneously occurs with measurement. Amazingly, distance is irrelevant. Quantum research has consistently demonstrated that two electrons will have the opposite spin, when observed, whether they are an inch apart or millions of light years apart.[6] This means that these electrons impact each other even though there is no known physical mechanism to cause any interaction between the two distant particles. Specifically, there is no known physical force, such as gravity, that would cause one electron to instantaneously affect another electron separated by millions of light years.

These and other quantum mechanical principles may have possible ramifications to the spiritual realm and the near-death experience. Quantum mechanics suggest that the particle-based existence of the universe depends on conscious thought. Furthermore, conscious thought can instantaneously influence the subatomic universe, no matter the distance. These quantum principles seem to be consistent with the interconnectedness of the universe described by NDErs, who also describe themselves as particle beings of energy. Quantum mechanics may also help describe the amazing instantaneous abilities of spiritual beings, which we will describe shortly in this chapter. It also could give context to how many NDErs report that every aspect of the universe is alive with God consciousness. In fact, without God consciousness, one might theorize that particles could not collapse into existence in the first place. If that is so, then nothing can exist without God.

Attributing sentience to daily, non-animate, physical structures appears quite foreign and counterintuitive. Yet, people can only observe a very narrow segment of three-dimensional reality. We do not see the universe through the subatomic quantum world. Nor do we see the universe from a point of interconnectedness. Along these lines, Dr. Alexander learned about the subatomic connectedness from divine beings in the spiritual realm. He wrote:

> We see the universe as a place full of separate objects (tables and chairs, people and plants) that occasionally interact with each other, but that nonetheless remain essentially separate. On the subatomic level, however, this universe of separate objects turns out to be a complete illusion. In the realm of the super-super small every object in the physical universe is intimately connected with every other object. In fact, there are really no objects in the world, at all, only vibrations of energy, and relationships.[2]

Interestingly, Alexander did not learn that the universe was operating under a system of divine miracles. Rather, he saw everything worked within the realm of science. He shared, "I feel confident in saying that, while I didn't know the term at the time, while in the Gateway and in the Core, I was actually 'doing science'."[2]

Quantum physicists have primarily studied subatomic action from energy producing objects, like stars. But what about quantum action in life forms? New discoveries have found that life forms may also act on quantum principles through the action of photosynthesis. In the study of green sulfur bacteria, researchers used a pulse laser to measure the transfer of particle energy within a billionth of a second. Researchers expected to see energy moving arbitrarily through various connective channels. Instead, they observed energy making impossible leaps, appearing in several places at once before collapsing in the most efficient location with an amazing 95% transfer of energy efficiency.[6] Quantum mechanics may not just apply to photosynthesis in the biological world. A team at the University of Arizona theorizes that brain cells, or neurons, may also operate on quantum principles. Specifically, they note that cylindrical protein structures called microtubules seem to operate in a quantum flux. They speculate that this quantum flux may play a critical role in consciousness.[6]

Quantum mechanics is a relatively new scientific field. Although I grasp some basic quantum principles, as described, I am not a quantum physicist. There are a number of books dedicated to this field for the curious reader. Yet, many physicists point out that no one really understands the underlying mechanisms that run the quantum world, even though experimental results are consistently reproducible. Thus, it is important for any writer to be cautious in explaining spiritual existence using quantum principles. There is more we don't know than we do know. It could be that the spiritual realm operates on quantum-like principles beyond human understanding. Or, it is possible that the spiritual realm operates on a completely unknown set of principles. At the very least, quantum principles may help humanity grasp complex concepts of interconnection and consciousness unbound by physical limitations.

Grasping scientific concepts, like quantum physics, is important to the understanding of interconnection through spiritual transformation. There are other scientific areas that help explain this process. Spiritual transformation impacts many of activities of the soul, including the interconnection of perception, communication, and knowledge. In the remainder of the chapter, we will review each of these abilities in some detail. We will begin with the soul's enriched interconnected experience of visual perception.

Visual Perception

The primary task of any sensory system is to detect the presence of energy changes in the environment. In the case of vision, our eyes help us "see" things by detecting changes in visible light. Yet, perception is only as good as the hardware. Let's define a couple of sensation and perception terms to better understand the meaning of hardware.

The term "absolute threshold," refers to the minimal amount of energy required for people to detect something. The term "discrimination," refers to people's ability to detect differences between stimuli.[7] The human's ability to detect and discriminate between sensory information has upper and lower limits that can be calculated and plotted on graphs. Suffice to say, the human sensory organs have limitations to what they can detect and discriminate. That is why scientists have developed a variety of instruments to measure all the things the human eye cannot detect, which includes most of physical reality. In terms of vision, we only see a small portion of light, called the visible light spectrum. We do not see other frequencies in the energy spectrum, like radio, ultraviolet, infrared, or gamma ray waves. Sensory barriers are not the only limitation. It doesn't help that we have difficulty perceiving those few things we can detect.

The human brain needs eyes to see. Unfortunately, these small organs just perceive the field of vision that exists in front of our bodies. Moreover, the eyes are crude visual instruments. Even with 20/20 vision, most of our vision is out of focus. To see how much of your visual area is blurry, experiment by reading out of the corners of your own eyes. You may notice that approximately 30% of your center vision is crystal clear while the rest is blurry. That is because the periphery of your eye consists of photoreceptor cells that specialize in movement rather than sharpness.[7] Further adding to the degradation, a pair of large nerve cords travel from each eye across the brain to visual center. Since there are no photoreceptors in the optic nerve, each of us carries two blind spots within our field of vision, dark holes filled in by imperfect inferences made by the brain.

The cells in your eyes use chemicals, or pigments, to absorb light. This detection process bears a surprising amount of blockage. Light first passes through blood vessels and is reflected by a mirror in the retina before being perceived by photoreceptors. Various transformations of physical energy occur before the human being sees anything: pigments pick up photons; chemicals break down pigments; neurons decode chemicals; pathways carry neural broadcasts; brain centers integrate and translate neural broadcasts; consciousness perceives brain center integration. How much is lost in translation? No one knows for certain. Yet, our vision is akin to looking through a dirty windshield. We do not realize that we see in such a muddied fashion because that is all we know from birth. NDErs, on the other hand, know otherwise.

Spiritual beings, made of energy, do not have physical eyes to see. NDErs experience vision directly through their interconnection with the particle structures around them. Thus, "seeing" really involves knowing as being. One NDERF writer described his experience of seeing by knowing:

> My own experience was that I was actually not "seeing." I tell others that the soul doesn't "see." The soul, or our consciousness, is in all things and is all things. I wasn't seeing, so much as I was being what I wanted to perceive. If I wanted to look at a pine tree, I wasn't actually "seeing" the pine tree, I was or became the pine tree - from whatever perspective I chose to observe it. I could either see it as a tree, or know it at the molecular level. Since I was also the tree, there was no limitation to my ability to "perceive" or "know" the tree. In fact, this is a better way of putting it. The soul (or the nub of consciousness that we become one with when we leave our bodies) doesn't "see" things - we "know" things. (NDERF #3265)

Knowing reality is a completely different than seeing reality. Not surprisingly, spiritual beings know everything within a 360 degree circumference. Spiritual beings can also know anything by simply being curious. One NDEr wrote:

> I had 360 degree vision, I could see above, below, on my right, on my left, behind, I could see EVERYWHERE at the same time! Secondly, I could zoom in on a particular point. (NDERF #1957)

Knowing is limitless. There are no obstacles to knowing, be it distance or the physical barriers between distances. Spiritual beings can know both the macro-universe and the micro-universe; from galaxy clusters to our own DNA. One NDEr wrote:

> Concepts like "near" or "far" are meaningless to the "soul" because we are one with all things and all things are one with us. We see distant things with the same perfect clarity as nearby things, because there is no such thing as near or far - those terms are only used to refer to the position of earthly things relative to each other. We don't "see" the spectrum of visible light, we "know" the spectrum of visible light because this facet of the universe is no different from any other. (NDERF #3265)

The ability to perceive by knowing erases the need for any perceptual medium, like a pair of eyes. In the spiritual realm, there is only one mode of perception: consciousness. There is no degeneration of information or distortion due to perceptual errors. Consequently, NDErs experience "vision" as brighter, completely in focus, and pristine. Spiritual entities are not subject to the absolute thresholds and discrimination limitations of our sensory systems. Thus, spiritual beings can perceive many types of extra-sensory perceptions that require sensory aids on earth - such as microscopes, radio telescopes, electronic spectroscopy, and so forth. By knowing all spectrums, new ranges of color are experienced and old colors are "seen" as intensely deeper, vibrant, and clear. One NDEr wrote:

> Everything was sharper, brighter, and surreal in that I saw many things very much like we do in time lapse photography. The clouds, the sun, the landscape - all changed color continuously depending on the cloud formation and the light. It was extraordinarily vivid and bright. (NDERF #2916)

Some NDErs also report experiencing synesthesia. The term synesthesia means the union of senses. In the physical world, synesthesia occurs when one sensory pathway is crossed with a second sensory pathway, probably due to an excess of neural interconnectivity.[8] There are at least 152 types of synesthesia that people experience involving every sensory system.[8] The most common form of synesthesia is seeing color in written shapes, like letters and numbers.[8] For instance, someone may see the letter "N" as brown or the letter "S" as blue. A written page, then, may look a bit like a kaleidoscope. However, there are many other types of synesthesia of differing levels of unusualness, such as tasting shapes, smelling temperatures, and seeing sequence in spatial configurations. Nobel-prize physicist Richard Feynman reportedly saw colored equations floating in front of him.[8]

Synesthesia can also be experienced in the spiritual realm. Sensation in the spiritual realm is not neurologically based, however, as spiritual beings do not have physical brains. Rather, spiritual synesthesia is likely due to the soul simultaneously perceiving different facets of interconnected reality. It is likely that the spirit experiences synesthesia on command, guided by the spirit's will and focus. One NDEr described a multifaceted system of synesthesia in the spiritual realm that included the feeling of color and sound, the entwined synthesis of color and self, and the sensing of sound and color in three dimensions. Her synesthesia was integrated into an intensely vivid, lively experience. She writes:

> At some point I was pulled into many colors, each getting more vivid or intense and colors changing colors from within. Sounds were heard too and I knew somehow that this was music. But both colors and music were far different from anything experienced in my lifetime. The colors were 3-D as well as the sounds, and there was by far a greater magnitude to the range of colors and notes than we experience in this realm. It was totally amazing and even though I was awed by what I was being shown, it still seemed so very normal and my heart drifted into the most overwhelming peace I have ever known. Sometimes the colors moved very quickly, other times I was able to feel them and feel them passing through my soul. I felt what each color had to offer, this is very hard to explain but I guess I would say that basically as each color flowed over me, or through me, I became one with that color. Again the notes of music and range of colors were far greater than what we use in our daily realm of existence here. (NDERF #2108)

There is a transcendent quality expressed in this NDERF submission. Her soul not only experienced the unity of various vivid sensations, but the interconnection of reality. The universe is not just filled with matter, as humans perceive, but rather a reality united by conscious existence, sometimes experienced as spiritual synesthesia. Dr. Alexander also experienced spiritual synesthesia between vision and hearing. He writes:

> Seeing and hearing were not separate in this place where I now was. I could hear the visual beauty of the silvery bodies of the scintillating beings above, and I could see the surging, joyful perfection of what they sang.[2]

NDErs emphasize vision when describing heightened perception. However, a few NDErs make quick mention of transcendent perceptions of smell and taste as well. The other 'big' area of perceptual discussion is "hearing." "Hearing" will be discussed in the next section within the broader context of communication.

Communication

Most people communicate through verbal language. Language, in turn, is supported by a complex auditory system. Like the visual system, the auditory system transforms energy from one state to another. The ear first perceives sound by detecting different pressure waves traveling through the air, called audio frequencies.[7] Audio frequencies are transformed into mechanical energy by three tiny, interconnected bones beating on the eardrum. Mechanical energy then travels down into a small snail-shaped organ called the cochlea. The cochlea is filled with a single row of 3,000 tiny hairs that bend by the mechanical energy.[7] Beneath these hairs, mechanical energy is yet again transformed into chemical and electrical activity carried by neurons. These neurons transfer signals to the auditory cortex, not far above the ears within the brain. Finally, people experience actual sound through the last transformation, consciousness.

Like the visual system, there is an inherent degradation of information with the repeated transformation of energy. Also, there are both upper and lower threshold limits when perceiving sound. A dog, for instance, can hear higher frequencies than a human. There are discrimination limitations, as well. To illustrate, you may hear a ringing in your ear following a loud rock concert. One or more of the little hairs in your cochlea just snapped. Unfortunately, it will never grow back, thus resulting in permanent hearing loss.

The imperfect auditory system is not the only source of interference we experience when communicating. Language inefficiently communicates ideas from the speaker to the listener. Have you ever struggled searching for just the right word to capture the fullness of an idea, only to feel frustrated by inadequacies of the English language? Language is like looking across a frozen lake without noticing the life teaming below the ice. When we listen to someone speak, only a crust of meaning can be understood. Words do not convey the whole meaning captured by the speaker's internal thoughts, hidden motivations, and quieted emotions.

Words are just symbols that only have assigned meaning. In other words, languages are abstractions of thought. As abstractions, language can never capture the full original, experiential meaning of intent. Thus, the listener never fully knows what the speaker actually means. Humans try to fill in blanks by searching for additional information, such as studying the speaker's tone of speech or body language. For instance, the statement, "You're so bad!" may have opposite meanings depending on whether the sender was smiling or grimacing.

A soul of energy does not have ears or a mouth. Consequently, spiritual beings cannot "hear" or "talk" any more than they can "see." Spiritual communication involves a deep and exhaustive interchange of both informational and emotional knowledge. Information is fully received directly through interconnectedness. Consequently, "my" thoughts do not exist. Only shared thoughts exist. With every nuance understood, spiritual communication can only be defined as pure. So in heaven, spiritual beings mean what they say. One NDEr described spiritual communication as telepathy:

> The communication system there is one of direct transference of thought and feeling. Words are not required for thought or communication. I found that my capacity to distinguish between 'ranges, shades, or nuances of affect' to be extremely expanded. (NDERF #3253)

The following NDEr tried to express her sense of awe regarding the inaudible tone of spiritual telepathy:

> It is the most wonderful language - perfectly clear, perfectly understood, perfectly liberating, perfectly perfect. I never heard a tone that could identify a specific voice. It's not like that. The tone is there. It's just a tone that identifies a specific soul, not something that's physically audible. (NDERF #1936)

Communication is not only shared between a receiver and sender. A soul can read another's thoughts through interconnectedness. One NDEr wrote:

> I heard people's thoughts. Even before they opened their mouth, I knew what they were about to say! Because I heard their thought! Besides, it was quite a cacophony in the room, but I just had to focus on one person and then, I just heard this person! (NDERF #1957)

Collective communication has no earthly parallels. There are potential implications of such direct, intimate communication. First, there is no such thing as privacy. This radical mode of communication may be disconcerting from the isolated, human perspective. We take solace in our private musings, perhaps embarrassed by our relatively uncontrolled, ceaseless stream of thoughts. For instance, the human brain often has particular difficulty controlling the rumination process when we are stressed or anxious. Regarding rumination, cognitive psychologist Albert Bandura notes that "painful repetitive, perturbing ideation accounts for much of human distress."[9] Sometimes the problem is not rumination, but the isolated, unruly thought popping into awareness. Often, these undesirable thoughts reflect uncaring attitudes toward other people. The individual may often try to hide these unexpressed thoughts through impression management.

The eminent sociologist, Erving Goffman, coined the term "impression management." Impression management theory submits that people try to influence others perception of themselves, usually slanting them in a favorable direction, much like a theatrical actor. According to Goffman, people act to impress in order to avoid embarrassing themselves or others.[10] People would be ashamed of sharing such brazen thoughts like as, "I wish you would screw up," or "I can't believe you sound so stupid." Whether conscious or unconscious, there is always a level of human deception in omitting or embellishing information. There is no opportunity for impression management in the spiritual realm. With direct communication, spiritual beings must always be themselves without deception. However, this does not appear to be a concern. According to the NDE experience, spiritual beings do not appear disturbed by the elimination of privacy. They seem to be in control of their baser thoughts because they are interconnected with the Whole.

In the spiritual realm, acceptance and understanding likely facilitates greater appreciation of fellow spiritual beings. This may, in turn, lead to greater caring and deeper compassion. Humans care more about those we know intimately. To illustrate, examine the following reverse hierarchy of people: Indonesian; American; coworker; friend; grandparent; daughter. Who do you care about most? Most people would say they care about their daughter more than a complete stranger from Indonesia. As interconnected beings, souls may care about all spiritual beings because they intimately know each other. Empathy may be yet further enhanced by the intense, interconnected emotions that souls exchange. On earth, people exhibit different developmental levels of partial empathy. The highest level of empathy might be the ability to empathize with someone's difficult life condition without any direct observation of distress, like those who generously provide food and medical aid to refugees in Africa. Such empathy may require the benefactor to visualize him or herself suffering through the same difficult situation.[11] Yet, such visualizations are only a crude approximation of the actual experience of the sufferer, often leading to only fleeting pangs of distress. Spiritual beings do not need to imagine another's pain in order to experience full empathy. The spiritual being understands another's plight completely through interconnectedness. They feel what the sufferer feels. Consequently, spiritual beings likely experience a level of interpersonal intimacy that far exceeds intimacy in the physical realm.

Many NDErs state that human words are not required to communicate in the spiritual realm. Others report hearing communication in their native human language, especially when first transitioning into the spiritual realm. One curious element of spiritual communication involves timing. Although thoughts are perceived in a linear, sequential manner, they are processed instantaneously. This perception of sequence in relative time generates somewhat of an unusual experience for the new visitor. One NDEr submitted these related observations:

> One of the souls who greeted me said to another soul, in a slow, pleading, pausing way, this sentence, "She's been through so much, she should be allowed to stay." In physical terms, this would take fifteen seconds to say at the speed with which he said it. However, it doesn't take time there. It's instantaneous, even though I know this sounds strange. The feeling of time is realized by an individual in communication. But, time doesn't exist in physical terms. (NDERF #1936)

People are limited to a plodding mode of symbolic communication called language. The receivers must slowly listen to one sender at a time because our brain can only process one stream of thought at a time. Obviously, the human brain cannot think out two sentences simultaneously. NDErs state that this is not the case in the spiritual realm. Spiritual beings use many different channels to perfectly communicate to a group. One NDEr used the term "meta-communication" to describe this process, which seems apt. Another NDEr described meta-communication in this way:

> Imagine having a thousand things and people talking at the exact same moment, and perfectly understanding every detail of all that's going on. I could understand all six souls speaking at the exact same

time with perfect clarity, as well as knowing the purest depths of their hearts, and a multitude of other things happening and information that I was privileged to receive, all at the exact same instance. There are no doubts about what is being said because of the dynamics of the form of communication (souls laid bare, plus you feel it, and know it's the truth). And you never question it. There's no need to. You know instinctively that it's the true form of communication. (NDERF #1936)

Similarly, another NDEr wrote about meta-communication on a larger scale:

There were literally hundreds of these stars "talking" with each other all at the same time yet there was not one single bit of clash of thought-feeling, not one single bit of misunderstanding of thought-feeling. (NDERF #3253)

One NDEr reported the experience of meta-communication was sort of like listening to a symphony. He wrote:

The totality of the communications produced nothing but harmony. There was no sense at all of any deviation from what might be best described as a meta-communication. It was as if the total of all the individual communications was in itself a single communication that had formed itself from the individual communications arising. It's like 'listening to music', meaning, there is a full range of feelings and thoughts like an 'orchestra'. (NDERF #2353)

Fond of classical music, I appreciate the orchestra metaphor. When one listens to a familiar piece of classical music, the listener will usually attend to the individual instrument parts as well as the entire symphony. At different moments, he or she may attend to the melody of the woodwinds, the counter melodies of the high brass, the bass of the tubas, and the rhythm of the percussion. At other times, he or she may be attending to the gestalt of the entire classical piece (gestalt means that the sum is greater than the individual parts). Although the music lover may be attending to only one perceived element at a time, the rapid flow of information may allow the listener to perceive the concert like a multi-layered musical communication. This is probably the closest that humans can experience meta-communication or meta-perception.

Spiritual communication knows no earthly bounds. The spiritual soul has the ability to know everything communicated, even if sent by multiple senders. Souls can process information using many different channels, simultaneously. Thus, spiritual beings completely know each other and themselves. This type of interconnected ability not only applies to communication, but to the acquisition of universal knowledge.

Universal Knowledge

Have you ever felt frustrated by the slow, labored pace of learning? I certainly wished for supernatural abilities during graduate school. Most final exams were based on my ability to concentrate and listen to three hours of lecture and read one to two textbooks a week. Late night study hours were required to grasp difficult concepts and encode information into memory. Although I generally learned enough to receive good grades, I have since forgotten some of what I learned. Most of what I learned now seems to be encased within a fog of generalized ideas and consolidated facts. Although I highly value learning, I don't miss those graduate school days of relentless work, especially since some of my learning has fallen as a victim to time.

Many NDErs suddenly obtain astounding intellectual powers in the spiritual realm, especially those who have a long NDE. They credit newfound abilities to their access to universal knowledge interwoven into the fabric of existence. As discussed earlier, this fabric of existence is tightly woven into the very essence of God consciousness. Because God is One with everything created, God knows everything. Through interconnectedness, God shares universal knowledge with spiritual beings in heaven. Every soul has access to that universal knowledge through a type of universal library bank; information flows freely with any inquisitive thought or question. Using a crude analogy, the library may be likened to a computer connected to the worldwide web.

The universe-wide web of knowledge was revealed in a tangible way to George Ritchie. For a brief historical backdrop, George Ritchie was one of the first individuals to publish a book about a personal near-death experience. He experienced his NDE during World War II. Because of the profound impact of his near-death experience, George Ritchie completed medical school in order to later practice as a psychiatrist. During his NDE, Dr. Ritchie was provided a partial tour of the spiritual realm. One of the levels consisted of a visual representation of universal knowledge manifested as a huge university complex. He wrote:

> Next we walked through a library the size of the whole University of Richmond. I gazed into rooms lined floor to ceiling with documents on parchment, clay, leather, metal, paper. "Here," the thought occurred to me, "are assembled the important books of the universe." Immediately I knew this was impossible. How could books be written somewhere beyond the earth! But the thought persisted, although my mind rejected it... Then abruptly, at the door to one of the smaller rooms, almost an annex: "here is the central thought of this earth."[12]

Dr. Ritchie's description of a heavenly library should not be taken literally. Rather, the library was manifested for the benefit of George Ritchie. Specifically, universal knowledge was presented in a manner that could be understood within a mid-twentieth century, human context. The manifestation was primarily meant to illustrate the vast scope of knowledge existing in the universe. Indeed, the scope of library appears vast, particularly compared to the paltry room that represented earth. All the knowledge accumulated on earth could never be learned by anyone in a thousand lifetimes. Yet, the knowledge of earth consisted of a small room, an annex, within an enormous library bigger than a major university. It seems quite amazing that you and I will have complete access to all that knowledge when we become spiritual beings. As spiritual beings, we will surpass our current level of knowledge by many, many orders of magnitude.

Not only do spiritual beings know everything from a storage point of view, but they also understand everything, no matter the complexity. Ponder the implications, the spiritual mind reaches far beyond any earthly brilliance. NDErs report that their souls can instantly comprehend the most complex of problems by understanding universal cause and effect. For example, one NDEr reports knowing complex mathematics far beyond the level of Einstein, even though she struggled with math in high school. Such NDE stories provide only a taste of soul magnificence. The true magnificence of spiritual intellectual capabilities exists far beyond human comprehension, because the human brain, with its hundred billion neurons, has a very limited processing and storage capacity. From a tired graduate student's perspective, existing as a spiritual being almost seems like cheating. One NDEr described the complete access to everything that he called "omniscient knowledge":

I further understood that the collective experiences are omniscient knowledge. Everything that has been spoken, heard, and experienced. These colored drops contained each experience down to the memory of every cell division, every thought. All experiences were known at once by the collective consciousness that was the stream. Any experience could be known as if it were a first person experience happening at the time it happened originally. (NDERF #815)

Dr. Alexander describes his staggering knowledge and intellectual ability from his own near-death experience:

A question would arise in my mind, and the answer would arise at the same time, like a flower coming up right next to it. It was as if, just as no physical particle in the universe is really separate from another, so in the same way there was no such thing as a question without an accompanying answer. These answers were not simple "yes" or "no" fare, either. They were vast conceptual edifices, staggering structures of living thought, as intricate as cities. Ideas so vast they would have taken me lifetimes to find my way around if I had been confined to earthly thoughts.[2]

If thoughts can be as intricate as cities, then spiritual beings can look at all facets of an event or a problem. Questions involving complex human behavior, or the meaning of human existence, are answered. Each thread within the fabric of existence can be analyzed instantly. Unlike the confusion that predominates on earth, there is no room for doubt in heaven. Without having doubt, spiritual beings always know how to make the right choices.

Humans are prone to make premature decisions because they often lack the necessary information to make good choices. Spiritual beings can formulate the very best decision by understanding all cause and effect interrelationships. In this manner, the present can be known by fully understanding the past. Let's take this line of thinking one step further. If every variable is known, then the future can be predicted. By knowing the past, present, and future, spiritual beings should have a singular understanding of how everything works and what is important to God. Imagine the ramifications. There are no political factions in heaven or major disagreements between spiritual beings. To know the right course of action, souls only have to understand God's universal design and future plan. After all, there is nothing else to know beyond God, for God is all. One NDEr wrote this about God:

The extent of the intelligence and wisdom of this being, of this light, was utterly indescribable other than to call it infinite. This intelligence and wisdom was of a magnitude that knew that there was nothing that was outside its compass, that knew there was nothing of which it was not aware, that knew there was nothing that was outside its scope. (NDERF: #3253)

Another NDEr wrote about understanding the past, present, and future:

I spent an eternity wallowing in a universe of knowledge that made me whole, connected, and an integral part of everything that had ever existed - past, present, and future. (NDERF #3339)

The following NDEr describes an experience of knowing everything while connected with the consciousness of God:

I instantly became all knowing. I became a part of the creator itself. I had no known memory of the feelings of separation of anything. I developed a strange mind in that it is accelerating faster than I could possibly keep up with. (NDERF #2437)

Learning from the God consciousness can fundamentally change the individual returning from life after death. Those NDErs who suffered deep emotional pain in the physical world often return with greater self-esteem and appreciation of life. What would you ask if you carried a library card to access the universal library of knowledge? Some might ask about the thornier mysteries of life, the type tackled by age-old philosophers and theologians. Specifically, one might inquire into the nature of good and evil, or even human suffering. Indeed, some curious NDErs receive answers to these difficult questions. Unfortunately, these age-old mysteries remain mysteries, probably by divine design, because NDErs have difficulty remembering and processing the information when they return to earth. Dr. Alexander writes, "It will take me the rest of my life, and then some, to unpack what I learned up there."[2] Many NDErs report the same frustration. Here is another NDEr talking about his difficulty retrieving information once returned to earth:

To this day, I cannot completely remember all that I talked with Him about...but I get a sense that it was a long conversation, one as if between friends. I do remember some parts of it, however – mainly that He told me directly that I would not remember much of what we talked about. (NDERF #2758)

Fortunately, many NDErs receive partial revelations to the "big" questions. Their revelations will be discussed in detail later in this book. Suffice to say for now, the NDEr is profoundly impacted by the mere perception that pressing questions were answered. Usually they report a great sense of relief and peace. To illustrate, one NDEr wrote this after talking with Jesus:

I was asking and crying about things that happened to me from the beginning of my life for the most part (incest, emotional abuse, physical abuse, mental abuse, running away starting at about 12 years old to get away from all the abuse, stranger raped me at 14). Countless things happened to me, but this might give the reader an idea as to where I came from. Frankly, I believe I was living a hell on earth. It was amazing and beautiful. My Savior answered and gave me knowledge that gave me peace about every single thing that had happened to me. Everything. However, He didn't allow me to come back with all that He revealed to me. What He did was send me back with peace in my spirit. (NDERF #2343)

Peace in spirit is not always easy to come by, especially when people have been hurt over and over again. This is the transforming power of divine knowledge, even if it is not fully remembered. This is the transforming power of God's love.

In this chapter, we have reviewed various transcendent abilities that the soul exhibits through interconnectedness; a benefit bestowed on spiritual beings through the unity of God and creation. Although we maintain the core essence of self as soul, the abilities of eternal spirit exceed the abilities of the mortal human body in regard to perception, communication, and knowledge. There are other soul abilities, such as the manifestation of reality that we will tackle later in the context of other topics. Endowed with all these amazing abilities, the soul is capable of almost anything in accordance with divine rule. In some respects, it has a tremendous amount of freedom to act within the universe. We have much to look forward to when we die and claim our inheritance as splendid spiritual beings. Truly, the soul travels within God's open road.

CHAPTER SIX

THE MISSION

Have you ever wondered why souls are sent to earth? What is there to show for this trip? At best, some claim that life is sweet; life's enjoyments trump the inevitable pain. These people consider gratifications and loving relationships to be the source of their joy. Others strongly argue that suffering predominates their lives. They may point to stretches of sickness, physical pain, emotional hurt, isolation, and ultimately death. Even in the best case scenario, human existence is a trifling comparison to our existence in the spiritual realm. As explored earlier, the nature of soul is comparatively majestic, with its commanding power and intelligence. The soul has been endowed with these expansive abilities by its interconnection with God and all of creation. So with this comparison in mind, why do souls reduce themselves to share existence with the human animal in the material realm? More simply, what's this "crazy" life all about? Philosophers and theologians have pondered such questions over human history. Fortunately, the NDErs have returned from life after death with some meaningful answers.

During her near-death experience, Kimberly Clark-Sharp, founder and president of the Seattle International Association for Near-Death Studies, shared her lessons regarding the eternal questions about life. She wrote, "I was learning the answers to the eternal questions of life questions so old we laugh them off as clichés. 'Why are we here?' To learn. 'What is the purpose to life?' to love."[1]

The purpose of all our lives is to learn and love; so simple, yet so profound. The term "mission" is apt. A mission refers to a specific task with which a person is charged. In this case, God charges each soul to learn through individual will and experience. In this chapter, we will explore several facets of mission. First, we will understand mission from the framework of the life review. Next, we will examine the evaluation process of mission through divine justice. We will then explore the role adversity plays in mission. Finally, we will discuss the universal mission to love.

The Life Review

Many NDErs return to their bodies realizing their mission is to learn and love. They learn through different venues; each NDE is unique. Perhaps the "life review" represents one of the more revealing methods for the NDEr to discover his or her general mission on earth. Again, a life review is a three-dimensional presentation of one's life lived prior to their NDE, which can serve as a source of both delight and regret. We briefly touched on the life review earlier. Let's now examine the topic in more depth.

NDE researcher Jody Long conducted the one of the largest studies on near-death experience life reviews. From a sample of 319 lucid near-death experiences, 26% of responders reported experiencing a life review during their NDE.[2] Similarly, Bruce Greyson reported that 22% reported life reviews in his research.[3] Clearly, a life review is not meant for every NDEr to remember. Additionally, the flavor of the life review varies, like most elements of the NDE, because it is tailored to the NDErs unique life history. Sometimes a life review occurs in the presence of God, who may serve as a director and commentator. For Western NDErs, the review may be conducted by Jesus. Reviews may also be conducted by other spiritual beings either known or unknown to the reviewer. Additional spiritual beings may also be present. On some occasions, God begins the life review process by simply asking, "What do you have to show me from your life?"

The life review process may cause anxiety for some NDErs, especially for those who bungled their mission in life. Despite their discomfort, the reel proceeds immediately and with very little intermission. The analogy between an NDE life review and a movie only goes so far, however, as the comparison lacks many shared qualities.

A movie typically consists of dramatized story depicted on a two-dimensional screen. Fictional lives are represented in fragmented scenes condensed within short blocks of time. A life review, on the other hand, depicts real events in three-dimensional space. The reviewer typically participates as a third person observer while their personal history is relived. Some NDErs report reviewing highlights of their life whereas others report reviewing their entire life. It is possible that everyone reviews their entire life, but that understanding may be lost on return to earth.

Because the soul has multiple levels of consciousness, as discussed in chapter five, different past events may be experienced simultaneously. This may explain why many NDErs report that their life review seemed to finish quickly, or all at once, despite reliving volumes of life material. Relatedly, George Ritchie wrote, "There were other scenes, hundreds, thousands, all illuminated by that searing Light, in an existence where time seemed to have ceased. It would have taken weeks of ordinary time even to glance at so many events, and I had no sense of minutes passing."[4]

Some NDErs report a single stream of realistic, holographic-like images throughout their life reviews. Others report experiencing multiple events simultaneously, sometimes in spectacular displays. For instance, one NDEr observed life scenes portrayed inside floating bubbles. Another described scenes simultaneously portrayed on different screens. He wrote:

> I'm suspended inside the center of an immense sphere, bigger than our high school gymnasium. The inside of the sphere looks like an enormous unending movie screen, with hundreds of movies playing in every direction at the same time. I am completely surrounded by images of my experiences. (NDERF #687)

Whatever the mode of presentation, the soul incorporates information with complete accuracy. More simply, the soul has the ability to "take it all in."

On occasion, an NDEr is shown one or more timelines that reflect major life choices. Amazingly, this process is akin to living different futures. Experiencing different timelines is only possible if every variable is known. Fortunately, the soul is interconnected with the bank of universal knowledge. One NDEr wrote about his life "possibilities":

I "felt" like the right side was reserved for when I actually did physically die. I would be privy to it then. It contained all the possibilities of all the angles of all the decisions I had made, played out in different realms. As if, let's say, I had decided not to get married when I did. What my life would have been—and it actually was played out, but not in a physical way. It was still acted out. It was all the "probables" in life. (NDERF #3098)

Reliving different timelines represents the special divine gift for learning. It also illustrates diversity inherent to the life review. Despite the variety, life reviews tend to have a common purpose. They are meant to teach us how to love. Based on many NDE life review accounts, most human accomplishments, such as wealth and prestige, have little relevance. Rather, the review focuses on our meaningful interactions with other people. When there is a director, such as God or Jesus, the reviewer may hear comments on whether life choices were harmful or helpful/selfish or loving. Although reviewers are third party observers, they are not passive, distant observers. Many NDErs actually witness interpersonal events from the other person's conscious experience. Specifically, the NDEr actually experiences the impact of unloving behaviors: embarrassment, humiliation, sadness, and dejection. On the flip side, the NDEr can also experience how others respond to their loving behaviors: appreciation, happiness, joy, or liberation from pain. In this manner, the reviewer can witness the long term cause and effects of their behavior.

All facets of the life review serve to teach the NDEr about what is important in human life and what is not. Howard Storm experienced a life review that illuminated why he had become spiritually lost. His review was directed by Jesus with participation from other spiritual beings. He shared:

We watched and experienced episodes that were from the point of view of a third party. The scenes they showed me were often of incidents I had forgotten. They showed me their effect on people's lives, thoughts, and feelings of people I had interacted with, which I had been unaware of at the time. They showed me scenes from my life that I would not have chosen, and they eliminated scenes from my life that I wanted them to see. It was a complete surprise to see how my life history was being presented.[5]

George Ritchie learned what was important in life during his review guided by Jesus. Jesus asked him, "What did you do with your life?" Because Ritchie's life was already laid bare, Jesus' question was rhetorical. George Ritchie further elaborates:

> It seemed to be a question about values, not facts: what did you accomplish with the precious time you were allotted?... It wasn't that there were spectacular sins, just the sexual hang-ups and secretiveness of most teenagers. But if there were no horrendous depths, there were no heights either, only an endless, shortsighted, clamorous concern for myself. Hadn't I ever gone beyond my own immediate interests, done anything other people would recognize as valuable?[4]

Prior to his NDE, George Ritchie equated meaning with widely recognized achievement; the glorification of self. He did not realize that acts of love, and all contributing values, were the greatest of all human accomplishments. Although George Ritchie was not proud of his young life, he felt no condemnation from Jesus. He only felt love and acceptance. This was somewhat unexpected for Ritchie, given his religious understanding of final judgment. In reality, God operates on a different standard, namely that of divine justice.

Divine Justice

God operates from a higher level of justice than humanity. From a fundamentalist religious perspective, God's final judgment only has two outcomes: eternal heavenly reward or hellfire punishment. NDErs are mostly unanimous in denying a "guilty" or "not guilty" justice in heaven. On earth, human justice serves a practical purpose; there would be anarchy without the rule of law. Unfortunately, human justice is prone to bias because the human brain engages in mental shortcuts. Practical and decisive efficiency is needed to make a multitude of quick decisions during daily life. Furthermore, judgments must be made on subjectivity of belief, or law, due to the absence of a universal moral standard. Unfortunately, the perfect rule book does not exist on earth. Rather, people rely on learned beliefs when they make personal judgments, even if the sources are questionable.

People often make judgments filtered through their "anchored positions." According to Social Judgment Theory, an anchored position is a type of internalized belief based on socially learned values, principles, and truths.[6] This anchored belief serves a type of schema, or mental filter, by which people make judgments on various right or wrong issues. A person can accept, reject, or be neutral on any issue. The more extreme the belief, either for or against, the less likely that person will change an opinion on an issue, regardless of any evidence to the contrary. Let's say, hypothetically, Jim is homosexual. People who believe homosexuality is a moral abomination may judge Jim's character based on his sexuality rather than on more pertinent personal factors. Human law is supposed to reduce stereotypes and over-generalizations based on erroneous anchored positions. However, even human law is also subject to human bias, as laws reflect the learned values, principles, and truths beholden to the surrounding culture. After all, law partly reflects the anchored positions of lawyers who are themselves a product of their environment. Furthermore, law incorporates retaliation into the criminal justice system.

Legal punishment is a type of retaliation in response to wrong doing. An "eye for eye" and a "tooth for a tooth" declaration represents an ancient biblical judgment based on the foundations of retaliation. One might argue that our modern judicial laws have evolved to a higher standard; legal punishments are written to teach the criminal pro-social behavior and to prevent future crime. Given the warehouse mentality behind many prison systems, as well as the death penalty, it could also be argued that punishment still largely serves as a function of retaliation. Psychological research suggests that people who tend to be more vengeful are motivated by power, authority, and status.[7] Humans feel powerless as victims. It is only natural that authoritarian oriented victims want justice served on their own terms. More specifically, the psychological motive behind retaliation is catharsis. Catharsis is an old psychological term that means a release of emotional tension from bringing conscious or unconscious wishes into reality. In other words, victims seek alleviation from pain using revenge. There was an interesting study completed by Kevin Carlsmith at Colgate University. He found that research subjects who were allowed to punish a "free-rider" actually felt worse than the non-punisher group. Yet, the punishers predicted that they would feel better. Moreover, even the non-punishers thought that they would feel better if given the opportunity to punish. In other words, both groups thought that revenge would be satisfying.[7]

Judgments involve mental discriminations that help people interact with others. These judgments also have survival value. One may prudently ask, "Do I trust this person?" For example, it would be unwise to offer money to a conman. To avoid exploitation, judgments are made. Religion teaches that God also makes conditional judgments. From their perspective, judgment entails an appraisal of an entire, complex life. Yet, NDErs state that God's love for people is unconditional. For the NDEr, eternal damnation does not appear to be a consequence of the life review. In fact, there is no condemnation or hostile rebuke in any form. Rather, NDErs report that the life review is conducted in a context of full understanding and acceptance. Many people may have mixed feelings about this revelation, especially those steeped in religious teaching. On one side of the coin, this revelation appears consistent with orthodox teaching that God expresses unconditional love and mercy. On the other side, many religions simultaneously teach about dire punishments attached to a "bad life." While the first part is consistent with the NDE, the latter part is not. The life reviewer has no reason to fear eternity in hell or any other type of punishment. Still, the reviewer appraises his or her own actions. Self-reflective judgment is meant as a learning experience, a means for the NDEr to return with a better understanding of mission. One eight-year-old NDEr reported:

> I could feel the pain that I had caused because of my actions. Then I remember thinking, "Oooh no! I'm in trouble!" My angel surprised me by saying "Don't worry, these are just lessons." (NDERF #1675)

Another NDEr shared how her life review, although painful, was liberating because she experienced God's love and forgiveness:

> You know how we are taught that we will stand before God and be judged one day? God was not judging me. I was looking at my actions with God at my side loving me while I was judging myself... My immediate thought, and I said it out loud, was "I'm ready. I belong in Hell. I don't deserve to go to Heaven!" But it felt like He took hold of my arm as I was making my way to Hell and said "Wait a minute young lady you get back here! You don't understand and I'm going to explain this to you." He was asking me, "What different choices could you have made? What are you learning from this?"... This was clearly not the punishing God I had been taught to believe in. The hardest part of this was realizing that He had already forgiven me. I was having a very hard time forgiving myself. He showed me how I couldn't let His love in without, first, forgiving myself. (NDERF #682)

During her NDE, this woman realized that God, despite contrary religious beliefs, had already forgiven her. The concept of forgiveness has central importance. With mission comes inherent choice. To the extent we fall short in mission, we are forgiven. In her book, *Soul to Soulmate*, Jody Long notes that guilt is an earthly construct, not a divine construct.[8] Guilt is a human emotion generated from our human separation from God. God understands that we are limited biological beings. It is only important that we learn by our mistakes and ultimately from our separateness. Because God's love is unconditional, forgiveness is automatic.

Even with automatic forgiveness, experiencing life from another person's experience can be a sobering experience for the reviewer. There can be no successful denial, rationalization, or minimizing during the review process. Attempts to psychologically maneuver against the life review lessons are gently refuted by clear and compelling evidence to the contrary. There is nowhere the reviewer can hide. Not surprisingly, the reviewer often experiences a mixture of very strong emotions as events unfold. For instance, they may feel deep empathy when they inadvertently hurt others. Or they may feel intense pangs of guilt when they intentionally inflict pain. Similarly, they may feel joy by giving hope to the hopeless or feel satisfaction when guiding others to make right decisions. God does not cause the reviewer to feel any particular emotion. Judgments and emotional reactions are the responsibility of the reviewer, dictated by his or her own conscience. Again, God understands our biological limitations and spiritual immaturity. God really loves us for who we are, which means we don't have to attempt to earn God's love. Rather, it is important to accomplish our divine mission in life by making good choices. Relatedly, one NDEr wrote:

> I felt and experienced all these events again and I also felt emotions I had raised in others. I was my only judge! This experience was very painful. I dare not imagine what Adolf Hitler underwent when feeling the pain of millions of individuals. God showed me when I had generously done things without thinking about it beforehand, and when I had done unloving things... This is what hit me the most: God does not judge, he just loves us with unconditional love. This love is indescribable, it is not like what we feel on earth, but rather a force-love. (NDERF #1957)

Another wrote about her response to positive feedback during the life review:

Reviewing my random acts of kindness gave me the most joy because I was able to feel the difference I made in someone's life that I hadn't realized at the time, and I didn't even know them. I was shown it is not the big things we do in life that make the difference. It's all the little things we do each day that make the difference. Little acts of kindness mean so much to God. (NDERF #682)

Important lessons can be learned from a variety of experiences, big and small. The life review serves as a measuring gauge that compares what has been done with what optimally can be done. As the reviewer monitors the gauge, a life lived can be measured against the original mission standards.

A life review is a special kind of life reminiscence. The elderly sometimes reminisce about their active years, feeling satisfaction or regret over deeds done, or not. Reminiscence, in this context, rarely serves a productive purpose, especially if regrets involve people who have already died. Regret only leads to states of frustration and despair. The life review, conversely, is not meant to foster frustration and despair. Rather, it is an instrument of hope. The NDErs life review serves as a learning tool for school earth, equipping the reviewer to better fulfill their mission upon return to earth. Sometimes, this gives the reviewer an opportunity for a second chance. I know a coworker who experienced a life review during an NDE. The coworker understood that she would be provided a second life review at the time of her final death from which her first life review would be compared. The coworker knows that she will be asked, "What have you learned since your last review?" She plans on having a satisfactory answer to this question.

Mission Possible

Almost all NDErs come to understand that they have a mission in life. Although the specifics are usually withheld, they at least understand that their mission generally involves loving other people. Howard Storm was surprised by what was reviewed and what was not. He was probably expecting his academic achievements to be acknowledged. They weren't. Rather, the events in life that appear to have the most relevance to God involve our interactions with people. There is a general question, spoken or unspoken, during each review: "Have you learned to love other people?" Ideally, the individual should be moving, ever so slowly and steadily, toward the divine by learning how to love. The following NDERF reference provides an excellent summation of our mission to love:

> Our purpose and goal is God and his perfect love, to continually learn and serve God, love and serve each other, love ourselves, grow spiritually but we have a free will to not be aligned with God at any point. We must understand God's love, understand the opposite of it and how destructive and wrong it is, then reach toward God to have a beautiful and completely loving existence. (NDERF #2037)

The life review serves as a primary venue for NDErs to learn about their mission to learn and love. But it is not the only approach. Some NDErs learn about mission through their interactions with other spiritual beings. This most commonly occurs when an NDEr is instructed to return to earth. Enamored by heaven, many souls resist returning. Specifically, they do not want to be disconnected from the divine and face life's many challenges. Their reluctance is understandable given their description of heaven. Their reluctance, or even initial refusal, is often discouraged by God, Jesus, or by other spiritual beings. Specifically, the NDEr is often presented with their individual mission to care for loved ones, usually ailing parents or grieving children. Sometimes the NDEr is even allowed to view how loved ones are impacted by their death. One NDEr wrote:

> He came closer to me and I was comforted and he calmly encouraged me to be strong. He told me to look to my left. As I did, I saw a school bus pull up in the distance. A small child was escorted out and brought to me. I recognized that it was my own daughter, who at the time was only four years old. She had been asked in her sleep to come in spirit to help me. She walked up to me, tugged at me a little and sweetly said in an encouraging voice, "But Mommy? Who will take care of us?" He said, "Look to your right." I looked to my right and saw a holographic figure. It was my own mother. It was a view of her in the future, and she seemed tired and in need of help... The hologram faded out and my Guide said, "You see? It is time. YOU want to go." (NDERF #2386)

The defined mission depends on individual needs. For many, the mission to love family appears to have particular importance. In fact, the needs of family often convince many NDErs to return to their bodies.

Obviously, we cannot know about those who did not choose to come back since their stories are untold. But for the souls that do chose to come back, they often realize that their mission to love family involves spiritual growth for many, not just for themselves. Moreover, the realization of mission often changes the person's outlook on life when they return to earth.

Every person has a choice to follow the divine mission to learn and love. Yet, the decision is not black and white. Mission can be accomplished by varying degrees depending on motivation and other factors. One factor includes the psychological concept of self-concordance. In psychology, the Self-Concordance Model looks at the sequence of steps a person needs to attain a goal. Motivation increases when a person integrates goals with their identity. When a goal is consistent with an individual's self-identity, the goal is said to be "self-concordant." Conversely, goals that are externally motivated are not internalized. Externally motivated goals are frequently abandoned over time.[9] In this manner, the success of a mission greatly depends on whether a goal is self-concordant or externally motivated. If an individual follows a life goal out of obligation, or fear of hell, then their mission on earth will probably not be optimally achieved. On the other hand, if people learn to love because they embrace the divine mission as an extension from true self, then the mission is more likely to be successful. This is particularly the case with love. Love cannot be forced or externally motivated. Love out of obligation is only obligation.

A tyrant might induce fear and force obedience on a beaten population, but a tyrant cannot force a single person to love by submission. Love must be a personal choice given freely. It should be pointed out that love is not a singular choice. There are opportunities to love every day. Each of us must diligently fight against our own selfish nature and make countless choices in every interactive moment. This can be difficult, as elevating ourselves above our own selfish desires, even our own biology, can be a daunting task. That is why love is imperfect, by default, in the material human realm. Rather, individuals grow by learning to love with sustained, mindful effort. This process takes time, even more than a lifetime. The "I am" part of our selves only becomes more loving after the realization of many loving experiences. Through these experiences, a new being emerges with the unfolding of existence, one that is closer to the divine ideal. This new being is not only closer to the divine ideal through connection with the divine, but as a result of many experiences and free will choices.

School Earth and the Purpose behind Suffering

There is a type of authentic learning that can only be internalized through experience, particularly adversity. Imagine you read a book about traveling across the African continent. You are enthralled by your imagination of exciting adventures, or misadventures, of traveling the third world. Yet, reading about Africa is much different than traveling through Africa. Experiential learning is deeper because it is real. The vicarious African trip by book, however, is not real; it is only an abstraction. One can only know Africa by actually trekking across the continent. Likewise, souls are limited in their learning in the spiritual realm, despite having universal access to knowledge, because they cannot learn through real, personal experience. Real growth, the type of development that involves adversity and choice, can only be experienced by getting "dirty in the trenches." This is why earth becomes so important. Souls come to earth to grow through experience. From the NDERF website, an NDEr wrote this about being on earth:

> I was told that the earth is like a big school, a place where you can apply spiritual lessons learned and test yourself, under pressure, to see if you can actually "live" what you already know you should do. Basically, the earth is a place to walk the walk and literally live the way it should be done. (NDERF #2932)

Note that this NDEr likened earth to a school. This analogy appears apt. A person cannot competently practice as a doctor without going to medical school. Likewise, a soul cannot reach higher spiritual vibrations without learning through experience. In this vein, another NDEr wrote:

> I learned why bad things happen to good people. If nothing bad ever happened to us we would all basically be the same. It is like metal in a forge; you have to heat it and strike it repeatedly to make a useful tool from it. (NDERF #1634)

Learning from difficult experiences becomes critical in our mission to love. Imagine that you are caring for a mother dying of advanced Alzheimer's disease. You quit your job to cook, clean, and bathe your parent. Meanwhile, you see your mother's faculties, memories, and personality slowly fade. This may be the most emotionally exhausting time in your life. You suffer because your loved one suffers. Yet, spiritual growth will certainly follow if you open yourself to care for that parent. You will have learned how to sacrifice with unconditional love, thereby passing an important lesson on earth school. Humans only understand the "small picture" of human existence because we misunderstand the eternal "big picture" of God. Our "good" actions, even our solid faith in God, do not guarantee smooth living. Numerous religious progressives, like the apostles of Jesus, met a violent death for their unorthodox ideas. Although difficult to accept, human tribulation is part of the learning process.

Although I understand the value of suffering from an intellectual standpoint, I still have difficulty appreciating the value of suffering from an experiential standpoint. I continue to dwell on the daily stresses and frustrations of life. Perhaps humans are largely confined to a material, finite perspective due to the illusion of being separated from God. Many people think that they are alone in their suffering, and feel like their discomfort will last forever. Yet, suffering does not last forever. After all, our human life prepares us for the eternal life. Howard Storm notes that our human perspective is completely wrong:

> Our perspective on life is wrong. We think this life in the world is important. It is only important as a preparation for our eternal life. The only importance of this life is the choice we make to love God or not.[5]

How do people make a choice to love God when God seems so far away? God desires our love but does not need our love. Due to this perceived connection, it is enough to show our love to God by loving others. In the Alzheimer example, the withering parent will transform into a magnificent spiritual being immediately after physical death. Her suffering will have not been in vain. Just like the caregiver, the deceased individual will have also learned important hardship lessons from earth school. She will have learned what it means to be frightened and helpless without God. She will have learned empathy for those who suffer. No matter what we face in life, we all learn critical growth oriented lessons. This point cannot be overemphasized. Dr. Kübler-Ross shared her understanding why humans need to struggle in order to accomplish their spiritual mission:

> All the hardships that you face in life, all the trials and tribulations, all the nightmares and all the losses, most people view as a curse, as a

punishment by God, as something negative. If you would only realize that nothing that comes to you is negative... It is an opportunity to grow. You will not grow if you sit in a beautiful flower garden and somebody brings you gorgeous food on a silver platter. But you will grow if you are sick, if you are in pain, if you experience losses, and if you do not put your head in the sand but take the pain and learn to accept it, not as a curse, or as a punishment, but as a gift to you with a very specific purpose.[10]

One NDEr noted that his choices, even bad choices, served a divine purpose for individual growth. He writes:

I knew my whole life, every event both good and bad, yet standing in the presence of divinity, I saw the pure love in all of it. There was NO judgement, only the 'knowing'; that it was all perfect. That my entire life was created in love FOR me. Even my choices, good or bad, had served my highest good in every way. For I was only here to learn and God, along with me, had provided the perfect path for my soul's progression. (NDERF #3304)

From a developmental perspective, discomfort is necessary for significant growth. Daily trials serve as motivators for ongoing change. Let's review a few examples: grounding a child for lying may motivate truthfulness; receiving a failing grade on a college exam may motivate dedicated study; feeling pain may motivate empathy; feeling alone may motivate interpersonal connection; feeling rejection may motivate genuine relationships; facing mortality may motivate appreciation for small blessings; falling to temptation may motivate reliance on God - and the list goes on.

From a human perspective, hardships are a tough sell. One rarely prays, "God, please send me more trials, and this time give me a long, painful disease to endure." Who seeks lessons filled with tribulation and nightmares? Well, according to some NDErs, we all do. Souls choose their human host with guidance, prior to birth, in order to learn specific lessons they need to learn. In other words, souls know their general future after being born. The soul, with guidance, then chooses whether to live those experiences. This is probably a difficult concept for the reader to accept given Western religious tradition. Yet, a number of NDErs report the same revelation. One NDEr wrote the following about choosing a life plan:

I came to understand that we all choose to come to earth to fulfill a plan of some sort or even learn about a particular interest. We choose our bodies and parents and life plan. (NDERF #1653)

Another NDEr wrote about how choosing a life plan relates to lessons learned:

He showed me why I had the parents, childhood, and life I had experienced. I asked Him for it!!! I chose this life because I wanted to learn those lessons. Everything was so clear to me...I had to go through it all to learn what I needed to learn and be able to continue my work here. (NDERF #862)

Still another NDEr wrote about choosing a life of hardships to promote spiritual growth:

Nothing at all sits in accident or chaos. Every single aspect of our lives are ruled by natural Laws that we placed ourselves in! That in a sense, we create our own worlds. I was shown how one can never assume either, that if someone lives a life of suffering that this is because of "evil" deeds. Many may choose a life of suffering because of what it awakens in them, or because of how they can touch others from that position, etc. (NDERF #2386)

These NDErs, and others, state that souls choose certain lives, even difficult lives, to fulfill their mission to grow in love. From this point of view, the human perspective has it backwards. We think that the world created our misery and made us victims. In truth, we created our own difficult world to learn and grow. The divine perspective challenges our very basic beliefs in earthly reality, partly due to our limited understanding of time. We perceive the human lifespan as lengthy. We measure our goals solely on earthly existence: school, marriage, work, children, retirement, etc. Compared to eternity, however, the human lifespan is a blip within an endless sea of time. As an extension of God consciousness, NDErs report that every soul is eternal.

There is an important ramification to the soul choosing a specific host. Namely, mission varies from soul to soul. Although there may be billions, or even trillions, of sentient beings scattered throughout the universe(s), you and I have a distinct mission to fulfill as unique beings. One NDEr wrote this segment about individual missions:

It was made clear to me that some people come to the earth to work on only one aspect of themselves, while others come to work on several aspects. Then there are others who come to not only work on their own nature, but also to help the world as a whole. (NDERF #2932)

Everyone presents with personal strengths and weaknesses. I can think of several personal attributes that need a little polishing. But do I have one predominant weakness? Perhaps I have two? Am I supposed to focus on my family, or my work as a psychologist? Unfortunately, we were not provided with an individualized mission statement at birth. Furthermore, individual missions are rarely overtly revealed by the divine, even during near-death experiences. It appears important, by design, for people to discern their own purpose through trial and error, insight, and serious self-reflection. Perhaps God wants us to select the right choices in life through personal aspiration, not out of obligation. Free will remains a pillar to every mission of the soul on 'school earth'. I speculate, however, that if we don't find our mission, our mission will find us. After all, we are born into circumstances that force our mission upon us. Perhaps if we try to learn and love in all that we do, we cannot go wrong. Our specific mission to love will follow a natural course of development in line with our unique circumstances, personality, and strengths. It is only when we choose not to love that we fail in our mission. That is not to say, however, that defining our mission wouldn't help. Fortunately, we can better define our mission by knowing foundations of our general divine purpose.

The Many Missions to Love

People have many divergent opportunities to learn to love. Some may need to learn to love themselves. Others may need to learn to love an individual, family, group, a society, or even an entire race. The mission possibilities are endless. Let's name a few: A chemist may help cure a wasting disease; an environmentalist may bring attention to a sickening planet; an angry person may work on forgiving; a psychologist may help the overburdened to cope; an animal enthusiast may promote animal rights; a clergyperson may provide moral compass for the lost; a mother or father may provide necessary child direction to succeed in his or her own mission; a depressed person may learn self-value; a person who has had a near-death experience may teach others that death does not exist. Some self-reflective individuals, such as Dr. Kübler-Ross, discovered mission through their life work. She wrote, "But my real job is, and this is why I need your help, to tell people that death does not exist."[10] I believe that teaching "death does not exist" has become my mission, and the purpose for writing this book.

Every soul comes to earth on a mission to become more consistent with the divine. More simply, the important choices in human life involve loving each other. We must embrace that mission to love, not out of obligation, but from the center of our being. The message of love should not be new for many religious seekers. Most religions recognize the spiritual importance of love, including Christianity. Jesus's greatest commandment reads thus: "Love the Lord your God with all your heart and with all your soul and with all your mind. This is the first and greatest commandment. And the second is like it: 'Love your neighbor as yourself'" (Matthew 22:37).

Knowing the human mission to love is vitally important. However, knowledge of mission is only a first step. As a psychologist, I have learned that knowledge is often a necessary but insufficient condition for change. It is not enough that people know that human mission involves love. People need to know *what* love entails. They also need to know *how* to express love in terms of choices and action. Given these critical components to our mission, defining love and how to love will be the focus of the next chapter.

CHAPTER SEVEN

LOVE

What do you feel when someone tells you, "I love you?" The term "love" often invokes strong responses, despite its lack of specificity in the English language. Some speak of familial love, romantic love, sensual love, love for a greater cause, love for humanity, and love of God. Teaching positive psychology to inmates, I have noticed that many students appear confused about the meaning of love. The ancient Greeks understood that love cannot be defined so generally. They tried to capture the complexity of love by breaking it down into four terms: Eros (sensual longing), Phillia (friendship), Storge (familial affection), Agape (spiritual love).[1] Love is repeated frequently throughout NDERF submissions. As noted in the last chapter, NDErs emphasize that love remains a central component to the human mission. What are the qualities of love discussed in the near-death experience? Are NDErs referring to agape love? Or are they referring to something else? Perhaps love simply amounts to a series of chemical reactions serving some evolutionary purpose, as biological scientist David M. Buss proposes. Buss writes that love evolved from our most recent primate ancestors for "long-term mating, concealment of female ovulation, and the heavy investment by men in their children."[2] A majority of spiritual people reject such a mechanical hypothesis. However, before anyone can say what love is not, one must first define what love is. By extension, before people can accomplish their spiritual mission to love others, they must work from an accurate definition of love. It is the purpose of this chapter to specify the attributes of love by examining psychological theory and the near-death experience. With greater clarity, it is hoped that the spiritually-minded person may be better able to plan their mission to love other people.

Defining Love

Many people believe that love is a feeling. Even in everyday language, people say they have "fallen in love". These words assume that love exists as an overpowering, irrational state. According to psychological models and the NDE, the emotional definition fails to capture the complexity of love. "Falling in love" refers to infatuation, a physiological byproduct to sexual attraction. Perhaps genuine love can better be likened to making intentional steps, somewhat like hiking up a mountain. Love reflects an orientation of being more than an emotion; a state that involves almost every facet of human psychology: thoughts, emotions, attitudes, motivations, and behavior. For each facet, the final loving choice requires action. Perhaps the Apostle Paul best captured the multifaceted nature of love almost 2,000 years ago:

> Love is patient, love is kind. It does not boast, it is not proud. It is not rude, it is not self-seeking, it is not easily angered, it keeps no records of wrongs. Love does not delight in evil, but rejoices with the truth. It always protects, always trusts, always hopes, always perseveres. (1st Corinithans 13:4-7)

Although Paul's definition of love encompasses a wide range of human behavior and emotional states, they all have one thing in common. Namely, love is "other" centered. Love requires putting other people first out of a position of care, respect, and compassion. That does not mean that people shouldn't love themselves. It just means that loving behaviors do not elevate the self over others. There is no room for jealousy, hostility, cut-throat competition, undermining deceit, paranoia, hoarding, grudges, hate, or destruction.

Intimacy can be achieved when two people put the other person first. Irvin Yalom proposed that intimacy involves creating an "I-Thou" relationship. The "Thou" refers to a bonded connection based on re-spect.[3] Conversely, the lack of intimacy involves relating to another as an "I-It" relationship. When relating to others as "it", people just be-come things to be strategically handled, used, and manipulated. "It" relatedness seems to pervade social interactions on earth. For example, most relate to a pan handler or the door-to-door salesman with strate-gic coolness. Some people, like the criminal psychopath, strategically relate to everyone as an "it." When a person relates to another pure-ly as a "Thou," their whole being becomes intimately involved in the interaction. Such relationships are defined by active listening, empa-thy, and caring. It is almost a magical state where two people become bonded by a single experience.

The bonding between humans can barely be attained. As previously discussed, empathy becomes severely hampered by our biological sep-arateness in the material realm. Whereas an imperfect bonding may exist on earth, spirits are perfectly fused in heaven. In chapter five, we explored how emotions, thoughts and perceptions are shared through interconnectedness. The difference between the spiritual and earthly realms appears stark. Still, even a weak fusion of "Thou" can be criti-cally important in the development of love on earth. Namely, humans can begin to learn need-free love.

Irvin Yalom wrote an excellent section about need-free love in his textbook, *Existential Psychotherapy*.[3] Quoting from Erich Fromm, Yalom differentiates between mature, need-free love from immature, need-me love. Mature need-free love follows the principle of 'I *am* loved because I love' whereas immature need-me love follows the principle of 'I love because I *am* loved'.[4] In other words, need-free love requires the act of initiating love without knowing the recipient's response. Yalom wrote this about his professional work with psychotherapy patients, "Patients complain of loneliness, of being unloved and unlovable, but the productive work is always to be done in the opposite realm; their inability to love. Love is a positive act, not a passive affect; it is giving, not receiving-a 'standing-in,' not a 'falling for.'"[3]

Mature love involves a variety of positive, selfless, giving behaviors. Mainly, it involves caring for another person, even if that other person doesn't always deserve, or return, that love. It requires that we love first because we want to love, not because we feel obligated to love. In other words, love becomes unconditional.

Unconditional Love

Unconditional love requires a deep caring without precondition or expectation for benefit. It is not associated with anger, revenge, or punishment. Unconditional love grates against our human biology, as evidenced by human social structure. In every society, the winners gain power by beating competitors with guile and strength. The entire world system seems to work on the "might make right" principle. Rich nations exploit poor nations, large corporations ingest small companies, banks lend to the rich but not to the desperate poor, and individuals align themselves with others that have resources and influence. If aliens investigated our social and economic structures, they might conclude that the human species lacks the capacity for altruism. Altruism is possible for humans, however, even if it is temporary. Take a look at the parent-child relationship. Parents may unconditionally love their teenager even when he or she rebels with an attitude of indignation and ingratitude. The parents may sacrifice for that teenager simply because they have always loved the child.

Although revered, unconditional love represents an impossible earthly ideal. Human attempts at unconditional love pale in comparison to God's unconditional love. Even the best attempts seem childish. One NDEr wrote:

> Our life here is only pathetic approximations of what we can achieve through God and His love. Our love is so immature. (NDERF #2037)

There are reasons for our immaturity. Biological drives lead to emotions that interfere with unconditional love: jealousies, anger, and greed. Although a hard truth to swallow, human adults often exhibit the same feelings, desires, and tantrums as toddlers; adults have just been trained to disguise their childish impulses through socialization. Unseemly behavior pours forth, however, when adults become frustrated. In the psychoanalytic tradition, Sigmund Freud noted that people tend to "regress" to earlier childhood states when placed under stress. For example, irrational thoughts may lead to bad choices when a person becomes furious. Any prior loving thoughts are squashed by the fury. For those who never learned self-control, emotional immaturity usually predominates much of their lives. Along these lines, one NDEr wrote:

I was able to enter the minds and emotional centers of many who had been around me, and understand where they were coming from in their own thinking - how their own personal views and life experiences had brought them to the places each stood. I felt their own struggle and their own fears, their own desperate need for love and approval, their confusion, and more than anything, I could feel how child-like everyone was. With every person I viewed, including myself, I was able to see and feel with a higher mind and eye. And the feeling I had toward everyone was nothing less than what a loving mother would feel for her own children at toddler age. (NDERF #2386)

Although God loves us unconditionally, we fail to appreciate that love is due to our disconnection from the divine. Unfortunately, one must experience unconditional love in heaven to know unconditional love. Imagine trying to describe the flavor of chocolate to someone who has never tasted chocolate. Despite the difficulty of the task, some NDErs have nevertheless tried to describe divine love by using metaphors. One NDEr describes divine love as a force:

The Power of Love created and sent out by that being was a force, like electricity is a force. I could feel it being sent out and touching everything around it. (NDERF #1615)

I can hardly imagine a love that has the power of an electrifying force. Another NDEr wrote about becoming fully encompassed by divine love:

This love was possessed of a personality of which I could feel with every fiber of my being flow into me, through me, touching every single part of me... I know of no sensation ever given to me, that in any way approaches the extent of the sensation freely extended to me by this being without reservation. (NDERF #3253)

Another NDEr became nearly overwhelmed by God's love. She wrote:

It knocks your socks off. When you receive this love, it is not comprehended with your mind. It is FELT by your soul. And that immense feeling of this perfect love shoots straight into your heart, as a feeling that you experience. It can bring your soul to its knees, in a sense, with a quick swoosh of sensation. Now, this is not overwhelming in a bad way. It is totally overwhelming in the best way imaginable.

Once you have a taste of it, you will forever be changed. It is total bliss. What you've always wanted, and then so much more. I was awestruck that I was so loved. I still am, and I forever will be. (NDERF #1936)

From a human perspective, it is hard to imagine every part of our being awash with love and bliss. Humans experience the *feeling* of love as a physiological reaction whereas souls experience love with every particle of their being. Humans fail to understand the intensity and inclusiveness of unconditional love due to disconnection to their soul and to the divine. However, there is no reason to despair. We will experience unconditional love again when our earthly sojourn comes to a close. But in the meantime, love can be given and received on earth, even if it pales before the unconditional love of God. It can be best expressed through acts of respect, forgiveness, and sacrifice.

Inherent Respect

Unconditional love becomes demonstrated when an individual cares deeply about the growth and life of another person. Investment in another person's growth can be facilitated by respect. Ideally, respect involves recognizing every person's inherent value as a soul created by God. In the heavenly realm, every spiritual being automatically respects one another on this basis. But on earth, basic respect usually must be earned, often through the appreciation of people's ability, knowledge, authority, and accomplishments. Correspondingly, people who seem to be the most respected include the professional athlete, the expert doctor, the policeman, and the inventor. Perhaps of greater merit, respect can also be given to people who give love freely. Mother Teresa may fit in this category, but so would a dedicated mother and father. These aspects of respect are some of the building blocks to love. Neil Peart suitably wrote, "Beyond basic survival needs, everybody wants to be loved and respected. And neither is any good without the other. Love without respect can be as cold as pity; respect without love can be as grim as fear."[5] What does it mean, "Love without respect can be as cold as pity?" Not every helpful action is motivated by love. Without inherent respect behind giving, aid becomes just acts of pity. I suspect that fear motivates acts of pity more than unconditional love; the uncomfortable thought, "this could happen to me." On the flip side, a criminally minded person will "respect" a more powerful criminal just to share in power. The respect of a criminal is based on fear and greed, not love. Again, love and respect are not much good without each other. Unfortunately, it is difficult to appreciate the value in those who do not command respect based on societal norms.

People often lose respect for those who are different. For this reason, non-conformists often become outcasts: the odd, the sick, the poor, the immigrant, and the mentally challenged. Yet, many outcasts have unseen, untapped worth. Perhaps their potential could be tapped if people noticed their value and interacted with them on an individual "I-Thou" basis instead of an "I-It" basis. A few people have developed the spiritual maturity to respect the outcast with need-free love. Unfortunately, many more have not. If people want to grow spiritually, they might consider respecting those who live outside the norm rather than demeaning them. Criticisms, back-handed compliments, barbed jokes, and gossip all serve to build the ego by undermining others. The underlying motive seems to be, "I'll feel better about myself if I cut you down." In a moment of weakness, even the kindest person can inadvertently disrespect others. Why is that the case? It seems that everyone is competing to be liked and respected by impressing the in-group. From my perspective, humanity has a long way to go to achieve a high level of spiritual maturity based on love.

Some people are disrespected because they disrespect others. A malicious, selfish person is almost impossible to respect, making it virtually impossible for people to love them unconditionally. Respecting the unlovable person seems to be the place where human love consistently falls short. God can love a habitual taker or even a heartless murderer. Humans generally cannot. A higher perspective may be gained, nonetheless, when one recognizes that each individual is a spiritual being created by God. As people glimpse this higher perspective, they may see the value in helping everyone's journey toward the divine.

Although we can guide others through their spiritual journey, we should respect their autonomy. Another aspect of love, then, includes the respect for individual free will. Respect and freedom go hand in hand. God respects humanity enough to grant us freedom to choose while living on school earth. Shouldn't people emulate such respect? Carl Rogers, the founder of the humanist psychology movement, would certainly agree. Carl Rogers asks fellow therapists, "Do we respect his capacity and his right to self-direction, or do we basically believe that his life would be best guided by us?"[6] According to Carl Rogers, disrespect occurs when a person becomes coerced to bend their will for another. There are many sources of coercion on earth, including propaganda, dogmatic religion, and despotic government.

The skeptic might argue that respect for autonomy is impractical on earth. To prevent anarchy, the masses must be corralled into obedience. Obviously, society cannot function without laws and rules. Respecting the individual does not exclude culpability. A person can be held accountable while still maintaining their dignity. I observe this dynamic frequently when working in prisons. Inmates caught breaking prison rules usually accept disciplinary sanctions if the rules are enforced fairly. If they become aggressive, it is usually because they are not treated respectfully.

Although there are limits to autonomy on earth, people would do well by expanding individual's freedoms. God honors human autonomy. Although God is all-powerful, the Creator allows for free-will. Evil could be wiped out instantly. Yet, God respects each individual freedom enough to tolerate evil. Rob Bell, a progressive Christian theologian, put it this way:

> Although God is powerful and mighty, when it comes to the human heart, God has to play by the same rules we do. God has to respect our freedom to choose to the very end, even at the risk of the relationship itself. If at any point God overrides, co-opts, or hijacks the human heart, robbing us of our freedom to choose, then God has violated the fundamental essence of what love even is.[7]

Have we earned God's respect? Only God can say. But God respects everyone through love, nevertheless. Humans are charged to do the same as part of our mission to love unconditionally. Yet, how do we respect the disrespectful, especially those who harm us? To see the inherent worth of the unlovable, we must overlook their transgressions. This feat requires the greatest and most difficult aspect of love, namely forgiveness.

The Gift of Forgiveness

Forgiveness may be the most stringent litmus test for pure, unconditional love. The act of forgiveness requires removing any bitterness or grudge toward the perpetrator, even if the transgression resulted in deep emotional injury. Forgiveness unlocks many doors to love by giving the victim an opportunity to respect and value a perpetrator, despite the perpetrator devaluing the victim. Obviously, it is easier to forgive those who sincerely ask for forgiveness, especially for the simple mistake made outside character. It is much tougher to forgive a habitual offender who displays little remorse. Tough forgiveness requires the victim to "turn the other cheek" and to be ready for more strikes. In other words, there is no guarantee that the perpetrator will even appreciate the act of forgiveness. In my experience as a psychologist, however, forgiveness has tremendous healing power, even for the relatively hardened individual. Despite its magnetic power in attracting good, forgiveness can be a difficult choice. In his book, *Authentic Happiness*, Martin Seligman[8] notes three reasons why it is difficult to forgive:

1. Forgiving is seen as unjust. It undermines punishment for the guilty and steals away justice for the victim.
2. Forgiving shows love toward the perpetrator but not for the victim.
3. Forgiving blocks revenge that may seem natural and right.

Many people do not hold forgiveness as a virtue, but rather a corruption of human justice. As discussed in chapter seven, human justice is motivated by our anchored positions, often entrenched, and also the need for revenge. Yet, there is always a cost-benefit to holding grudges. Benefits may include restitution and other external rewards. The costs to holding a grudge are typically psychological in nature. Psychological costs include embracing the victim role, a commitment to remain angry, and termination of relationships.[9] Grudges can particularly cause havoc in intimate human relationships. Take a look at marriage, for example. The self-identified victim may become completely disinterested in the perpetrator. Consequently, the companionship, gratifications, and pleasures derived from a healthy marriage may be severed over time, leading to sustained marital conflict and even divorce.

Human justice appears discordant with God's justice. Almost every NDEr describes God's forgiveness as boundless. Human beings, despite our multitude of transgressions, are automatically forgiven through God's unconditional love. This point cannot be understated. People do not always make the connection between unconditional love and total absolution. They fail to make the connection because human love is incomplete; there always seem to be conditions and upper limits. Religion often claims that God's love is boundless and unconditional.

Yet, even strongly religious people tend to project human conditional attributes on to God. For example, some may believe that they have sinned too much to go to heaven. Yet, humans are found faultless *because* of complete love. Our transgressions are washed away leaving us pristine in the view of God. One NDEr wrote:

> I had spent a lifetime of fear of judgment and now, standing with God, I had been known completely and found faultless. I knew God regarded me as perfect. God loved me because love is the totality of God. God loves without limit. Finally it all made sense. God could only love me because God is only love, nothing other than love. (NDERF #1011)

God loves and forgives everyone even though we do not love or forgive ourselves. As Anita Moorjani wrote, "When there's no judgment, there is nothing to pardon."[10] Along these lines, an NDEr described unconditional forgiveness after attempting suicide:

> That being knew all of everything I ever was and loved me. Not just loved me but everything that defined me as myself, unique from any other bit of creation, was wonderful to it. It loved the way I was made. It loved that we were meeting. It loved me with all the love It had in it. Its love overpowered me. I knew that I was precious to It and treasured by It. I was perfectly what I was supposed to be and It loved me just that way. If I was a diamond, I was flawless, perfectly cut, beyond beautiful. I could not be loved more by that being. (NDERF #1615)

This individual NDEr, who suffered debilitating depression, was radically transformed by God's love. Finding self-affirmation and worth, he no longer sought peace in death.

Human love can never measure up to God's love. However, it is our mission to try. Thus, we are likewise charged to forgive. Shortly before the time of this writing, an inmate died at the hospital and was revived. Learning about his recovery from medical staff, I asked him if he had a near-death experience. Answering "yes," the inmate shared that he spoke with Jesus. Jesus asked him to recite the greatest commandment during their exchange. The inmate answered, "To love others." Jesus replied, "No, it is to forgive others, from which your love will spring and develop." This NDE message, as all NDE messages, was uniquely tailored to this particular individual's spiritual mission. The inmate admitted to me that he struggled with forgiveness; he simmered in a state of anger from grudges long harbored. After he returned from the hospital, the inmate promptly resolved several conflicts both at the institution and at home by offering forgiveness. This process not only worked to resolve most of his conflicts, but it provided him additional peace and happiness. This person, named David, shared with me his understanding of forgiveness as revealed during the NDE:

> Let me forgive all men of their anger and hatred towards me, and all men their differences, so that they may forgive me mine. Through forgiveness each of us is blameless so that we may be joined as equals in the unity of forgiveness and love for one another. May we walk a path of forgiveness until our worlds become One.

Just as there is a strong relationship between love and forgiveness, there also exists a strong inverse relationship between anger and forgiveness. A significant number of people who complain of chronic anger have suffered appalling abuse during their childhood. Should they forgive their perpetrator? Many believe not. Yet, forgiveness may be the only relief from bottled anger. Otherwise, anger, the most corrosive of emotions, will simmer or grow into a toxic monster. Ironically, the person who holds grudges may suffer the most. Humans can only experience one emotional physiology response, or strong emotion, at a time. If the grudge holder exists in a perpetual state of anger, then there is no time to feel any other emotions, such as joy, happiness, or love. So, how does one turn their back on anger and embrace forgiveness? In his book, *Dimensions of Forgiveness*, psychologist Everett Worthington[11] wrote a five step process to forgiveness he called REACH:

> Recall the hurt: After a person becomes victimized, fear, anxiety, anger may be experienced whenever the victim is near the perpetrator. Consequently, victims avoid perpetrators and anything associated with the hurtful event. Unfortunately, avoidance sabotages the possibility for forgiveness or reconciliation. By repeatedly recalling the hurt in a safe environment, the memories are paired with neutral consequences leading to a partial reduction of negative emotions.

> Empathize with the perpetrators point of view: Empathy involves knowing the thoughts and feelings of another person. Usually there are reasons why the perpetrator acted the way he or she did. For a victim to empathize with the perpetrator, it is important for them to speculate

what the perpetrator was thinking or feeling during the hurtful event. It is also important for them to recall the good experiences with the offender, if possible, during better times. By generating empathy, the victim may begin to show compassion for the perpetrator, which primes them for the next step.

<u>Altruism, or selfless regard, for the perpetrator:</u> Altruism entails deciding to forgive the perpetrator, whether it is deserved or not. Thus, altruism is a gift. The act of forgiving is usually difficult, but can be eased if the victim understands that he or she may have a role in the hurt. In other words, responsibility is rarely completely one-sided; harm is usually reciprocal. In this stage, it is also helpful for the victim to remember a time when he or she was forgiven by someone else and recall the feeling of release after being absolved.

<u>Commit by forgiving publically:</u> A public declaration of forgiveness can strengthen the commitment to forgive. This can be done in a variety of ways, such as making a public announcement or writing a letter.

<u>Hold onto the forgiveness:</u> Forgiveness may weaken over time. Hurt may increase with further rumination, especially if more hurtful events are recalled. Additional forgiveness may be needed in some cases. Thus, the REACH process may need to be repeated.

Displaying altruism for the perpetrator may be the hardest part of REACH. Altruism seems to be almost mystical. A psychologist, for instance, cannot instruct a client how to make the switch from grudge to forgiveness. However, a psychologist may encourage a client to forgive by an act of "letting go." Letting go must be a decisive act of free will. Although difficult, it can be, and it has been, done. Unfortunately, reconciliation sometimes becomes impossible. Even in these unresolvable situations, forgiveness may usually be the best choice, if only to liberate the grudge holder from a cycle of anger.

Acts of Sacrifice

Forgiveness requires a dramatic shift in attitude and belief. Yet attitudes and beliefs add to only one dimension of unconditional love. How do we apply unconditional love and forgiveness to our lives? The principle action component to unconditional love is sacrifice. Sacrifice has several meanings. For the purposes of this book, sacrifice may be defined as surrendering something personally precious for the good of another. Sacrifice can include the intentional loss of pleasures, comforts, wealth, time, goals, and possibly life itself. Sacrifice is where the spiritual muscle lifts the heavy weights of life. Imagine a young man walking down the sidewalk. What action best represents unconditional love for this young man, to help a beautiful woman carry groceries across the street, or to help a struggling old lady carry groceries across the street? Both represent giving behaviors. But only the latter involves the sacrifice of time and effort for a stranger in need. Ulterior motives, such as flirting, may better explain the man's eager desire to help the attractive woman. There appears to be no ulterior motive helping the elderly woman, however, other than maybe receiving a word of appreciation. Although this example demonstrates a small sacrifice, there are opportunities for much larger sacrifices in life: donating one's inheritance to charity; caring for an elderly parent; resigning from a lucrative job to care for a sick child at home; giving up valuable Saturdays to work at shelters; giving up the easy life to work overseas missions; dying for another during war.

The science of psychology has barely given passing notice to sacrifice. When the subject is broached, sacrifice is mostly studied from an evolutionary perspective. Some evolutionists are perplexed because sacrifice does not increase an organism's chances for survival. What possibly could be the survival benefit for an individual to give up resources for another? To explain this inconsistency, some evolutionists propose that individual sacrifice increases the survival chances of the community. They call this concept kin selection.[12] Evolutionary theory may contribute to the understanding of genetically based behavior. However, genetics explains only one small dimension of sacrifice. Evolution fails to explain how sacrifice impacts human thoughts and feelings from a personal growth perspective. More pointedly, it fails to incorporate the experiential impact of changed lives, nor does it say anything about the larger purpose sacrifice has on divine mission.

Sacrifice has been a central tenet in many religions, both East and West, as a means to express need-free love. In the Christian book of Romans, the apostle Paul instructs new Roman devotees to sacrifice for the faith. He writes, "Therefore, I urge you, brothers, in view of God's mercy, to offer your bodies as living sacrifices" (Romans 12:1). Sacrifice also plays a central role in Hinduism. In the fourth chapter of the

Bhagavad Gita, the Hindu god Krishna teaches, "Know that all sacrifice is holy work, and knowing this will set you free."[13] Sacrifice is also a repeated theme in the near-death experience. Similar to the Hindu text, NDErs report that sacrifice helps set a person free.

An NDEr asked God why people are born with disabilities. God answered that the disabled taught people how to love through sacrifice. It is difficult to reconcile the message of pain and suffering with a benevolent God. Why must people suffer permanent disabilities or struggle as caretakers? As discussed in chapter six, the answer is embedded in the soul's mission to learn love. Sacrifice shifts, or even jolts, a person from a "self-centered" position to an "other-centered" position. Let's review the growth process from the perspective of the caregiver for a disabled person. By working with the disabled, a caregiver learns empathy through a fusion of experience. Empathy, in turn, leads to compassion. By acting with compassion, the person learns to appreciate their own comparative blessings, big and small. Next, gratitude teaches humility through our own powerlessness. Collectively, all these lessons generalize to loving other people. People start to matter more than things. In the end, the soul has learned important lessons on school earth through acts of sacrifice. Namely, the soul has been set free from the insidious chains of self-absorption.

Unfortunately, sacrifice often involves hardship, sometimes even prolonged suffering. People usually despair over suffering and view it as a curse from God. Some even throw out their arms and plead in desperation, "Why God!?" People may interpret God's silence as uncaring. Others may reject God completely. It has been my observation that many atheists reject God because of suffering rather than evidence-based science. Regardless, NDErs report that God deeply cares about our suffering. Yet, God also knows that suffering serves a purpose on school earth and is only a temporary situation during the soul's existence on earth. Sometimes spiritual growth must be forged by fire.

The Ego versus Self-Love

The term "spiritual growth" has a specific meaning within the context of love. It is not enough to know our mission. Love is a verb that requires action. Spiritual growth depends on moving toward God. Eben Alexander noted, "Our life down here may seem insignificant, for it is minute in relation to the other lives and other worlds that also crowd the invisible and visible universes. But it is also hugely important, for our rule here is to grow toward the Divine."[14]

If our life mission is so important, how do we know whether we are on a good track? Ignorance clouds the journey, leading the bumbling wanderer into a briar bush. Thus, we should not only discuss "what to do" but also "what not to do." Knowing the difference keeps us on the right path. After working with prisoners for many years, I have concluded that the "root of all evil" is selfishness. Criminal thinking boils down to "I want, what I want, when I want it, and I don't care what I have to do to get it. If someone gets hurt, it is their fault for getting in my way." Exploitation demonstrates how self-centeredness is inconsistent with need-free love. One cannot fulfill one's mission to love and glorify the self. In other words, one cannot serve both God and ego. The typical preoccupations of ego are of little concern to God. Our mission involves learning and loving, not the acquisition of wealth, power, or personal prestige. One NDEr wrote:

> It was not what I did in physical life that mattered most. It was who I was, who I am inside, my soul that was more important than any physical thing I did. (NDERF #1936)

Have you ever observed that escaping problems only leads to more of the same? A person trying to escape a bad marriage, for example, may eventually enter another loveless relationship. Some mistakenly interpret a cycle of unfortunate events as "bad luck." Worse, they may blame everyone else. Yet, problems cannot always be blamed on the environment. Rather, the deeper causes are often spiritual. When this is the case, chronic unhappiness may serve as a warning to get back to mission. Unfortunately, many people miss the warning. They are too wrapped up in ego to see beyond themselves. Over-reliance on ego was a lesson that Howard Storm learned during his near-death experience. After being saved from a hellish environment, he wrote:

> My life was devoted to building a monument to my ego. My family, my sculptures, my painting, my house, my gardens, my little fame, my illusions of power, were all an extension of my ego...all those things that I have lived for were lost to me, and they didn't mean a thing.[15]

Relatedly, Storm later wrote about pride and selfishness:

The delusion of independence is pride, and pride is the source of all sin (that which intentionally separates us from God). To know God's love, we have to rid ourselves of the delusion of independence. We create our ego in response to the experience of our life. Tragically, we create egos that eliminate our relationship with God. Even people who think they are religious often attempt to manipulate God for their own self-centered purposes.[15]

People seem amazed whenever wealthy celebrities die by suicide. Many wonder how they could not be happy. After all, the rich and famous appear to have gained everything desirable: wealth, adoration, fame, influence. In reality, fame leads to a downward cycle on a path of self-absorption, excesses, destructive behaviors, and addiction. The pampered never learn the hard lessons of love because they are too busy building monuments to ego. A self-described celebrity wrote about the impact of his NDE:

By the time I was twenty I had started on a path that would lead to fame and riches for all the wrong reasons. And after twenty-five years of this, I had succeeded in accomplishing most of my goals. The way up the ladder was not always easy nor did my survival have anything to do with my own design. It seemed that my curse was that I was as untouchable as I was unhappy no matter how the stories and wealth accumulated.

My first thoughts were about how and when my family would find out that I had died and how would my dog get fed and taken care of. Then it got more serious as I realized that it did not matter whether I was wealthy or poor, or whether I was driving a luxury car or a junker, because I was about to leave this earth. I did not feel qualified to pray for my life at that time. However, I had a one-way conversation with God and I acknowledged to him that my life had been one of foolishness. (NDERF #1113)

This NDEr expected to be sent to hell for his foolish life. Rather, he was given a second opportunity to orient his life toward love. Although this transformation was gradual, it did eventually happen.

Some might equate the building of ego with loving the self. Some even claimed that loving the self is sinful because it supersedes our love of God. I view such spiritual teaching to be highly questionable.

Ego refers to loving the self *at the expense of loving others*. A healthy self-love involves loving everyone, including the self. It is practically impossible to love others if we cannot reach them from a position of self-respect, confidence, and spiritual strength. People who dislike themselves lack these qualities because they are blinded by negativity. Feeling worthless, they believe that others dislike them as well.

Anita Moorjani wrote extensively about the devaluation of self. In her case, she learned how personal devaluation caused her terminal cancer. She wrote:

> In my culture, I was taught to put others first and myself last or not at all. I wasn't taught to love myself or to value who and what I am. As a consequence, I had very little to offer others. Only when we fill our own cup with regard for ourselves, will we have any to give away... Cherishing the self comes first, and caring for others is the inevitable outcome. Selfishness comes from too little self-love, not too much, as we compensate for our lack.[10]

Some self-absorbed people have difficulty recognizing the value in themselves and others. Narrowly centered, they become mired in a glut of problems. Not only do some people fail to cherish themselves, but they actually despise themselves. Too many have escaped self-inflicted pain through suicide. According to Acceptance and Commitment Theory, people kill themselves by formulating negative self-assessments.[16] In other words, suicides occur when people slice into their self-image with barbed thoughts. They fail to practice love - first toward themselves and then toward others.

The Practice of Love

The practice of love has psychological benefits beyond fulfilling divine mission. Psychological research indicates that practicing love leads to greater happiness in life. In the book, *Authentic Happiness*, Martin Seligman noted several environmental and personal factors relating to human happiness based on a broad array of research. These factors include: living in a democracy; marriage; avoiding negative events and emotions (moderate effect); maintaining a rich social network; realizing strengths and virtues; raising children; unconditional love. Environmental and personal factors that do not relate to human happiness include: making more money (beyond meeting basic needs); constantly pursuing pleasures; staying healthy (surprisingly); higher education; moving to a sunnier climate.[8] It appears that happiness may be strongly correlated with our mission to love other people. Note that becoming "flawless" was not on the list. We do not need to be perfect to effectively love. In fact, we may actually stifle our love in our efforts to be perfect.

Accepting personal frailties enhances our ability to practice love in the long run. Recognizing imperfection leads to faster growth because we learn from making mistakes. I tend to think of mistakes as classwork on school earth. When Howard Storm was faced with return, his spiritual guides said, "When you go back, you will make mistakes. That is how you learn and grow. If you didn't make mistakes, you would be either perfect or dead (in heaven). God created a world where you learn by your experience. The important thing you need to learn is to stop repeating the same mistakes over and over again."[15]

Making mistakes is part of being a fallible human being. What is important is that we recognize our mistakes, take responsibility, and seek better alternatives. In this manner, we respect ourselves through self-forgiveness. Rather than attacking ourselves, we should simply blame the behavior. For example, instead of saying, "I am so stupid", it would be more rational to say, "I should have planned better" or "I should have made a better choice." Blaming behavior may cause some guilt, but guilt can be healthy as the discomfort it produces motivates positive change. By attacking the self, however, the person tears down their personal integrity. They do not feel guilt, but rather shame. This shame leaves them feeling hopeless and depressed. They may ask, "What's the point in even trying if I am going to fail anyway?" Shame sabotages our divine mission to love. Thus, it is vital that people recognize their mistakes as a source of spiritual growth rather than a source of humiliation.

Individual Value and the Personal Love of God

Some individuals believe in the words and actions of negative people. Mistreated children often internalize the terrible messages communicated by their adult abusers. Who is at fault, the child or the adult? From a third person perspective, obviously the culprit must be the adult. But from the child victim's perspective, he or she might think, "If only if I tried harder I would not be hated by my parents. If I was good enough they wouldn't hit me so hard." Traumatized and scarred, victims understandably doubt the existence of a loving God, especially when they grow into adulthood. They conclude that a loving God would never allow such terrible suffering to happen to them, or anyone like them. Indeed, a loving God does seem absent during the darkest hours of life. Yet according to the message of the near-death experience, God is fully present in the background of our traumas, even helping us in subtle ways. There are several NDE submissions that deal with this topic. I have included one special NDE submission that touched me personally. Having attempted suicide, the NDEr meets with God in a courtroom type scene. However, the purpose of the trial is not as it first appears. The NDEr is very angry at God for allowing horrendous abuse since the age of four. God does not respond as she expected while her anger is unleashed. Reconciliation ensues. She wrote:

> I could no longer conceal my anger. Without thinking I started yelling about the injustices that had robbed me of wholeness all of my life...I asked, "Where were you? The first time I was molested, I was four years old. Violently molested, held down against my will and violated! Four! Where were you then?"

> My hands covered my mouth with lightning speed. Had I really just yelled at the judge, at God, creator of the heavens and the universe? I waited in horror to be smote to ash and dust. No lightning bolts blazed from his eyes, no hate came from his lips. I remained where I was in the judgment seat, no ash, fire, or flame. "Look at me," his voice was low and gentle. "I can't," I squeaked. I was too ashamed and too afraid to move. "You can," he said in a soothing voice, engendering so much love and trust to me in that moment. He reached over the bench with his hand and gave me his strength. "Look at me," he urged again. When my shallow and tear-soaked eyes met his, I saw that moment of violation from his view. I saw his heart swell to its brink with torture and pain. I saw the Creator of the Universe cry out with pain. He reached out through time and distance toward me, and took my little hand in his. In that moment of violation, he sent his love and his comfort radiating through my little four year-old body. His giant hand, so full of light and radiance, dwarfed my smallness. We endured that moment together, the Creator and I, both tear-soaked and full of heart wrenching pain. Through my weakness, he gave me His own strength. (NDERF #3169)

Perhaps this NDE submission well captures the personal loving nature of God. God is often viewed by people as a background cosmic puppeteer; an entity more busy running the universe than helping the individual through the mundane struggles of daily life. Thus, people see God more as an abstraction than a spiritual mother or father. Yet, this submission demonstrates that God's love is strong, unconditional, and very personal. Even though people are temporarily separated from that direct love while living on earth, there is no mistake that God feels and cares greatly about our worst pain and most endured period of suffering.

No doubt many people will continue to doubt God's love as long as there is suffering. Perhaps it would be easier for people to endure suffering if they understood that the soul is eternal. In its natural state, the soul, or true self, is impervious to suffering and death. Every soul goes back to the Source just as every finite mission leads back to the infinite. The human life is a biological vehicle to move the soul, the true self, closer to divine unity. Our human lives are not accidental. Our lives have been carefully customized to maximize growth. This human life, then, has great value. Howard Storm wrote, "Everyone begins their journey toward God in their own way according to their spiritual need. Those paths are unlimited and the end is the same, which is God"[15]

Using an earlier analogy, every soul can be conceived as a thread weaved into a splendid tapestry. Each life is interconnected with God consciousness. Collectively, we all share in a mission to co-create, grow, and love. As time goes forward, we all become complete as individuals in harmony with the divine. In the end, when every thread is woven into place, everything will be of God. Still, every thread will remain unique. Indeed, God's tapestry is very diverse and colorful. We all are loved. We all are important. We are anchored in a purpose embedded in our cherished individuality, our interconnection, and our shared mission.

All children of God, loved and cherished beyond measure, will experience the incredible unconditional love that awaits them after graduation from school earth. Human life is the soul's opportunity to love through expressions of free will. This is a gift that God has freely given to each soul. It may be foolish to waste this gift by discarding life's precious opportunity to love by embracing the selfish ego. Thankfully, if we *try* to love others at every opportunity, even imperfectly, we cannot flunk school earth. As we have explored in this chapter, that means that we need to work on developing unconditional love of self and others through acts of respect, forgiveness, and sacrifice. God helps us learn these lessons through adversity and by making mistakes. In order to love others, people cannot complete their mission by filling life with superficial interactions. The more we connect with other people in a genuine loving way, the more we will have opportunity to succeed in our mission to learn and love. Connecting with other people is so vitally important, in fact, that it will be the topic in a soon to come chapter. But let's first apply the concepts of love and mission to a real life, personal story. The next chapter shares the NDE and life experience of a woman named Candy.

CHAPTER EIGHT

CANDY

(TESTIMONY NO. 1)

Clinical psychologists deal with human pain, regardless of the target population. Working as a prison psychologist, I have found that inmates have their own clinical presentation. I am sometimes asked, "Aren't all those inmates depressed? I certainly would be depressed if I were in prison." I respond that, although some inmates struggle, the prison population actually has a lower suicide rate than people who live in the community. Do prisoners enjoy incarceration better than freedom? Probably not. Many complain about food, noise, cramped quarters, and being told what to do. Almost everyone looks forward to release. Thus, it is unlikely that their relative contentment has anything to do with prison. Rather, many inmates are relatively content because they have been saved. The legal system has removed them from their self-destructive lifestyles filled with violence, drug abuse, and fear. Some are even transformed through prison programming. I have often heard inmates say, "Going to prison was the best thing that ever happened to me."

Why are some people happier in prison than in the community? It is the state of soul that brings joy, not external circumstances. This seems contradictory to conventional thinking. Yet, I see some inmates experience joy in prison. I often ask inmates, "How do you find freedom within when your body is locked up?" The current chapter addresses the very heart of this question by sharing the struggles of a woman who learned to be free of spirit despite being trapped, literally, in her body. It is a story about Candy.

Candy seemed to have it all, by earthly standards, prior to her accident about 25 years ago. The day was June 18, 1989. It was a beautiful, cloudless day over San Diego bay. Candy was having "a blast" waterskiing under the warm Southern California sun. Why wouldn't Candy be having fun? She was a young attractive woman advancing her career as a pediatric nurse. She was married to a wealthy real estate tycoon. She dined at the finest restaurants, socialized at lavish parties, and traveled around the world. She was raising a beautiful daughter, an energetic toddler, whom she adored. What a thrill it was to be gliding over the water, as a vibrant young woman living life, when disaster struck.

Candy splashed into the water after a routine fall. Moments later, another boat turned toward her and plowed into her body. Within less than a second, Candy's entire life changed. Such a blow had the force to sever her body in two. For whatever the reason, the keel of the boat only severed part of her body, mostly below the rib line. Although it was a miracle that Candy did not die instantly, the collision caused catastrophic injury. The speeding boat completely severed her spinal cord, ripped-out a kidney, destroyed part of her intestines, damaged her liver, and partially crushed one arm. How did she survive? The cold water and wetsuit kept her from "bleeding-out" long enough to be transported to the hospital. Arriving at the emergency room, doctors administered seventy units of blood to try to stabilize her. It was not enough. Candy's lungs began to fill with fluid and she slipped into death.

Candy experienced a seamless and immediate exit from her misery. Rising above her torn body, she suddenly found herself floating in a realm of blackness punctuated by a bright orb of light. Candy had been instantly transformed into a bodiless essence of spirit. She knew that her essence had become healed; the pain and terror were gone. There was one primary quality that defined her new discovery of being, complete love. This love had little parallel to the mundane earth experience. Rather, it was a love so pure and intense that it washed over every particle of her being. Fumbling to provide a description, Candy used a metaphor to describe how she felt. She stated that divine love was like looking into the eyes of a newborn baby, innocent and untainted by the world. Unlike an artificial high, Candy experienced no elation, compromised judgment, fluctuating emotions, or altered states of consciousness. Rather, the love she experienced was pure, steady, and authentic. Candy quickly realized that death was built on a foundation of love.

Candy immediately focused her attention on the brilliant orb pouring out pure light in the distance. The orb was unlike any earthly light, such as a strobe flash or even the sun. Although it was indescribably intense, it was not painful to perceive. The light had a kind of conscious solidity to its rich essence; it was vibrant, expansive, and infinitely aware. Candy saw two vague shadowed figures hovering in the foreground, dark relative to the light behind them. Despite their undefined shapes, Candy knew their identity as her deceased mother and aunt. They only communicated love. In the background hovered an infinite presence. Candy calculated that if one added all the love experienced in a human lifetime, it would not compare to the love she felt in those few moments floating before God.

God began to review Candy's life. Interestingly, Candy does not recollect participating in her own review. However, she understood that she would have to return to her mangled body, but that her final home would be heaven. Candy resisted return despite knowing that her family was pleading for her return. She could actually "see" family hovering over her lifeless body lying in the ICU. She witnessed her brother plead, "Come back! Your daughter needs you! We need you!" Although the pull to return was strong, it was not nearly as strong as her desire to stay. Candy tried to push forward, but her way was blocked. She implored to continue into heaven. Candy communicated telepathically, "Please, can I go forward? I am in tremendous pain on earth!"

Candy received a clear answer. A strong "voice" communicated, "The book of your life is not finished. You have completed the first half of your book. Now you must finish the second half." Candy was immediately slammed back into her body. Excruciating pain subsequently seized her mind. Lungs topped with fluid, she painfully labored to take her first two breaths. Yet, the breathing continued and became easier. Candy was back on earth to live the second half of her life book. For better or worse, the second half would be nothing like the first.

Recovery was incredibly difficult. Candy remained immobilized in the hospital and suffered constant, indescribable pain. Looking back, she had never forgotten the smell of blood in her hair. Time slowly ground on as Candy made it from one day to the next. Days became weeks and weeks became months. In all, Candy spent over a year in the hospital, slowly recovering from one surgery only to prepare for the next surgery. She had her arm reconstructed, an eye repaired, a thyroid removed, rods placed in her back, and so on. Candy underwent over 40 surgeries during that arduous first year. There was nothing liberating about her recovery. For the first two months she could not sit up beyond five degrees without passing out. In addition to the physical trauma, Candy had to deal with the emotional trauma stemming from her accident and ongoing hospital experiences. The surgeons told Candy that her spine had been completely severed below the T-10 vertebrae. Without neural communication traveling up and down in her spinal column, Candy would never feel the touch of a hand or move a muscle below her rib cage. She would remain a paraplegic forever. One can only imagine the shock of suddenly losing mobility, bladder control, and bowel continence. Candy's future seemed grim.

Candy's life was turned upside down by the accident. She could no longer work as a nurse or act in the role of "trophy wife" for her wealthy husband. Running had been her primary means to cope with stress. Even that was taken away from her during a long period of immeasurable stress. Every hope and plan in life was now in doubt. However, two truths were never in doubt. One, Candy knew that God loved her. Second, Candy knew that she had a special purpose on earth, even as she faced a very uncertain future. Somehow, she kept focused on the brilliant light shining in the darkness. Rather than wallowing in despair, she developed a sense of new mission that would flower in accordance to God's plan. Candy worked to rise above the negativity, let go of her need for control, and learned to trust without having any life map to guide her forward.

During the interview, Candy told me, "I don't have a poor me attitude." Indeed, she never showed any self-pity or sign of depression. Although Candy admitted to periods of sadness, she claimed that she never despaired for long. She admitted to periods of frustration, but rarely became angry. Although she questioned the future, she never gave up hope. Although she sometimes felt abandoned by people, she maintained faith in God. Candy decided to live free in her mind even though she was trapped in a broken body. She would find a way to live fully, despite all the odds against her. True, she could no longer cope with stress by running. But now she had a new coping mechanism, prayer.

The power of prayer helped heal Candy's spirit and body. Candy was provided spiritual assistance during her grueling recovery in the hospital. For instance, she received divine intervention during two risky surgeries. Both operations were risky enough to place her life in danger, yet were necessary for any hope of recovery. While under anesthesia, Candy witnessed a large angel during her first surgery. Although the angel displayed no particular form, Candy understood that the being wielded a great deal of power and authority. Through telepathy, the angel imparted two messages. The first message was, "I am with you." The second was, "You have more to do." Candy interpreted these messages to mean that she was to continue living in hope and with God's protection. On the second surgery, Candy witnessed a beautiful, perfect garden. Standing in the garden was a large spiritual being she felt to be Jesus. There were approximately fifty less-powerful spiritual beings in the garden as well. Candy heard them say, "We are here to help you." She marveled that there were so many spiritual beings working on her behalf.

Candy eventually healed enough to be released to the care of her family. Her challenges did not lessen at home. In addition to dealing with pain and the lack of mobility, Candy now had to cope with an abusive husband. As a trophy wife, Candy's husband remained civil provided she attended to his every need. Candy had assumed the role with a measure of success. She dutifully attended all of her husband's parties, work functions, church activities, and Bible studies. Candy's selfless service only enabled her husband to live a self-absorbed lifestyle that he had expected since early childhood. Raised by servants, her husband only knew how to take, never to give. After the accident, circumstances demanded that their roles be reversed. Unfortunately, her husband never intended to fulfill the role of a caretaker. He became increasingly angry and resentful that Candy could no longer fulfill him. He began to berate and curse her, calling her "half a person" and worse. On one occasion he threw her out of the car by a roadside field. Candy was left lying in a ditch, wondering how she could maneuver past the barbed wire fence in order to crawl to the nearest farmhouse. The husband eventually returned after two hours, but only in response to the pleading cries of their children. He stated that he would "punish her for days." This was one promise that he did fulfill. Candy finally left him after he cut a big gash in her forehead. It no longer mattered that she lived in wealth. She fled and never looked back.

Candy states that her ex-husband legally owes her a quarter of a million dollars. He reportedly has not paid a cent. According to Candy, the courts refused to enforce any legal child support arrangements. In like manner, they reportedly did not hold him accountable for four subsequent felonies beyond slapping him with probation. Candy believes that her ex-husband, wealthy and politically connected, paid off the judges. It would have been easy for her to remain embittered by the ongoing abuse and subsequent injustices. Yet, Candy chose a different path – a path of forgiveness. She chose to forgive her husband by "letting go" of resentments and plans for justice. Accordingly, she has no intention to pursue further lawsuits to reclaim owed money. Although Candy could certainly use the financial assistance, she believes a prolonged battle in court is not worth the expense of generating anger and bitterness within her. Candy absolved her ex-husband despite knowing that he would never appreciate or acknowledge her act of forgiveness. She would rather spend her time and energy loving other people. In other words, she would rather forgive him than veer off mission by restricting her mind and spirit. In retrospect, Candy believes that her abusive marriage actually served a larger good. Candy's recovery required ongoing character development based on fortitude, resilience, and determination. Candy believes that she would have failed in her mission to achieve any level of autonomy if not for her sheer tenacity. This level of tenacity would have been absent, she believes, if she was served by a doting husband.

Miracles started to occur not long after Candy left her husband. Specifically, Candy began to perceive tingling sensations below her spinal-cord injury. Tingling sensations were followed by small movements, then larger movements, and eventually bladder and bowel control. These early milestones opened a new world for Candy that most people take for granted. Candy could now learn to drive, seek employment, and recreate. With every new sensation and movement, Candy pushed herself ever harder and further. She developed a passionate and relentless drive to prevail over her disability, living life with respect and without compromise. As Candy developed feeling, strength, and muscle control, she started doing all her own cleaning, shopping, and yard work. For recreation, she began riding a bicycle with her feet duct taped to the pedals, obtained her scuba diver license, and even made short hikes with crutches. Candy even celebrated her accomplishments by entering the 2002 Miss Wheelchair competition.

The doctors continue to be baffled by Candy's ongoing recovery. According to the original medical tests, Candy's spinal-cord had been completely severed. She even showed me the X-rays to prove her point. Although heavy scar tissue prevents doctors from imaging everything around the spinal-cord injury today, recent imaging supports the original diagnosis that Candy's spine remains severed. In other words, there are no medical explanations as to why Candy can hike on crutches, much less exhibit any motor function below the spinal cord injury. Candy is proof that there are modern miracles of healing. In this manner, she continues to serve as a testimony for others.

Candy's story did not go unnoticed. She won the 2002 Miss Wheelchair competition and was invited to the White House. Unfortunately, the summer of 2002 coincided with the ongoing military response to the 9/11 terrorist attack. President George W. Bush had cancelled most public recognition events, including a meeting with 2002 Miss Wheelchair. Out of tenacity, Candy called White House staffers asking them to reconsider. Amazingly, they did reconsider. During my interview, Candy pulled out an 8 x 10 color print of herself sitting next to President Bush inside the oval office. Candy was scheduled for a ten minute meeting with the president. The meeting continued for over an hour, to the surprise of the president's aides. Candy observed that President Bush seemed enthralled by her story, including the ramifications of her miraculous recovery. Although Candy did not share the details of their discussion, she did offer an opinion that President Bush was earnestly searching for spiritual direction at this juncture in his presidency. Candy hoped that God worked through her, in some small way, in furthering the president's spiritual journey.

Today, Candy continues to exert herself in every way possible. She currently works seven days a week, mostly in a retail store, trying to make ends meet. She attends church regularly and considers her circle of Christian friends as her family. Even after 25 years since her near fatal accident, Candy still experiences miracles. Just last week she experienced feeling and strength for the first time in her quad muscle. Despite her past and current struggles, Candy displays gratitude for life and love for God. Her life philosophy can be summed up by her statement, "Every day is the best day of my life." Today, Candy is looking forward and the future looks bright. She believes she is entering a new phase in life, one that may be even more spiritually centered. When asked if she could change the day of the accident, she said, "No." It is not that Candy enjoys being partially paralyzed. Rather, she recognizes that her soul has been polished by all her experiences subsequent to the accident. For Candy, no earthly comfort or pleasure can replace the importance of the soul. Moreover, her focus on the soul has opened new spiritual doors in her life.

Candy reports heightened sensitivity to the spiritual realm ever since her near-death experience 25 years ago. According to NDE submissions, once spiritual doors are opened in heaven, they rarely completely shut upon return to earth. What may appear uncommon in Candy's case, however, is the breadth of her paranormal abilities. For instance, Candy reports seeing spiritual beings in the form of colored flashes of light, especially blue. She also experiences dreams about the future, usually pertaining to friends and strangers. Fearful that this power might be destructive, she shares these dreams with caution. Moreover, Candy has become very sensitive to the synchronicity of unusual events; seeing spiritual connections where others do not look. But with all these abilities, perhaps she relies most on spiritual intuition to guide her toward people in need.

Candy states that she is nudged into loving action, via divine inspiration, almost on a daily basis. Specifically, ideas are inserted into her mind propelling her to act. She shared a recent example where she was compelled to comfort a little girl by saying, "You are beautiful." The mother cried in response. Candy did not know the little girl, or her needs. The message, rather, came from a "deeper" source. Candy values these intuitive moments beyond any other. They are integral to her mission to serve others in love. Candy hopes to do more.

The life of a partial paraplegic still has limitations. For example, Candy can no longer practice as a nurse. Candy once disliked working retail jobs back in college. She loves working retail now, not because she enjoys sales, but from gaining opportunities to interact with people in need. Her service is not limited to her job. Candy tries to connect with many other people in a personal way. By the establishment of genuine rapport, Candy tries to help people navigate around adversity. Given her attitude and resiliency, it is no surprise that people naturally gravitate to her for inspiration. Through her experience of real life trauma, Candy inspires people to find hope when dark clouds mushroom.

I asked Candy what she has learned over these 25 turbulent years. Thoughtfully, she answered that everything in life has a purpose, even our darkest moments. Sometimes, she observed, people do not know why things happen until many years later. The timing of God's revelations teaches patience. To accomplish mission, each individual needs to let go of controlling everything. It is critical that people follow God's will, not just their own selfish drive. Candy has also learned that people need to live for today and appreciate the details in life. There is no point, she reasons, to dwell on the future or the past. She advised, "Look for today's miracles. The journey will take care of itself, as God meant it." Candy ended our interview by sharing the following story, "I was driving up to a lake to meet my ex-husband with my daughters. As typical, he did not show up. We opened the car trunk to have lunch by the lake. We had an open sugar container in the trunk, which attracted hundreds of butterflies. We caught the butterflies and put them in the car, so we had our own butterfly pavilion. This trip was one of my most memorable, positive experiences because it transformed our perspective from one of disappointment to one of hope. My life has been like that. When things go wrong, somehow beauty prevails."

Candy believes that there is beauty all around us, if we know where to look. So many people become mired down in their personal troubles and pain. They look down at their shuffling feet and ignore the light shining all around them. Their attention becomes impaired in two ways. First, they do not see the "big picture" beyond the graveled road beneath their feet. Blinded by negativity, they fail to recognize their mission to serve God. Second, people fail to notice the beauty in the details of life. Joy comes from the flow of experience, by perceiving the order and complexity of God's creation in the here and now. Personally, I have never experienced a more sacred serenity than when sitting on a mountain top, clearing my thoughts to see jagged peaks jutting into the blue sky, hearing the silence, and feeling the cold wind tingle my cheeks. As for Candy, she notices the hug of a child, the smile on a face, and the warm feelings moving down her legs.

Through her near-death experience and life struggles, Candy has learned to see beyond the pain of the here and now. Her vision extends beyond the self; she has learned to focus on others. At the same time, Candy has trusted that God will provide for all her daily needs. No matter how bad things are, Candy knows that she is surrounded by love in both the big and small. After all, the fabric of the universe is made of sacred love. In turn, Candy has taught me that it does not matter whether you are imprisoned or disabled. God's love shines brightest in some of the most unlikely of people; individuals who are imprisoned in body but who are free in both mind and spirit.

CHAPTER NINE

THE END OF ISOLATION

I solation becomes part of everyone's life to different degrees. Existentialist psychologists claim that all people are alone as part of the human condition. It doesn't matter that we interact with friends, family, and acquaintances. Each human being exists as an island of conscious thought separated by the encasement of the brain. No one knows exactly how you feel, how you think, who you really are. Irvin Yalom writes that existential isolation refers to "an unbridgeable gulf between oneself and any other being. It also refers to an even more fundamental isolation, the separation between the individual and the world."[1] Existentialist psychologists propose that all people experience a constant uneasiness that often goes unrecognized. At a subconscious level, isolation reminds us that that we all exist in a cold, meaninglessness universe. We are alone when the world inflicts pain. We are alone in the inadequacy of our choices. Finally, we are alone in facing death. How do people cope with the subsequent anxiety? Some seek solace in frequent socializing and the physical touch. Others bridge the gap by the higher social pursuits, such as encouragement, empathy, and altruistic giving. Yet despite these attempts, we all must return to the shore of isolation. Intimacy is fleeting. Ultimately, we are left with the self, particularly at the time of death.

There is comforting news from those who have had a near-death experience. The existentialists are dead wrong. The overriding message of this chapter is that people are never isolated. Reality is not governed by a cold, indifferent universe. We are eternally interconnected under the conscious umbrella of God. God has always been, and always will be, completely with each and every one of us throughout existence. Let's first take a look at the end of isolation in the spiritual realm.

The Blissful Welcome Home

Dying is not a cold, lonely event as proposed by the existentialists. NDErs are often greeted by a host of spiritual beings that serve as a welcoming committee to celebrate a soul's return home. Although some report a brief period alone when they first cross, NDErs are never alone for long. They are surrounded by loved ones from the welcoming point forward. The greeting is tailored to the spiritual needs of the individual. Some are greeted by deceased family members, others meet spiritual guardians, and still others encounter religious figures like God or Jesus. In all cases, the soul is greeted in an atmosphere of love and acceptance. One NDEr wrote:

> It was clarified that we are not alone. We are always surrounded by loving beings when we cross over and even now in this existing dimension. I know that we are always safe and protected. And I know that no matter what our circumstances, who we are perceived as or judged by the world, or what we have done in this lifetime, that we are all pure love. (NDERF #2969)

Alienation grates against the eternal nature of the soul. Souls are part of the collective consciousness of God; individual yet always simultaneously interconnected with each other. In chapters four and five, we examined how communication and emotions are purely experienced in the spiritual realm. We also explored how communication and emotions are always expressed in the context of caring and acceptance. Our relationships are built on a divine foundation: eternal, powerful, and loving. As we have explored in chapter seven, spiritual love is not just an emotion, but rather a complex set of attitudes, motivations, and behaviors. Although love is more than emotion, there are positive emotional by-products to love. The soul's emotional response to divine love is the experience of *bliss*.

Bliss can be defined as complete happiness. What creates complete happiness? Many a philosopher and sage have contemplated that very question. Fortunately, the NDErs has returned from heaven to share their answers. In the spiritual realm, complete happiness appears to be the soul's response to harmony, affection, peace, and unconditional love. One NDEr explained:

> I was bathed in bliss and harmony, I felt more love than I could even imagine and everything emanated positive energy, affection, every single positive word in the dictionary could not capture the feeling of eternal bliss that I felt. (NDERF #2916)

Another NDEr tried to capture the everlasting feeling of bliss in heaven through using earthly metaphors:

> The most important thing in this place was the feeling of bliss. The only thing different about this was that the feeling never waned, it stayed constant. It was the feeling of falling asleep on a summer's day on a hammock in the light of a warm sun. It was the feeling of drawing your child close to you out of love. It was the feeling of seeing a loved one for the first time in a long time. It was all good feelings, and it was ever present in this place. (NDERF #2927)

If bliss is a byproduct of constant love, then it stands to reason that the loving presence of God is always present in heaven. In sharp contrast, there are dark spiritual places where there is an absence of God. These places are empty of love, leaving occupants in utter isolation. Kimberly Clark-Sharp reportedly endured a revelation about experiential existence without God. She was briefly transported into a dark spiritual realm during a period of great doubt. Ms. Clark wrote in her book, *After the Light*, "Instantly, I was plunged into a formless dark void. There was an absence of everything, including time and space and God. I floundered there for what seemed like forever, in the emptiness that signifies the absence of love and faith and purpose."[2]

Although not technically an NDE, Ms. Clark's experience appears consistent with the rare near-death experience accounts of hell. The following NDEr wrote about a hellish NDE:

> My only sensation was that of being taken downward in total darkness, total silence. When the descent ended I was in the deepest, darkest void I had ever experienced. (NDERF #1734)

Fortunately, this NDEr pleaded to be saved. Jesus lovingly granted her request. She was immediately taken out of the pit of isolation and became reconnected to the loving Source. She too felt bliss.

Who Creates Isolation in the World?

Some people demand proof of God before they choose to believe in God. Their wait may last until death. Whereas God can be experienced in full glory in the foreground in heaven, God can only be experienced in the intangible background on earth. Although some feel separated from the divine, this does not preclude God's presence. Quite the opposite, God is present everywhere. Furthermore, God may be perceived ever so subtly when we earnestly seek the Source. Our partial separation is not accidental. We are meant to freely choose God. Most unbelievers would bow in obedience if God made a dramatic entrance in their lives. But would their obedience come from a state of love, or fear? God prefers relationships to be based on love and faith. Moreover, God wants people to choose their paths freely, even if destructive, so that we can evolve without coercion.

Individual spiritual development varies greatly. Some choose a path of service whereas others choose self-indulgence. With every collective effort to love, humanity decreases a small proportion of isolation in the world. With every collective effort of self-indulgence, humanity increases a small proportion of isolation in the world. The world is what we make it. Thus, it serves no purpose to shake our fists at God when we experience evil in the world. A more responsible response would be to collectively drag evil into the light and shake our fists with solidarity and say "No!" Although the task may seem too difficult, we have access to all the help needed to succeed. God will be there in the background, providing guidance for those creating a better earth. With God, everything is possible. Should this not be a part of everyone's mission, to decrease isolation through need-free love? Unfortunately, only a few people take their divine mission seriously. Too many are focused on indulging the self.

Many societies choose a predominantly self-centered approach, leaving vast segments of the population wanting. Alienation is so pervasive that it appears to be integral to the human condition. I have seen loneliness working as a psychologist. People believe they are alone because they feel that alone. They act according to these painful feelings, sometimes by lashing out in self-destructive ways. Yet, isolation is only an illusion. Our birthright is a state of bliss through interconnected love. Although human beings are not spiritually mature enough to create a state of bliss, we can certainly do better in decreasing isolation. After all, our souls have the power to connect and heal. If people reach out with caring, then they give hope to the hopeless and sanctuary to the wounded. It is our collective mission to reduce isolation in the world through need-free love. Unfortunately, humanity seems to be retreating from love rather than moving toward love. In the remainder of this chapter, we will explore an immediate crisis of isolation and then examine a few possible solutions.

The Isolation Crisis

Isolation has been eloquently illustrated through age-loved literature and verse. Isolation has been, and always will be, an anchor weighing on the human condition. Although isolation is not new, it has reached epidemic proportions in Western society as evidenced by a massive decline in social participation. Relatedly, Irvin Yalom writes:

> The decline of intimacy-sponsoring institutions - the extended family, the stable residential neighborhood, the church, local merchants, the family doctor - has, in the United States at least, inexorably led to the increased interpersonal estrangement.[1]

Yalom's statement does not just reflect personal opinion. Research strongly supports the position that isolation has elevated to crisis levels in the United States.

Robert D. Putnam's national bestseller book, *Bowling Alone*, methodically establishes the collapse of the American community. Putnam references a quarter century's worth of data spanning from the 1970s through the late 1990s. During this time period, participation in clubs and organizations plummeted 42%, volunteers working for a political party dropped 42%, and the number of citizens participating in public meetings and school functions dropped 35%.[3] Even Christian church participation, historically a robust American institution, has declined. Church attendance plummeted 50% between 1957 and 1976. Attendance suffered an additional 20% decline between 1974 and 1996.[3] Many other social and civic venues show similar decline. Are these percentages meaningful? In statistics, even a 0.1% change may be significantly meaningful when evaluating large populations. Consequently, a rapid 35% to 50% decrease of civic participation represents an enormous shift in American culture.

A severe decline in social participation has negatively increased isolation in the United States. The fewer the people who choose civic participation, the less will remain connected to the larger, caring community. Churches and organizations not only facilitate friendships, but they provide cooperative pro-social opportunities that help the community. Such opportunities foster the finest human qualities, those consistent with God's mission for us to "love thy neighbor." Churches, in particular, offer members avenues to minster to each other through teaching, pastoral care, peer outreach, children's ministries, and support groups. They offer human connectedness through social activities like gatherings, fellowship, music, and drama. Finally, they offer cooperative philanthropic opportunities that allow church members to engage in acts of altruism. Philanthropy not only connects church members in a loving way, but also the broader community that is being helped. How much impact does the American church have on society? Currently, churches provide 15-20 billion dollars in charitable services each year.[3] According to Putnam, 75-80 percent of church members volunteer, while only 30-35 percent of non-members volunteer.[3] Based on these statistics, any reduction in church membership significantly reduces philanthropy. There are many other civic organizations to connect people to work for the common good, although these groups tend to be narrower in scope. Some better known institutions include the Rotary Club, Lions Club, and Knights of Columbus but there are hundreds of other organizations serving almost every cause. Unfortunately, many of these organizations are also in severe decline. Consequently, the most marginalized groups, or society's outcasts, are most impacted. Collectively, less philanthropy leads to an increasingly isolated society. From a spiritual perspective, many people in society are steadily abandoning their mission to love each other by *doing* for each other.

One might counter that people can love each other on an individual basis. Granted, it is unnecessary that every person join an organization to love and be loved. Yet, research suggests that many Americans are also isolating themselves from friends and family. Consider the family meal, for instance. Historically, many families employed the family meal as a period to share the day's events. From 1977 to 1999, the number of families eating together decreased from 50% to 34% percent.[3]

Similarly, family vacationing decreased from 53% to 38% during that same time period. People visiting friends sunk 45%. These numbers are very high, yet people do not seem aware of these alarming statistics. Like a lobster contentedly boiling in a pot, we are simmering in isolation and we don't even know it!

What incredible force could cause such a dramatic shift in American culture within a single generation? As always, complex behaviors are caused by many factors. But there does appear to be one primary cause. That primary force is television. Putnam shares some startling research data. According to the Bureau of Labor Statistics, an American spends about three hours a day, on average, watching television. He notes that the average viewer spends three to four times the duration watching television than married couples spend talking to each other.[3] Arriving home from work, at least 80% of people watch television between dinner and bedtime while 50% also watch during dinner.[3] Interestingly, edifying television programming does not appear related to heavy television use. A full 43% of people admit that they turn on the television without any particular show in mind. It has been my observation that most entertainment programs, especially reality shows, have little to offer in substance.

Television rarely motivates, teaches, or gratifies. Neither human movement nor interaction is required. All that watching television requires is that the viewer sits quietly with eyes open. Although the broadcast industry calls television entertainment, most people do not find television particularly enjoyable. Researchers Robert Kubey and Mihaly Csikzentmihalyi[4] instructed study participants to carry a beeper while watching television. Participants were signaled six to eight times a day, randomly, where they documented their activities, level of alertness, and associated emotions. Not surprisingly, television watchers reported feeling relaxed and passive. More surprisingly, participants also reported feeling tired and listless, even mildly depressed, after watching television. T.V. watchers rated television to be about as enjoyable as house cleaning or cooking. Perhaps the critical term "couch potato" has some merit. As a passive, solitary activity, television dulls both mind and body in addition to decreasing connectedness. The result is that heavy television use likely increases both isolation and unhappiness.

Out of a 24-hour day, about 14 hours of my day is consumed by sleep and work (taking in account weekends). Grooming, cooking, eating, commuting, chores, and running errands eat up about another five of the remaining ten hours. If I watched an average of three hours of television, then I would be left with an average of about two hours a day to engage in my list of meaningful activities: investing in my children, sharing with my wife, visiting a friend, helping a neighbor, contributing to civic duties, engaging in charitable activities, exercising, attending church, learning something from a book, playing a musical instrument, writing. This book, for instance, would have never been written if I watched three hours of television each day. Research on civil engagement supports similar conclusions. Dependence on T.V. is the single most consistent predictor of civil disengagement - not poverty, morality, education or intelligence.[3] With television, there is little time for anything else. Unfortunately, what little time people have left has often become dedicated to Internet use.

The typical American spends, on average, 160.2 minutes a day, or two and a half hours, surfing the Internet for their personal use.[5] This two and a half hour duration roughly equates to the difference of discretionary time left over from watching television. Obviously, the average amount of discretionary time away from television and the Internet is not zero. There are other factors to consider, such as people watching television while they eat or dress, using the Internet at work, sleeping less, and so forth. The point is this, most people are spending the majority of their discretionary time either watching television or using the Internet. One might point out that people use the Internet to interpersonally connect by using email, texting, tweeting and Facebook. Granted, emails and social media enhance rapid communication, but electronic social exchange lacks the level of intimacy of face to face interaction. Absent is the touch of a handshake, the soothing tone of a voice, or a smile. Perhaps more importantly, there is an absence of mutually shared life experiences; people aren't doing things together. Dr. Sherry Turkle, a psychology professor at MIT, noted this concerning trend in her excellent book, *Alone Together: Why We Expect More from Technology and Less from Each Other*. In one example, she observed several people texting during a funeral memorial service. To hide their crassness, mourners texted behind funeral program flyers.[6] Although this may seem to be an extreme example, this case demonstrates that some people choose to live in a virtual world, even when social expressions of love are most critical in the real world.

Electronic communication, although more socially interactive than television, can contribute to isolation. Texting can relay important information, but often conveys the mundane. Texts like, "I'm in class. I'm so bored." does not increase intimacy. Chatter only creates an illusion of interconnection. For some chronic text users, they feel emptiness as soon as they are done texting. In order to self-soothe, they begin to text more. With so much texting instead of talking, people increasingly rely on technology to keep them connected instead of face to face social interaction. Dr. Turkle writes the following about electronic communication on a mass scale:

> Being alone can start to seem like a precondition for being together because it is easier to communicate if you can focus, without interruption, on your screen. In this new regime, a train station (like an airport, a café, or a park) is no longer a communal space but a place of social collection: people come together but do not speak to each other. Each is tethered to a mobile device and to the people and places to which that device serves as a portal.[6]

Living in the virtual world keeps people from feeling lonely while avoiding social risks. Thus, the over-use of electronic communication and entertainment may be viewed as a trouble-free defense against isolation. Television has been designed for us to feel as though we are sharing in real friendships and exciting lives. A laugh track, for instance, helps viewers feel like they are sharing humor with an audience. This entertainment media strategy works well, as the modern day hero often seems to be the television actor or the professional sports player. An entire industry has been enriched by bringing the glamorous stranger into our living room. Why do people care about the destructive, selfish behavior of the Hollywood star? Why do they care whether actors are marrying, fighting, drugging, birthing, cheating, and divorcing? Perhaps at a subconscious level, viewers incorporate strangers into their own personal identity. In this manner, these special strangers become idols. From the existentialist position, people create fictional associations with celebrities as a defense against isolation and meaninglessness. People don't really love celebrities, they only love the idea of them. Yet, many celebrities, with a few notable exceptions, have done little to further God's mission on earth. Their main contribution has been to entertain us. What if the opposite were true? What if our heroes consisted of rescuers, healers, philanthropists, and scientists? Perhaps these role models would encourage others to embark on similar missions of love and purpose. If that were so, humanity might embark on a new direction of growth.

Humanity does not appear to be embarking on a new direction of growth any time soon. I frequently listen to people lament about not having the *time* to maintain intimacy. However, this may have more to do with priorities rather than an issue with time. Many therapy clients complain of loneliness. The following is a hypothetical monologue from a depressed patient based on my experience as a therapist:

> Everyone in the house is so busy doing their own thing. Both my husband and I work hard during the week, sometimes coming home late at night. During the evenings, we are both so tired. We get some fast food so I don't have to cook. My husband eats while watching sports. I eat a little and then go up into the bedroom so I can watch my favorite television shows and relax. Our youngest boy plays video games in his room. Our oldest daughter texts her friends with her headphones on, listening to who knows what? We do errands on the weekends, trying to get them done in-between taking the kids to soccer, basketball, and karate classes. We can't really afford vacations anymore, but sometimes we eat out. I wish I could talk to my kids more, but they always seem so wrapped up in their own lives. All my friends say the same thing about this new generation. I don't understand it. My daughter even texts her friends while in the same room. But it is not just them. It seems that my husband and I are complete strangers. I understand that part of the problem is that he is so tired. I'm tired too. There doesn't seem to be enough time anymore. Sometimes I feel so alone.

Why would anyone abandon the very social institutions that keep us interpersonally connected? Why would anyone choose isolation? More to the point, why would anyone choose electronic soothing over social engagement? The difference between entertainment and meaningful social interaction reflects the difference between pleasures and gratifications. Martin Seligman, an important contributor to the field of Positive Psychology, notes that pleasures stimulate an immediate, enjoyable sensation or emotion. An ice cream cone, a back rub, a T.V. murder mystery, winning up to the next game level – these are all pleasures.[7] Pleasures only provide a temporary sensation of enjoyment. Shortly after the pleasurable stimuli are removed, however, the "feel-good" sensation quickly dissipates. The creamy sweet taste of an ice cream cone evaporates in seconds. The thrill of a murder mystery disappears by the time the credits reel. Ironically, the body inevitably adapts to pleasures. In other words, it takes more of the same pleasure to achieve the same effect. Eat three ice cream cones after every meal and you will probably be looking for another dessert. Psychologists call this biological process habituation, which even works on the cellular level.[7] The occasional pleasure, spaced out over time may add a little spice to life. But a life full of non-stop pleasures is unhealthy. People who continuously seek pleasures are constantly looking for the next fix, like a junkie looking for the next high. Seligman calls this process the "hedonistic treadmill." There is evidence to suggest that pleasures are inversely correlated with happiness. Research demonstrates that passive pleasures, like television, actually decrease overall happiness.[8]

Electronic communication devices were created, in part, to make communication instantaneous. There is enormous value in enhancing communication efficiency in various business, home, and emergency situations. Electronic communication can be a powerful adjunct to face-to-face communication. Yet, many people use electronics as a primary source of communication, often as a source of immediate gratification. Even using Facebook and texting can be an act of immediate gratification. Many "latch-key kids" growing up in the technology age report feeling isolated from parents who work several jobs. Computers and cell phones provide social communities that may otherwise be lacking. As a professor, Dr. Tuttle noted that many of her undergraduate students complained about feeling alone. Many stave off their loneliness by texting home fifteen to twenty times a day.[6] There are few shared activities in texts, most represent the mundane. Texting becomes a Band Aid solution that temporarily staves off isolation in order to fill an unfillable void.

According to Seligman, the difference between pleasures and gratifications represents the difference between the good life and the pleasant life. Gratifications, unlike pleasures, have a meaning beyond the immediate sensation or emotion. Completing a work project, raising a child, feeding the homeless, helping a neighbor, giving money to someone in need – these are all gratifications.[7] The positive effects of gratifications are long lasting. In fact, research suggests that gratifications, unlike pleasures, are very highly correlated with happiness.[8] Small gratifications may allow people to feel satisfied. Important gratifications may even allow people to temporarily feel blissful. From a spiritual point of view, gratifications edify the soul through learning and giving. In this manner, gratifications are integrally tied with our spiritual mission. Unfortunately, the heavy use of electronic gadgetry negates opportunity for gratifications. God did not send souls to earth to escape life by living in a virtual fantasy. Rather, we were sent to earth to live life in a meaningful way.

Easing Isolation

How does the near-death experience relate to isolation? The near-death experience serves as a model, or an idealized example, on how to reduce isolation on earth. Spiritual beings are never isolated. They are communally focused on completing God's work. Not a single person who has had a near-death experience observed a spiritual being watching television or tweeting God. Although I write this tongue-in-cheek, the notion underscores that what is important in heaven may have parallels to what may be important on earth. As discussed in chapter seven, our assigned mission in the material world boils down to making choices in concert with the divine plan, namely to learn and love. The more we become distracted by electronic idols, even those that seem benign, the more we move away from our divine purpose. If our life compass is set by a steady stream of pleasures, electronic or physical, we can never know the profound satisfaction, or even momentary bliss, that accompanies gratification of a mission well-accomplished.

Sometimes learning involves adversity. At other times learning involves savoring the sacred moments in life: graduation, marriage, the birth of a child, peering off a mountain top, learning about God. These sacred moments rarely come from electronic entertainment. Life comes from doing. Habitual television voyeurs cannot learn anything consequential by watching gossip entertainment, "on-scene" crime shows, or reality television.

Technology is not inherently good or bad. Only human choice merits judgment. Television, Internet, smartphones – they all have positive uses. Television keeps the savvy voter informed. Facebook reconnects old friendships. Texting provides people immediate critical communication, especially during emergencies. Even mindless entertainment has its place; one can enjoy passive distraction from the rigors of life *once in a while*. Our mission only becomes lost when we elevate electronic devices over people. Divine mission requires a degree of mindfulness, lest we lose what is important by focusing on senseless fillers.

In the effort to be mindful, how do we achieve a healthy balance between mission and entertainment? The question boils down to "who is in control?" Do we thoughtfully control our entertainment media choices, or do the media control us? More pointedly, do we watch television with discernment, or do we simply watch television to be soothed? These are important questions that have spiritual ramifications. We cannot fulfill divine mission if distracted by habits. First we make our habits and then our habits make us. A drunk husband can no longer be a loving husband. Likewise, a person addicted to electronics can no longer participate effectively in their mission.

Following the divine plan to accomplish mission is a stepwise process. The first step is to develop a desire to serve. From this desire develops a personal vision of service. Some visions are grand and visible whereas others are small and quiet. No matter the scope, all have great value. Furthermore, all visions are realized by the collective efforts of the community; people working together for a greater good. Collectively, people have the power to transform the world.

As mentioned early in the chapter, bliss is the emotional by-product of eternal intimate relationships. Loneliness will remain a part of the human condition because good and evil mix on earth. Although everyone experiences loneliness from time to time, no one needs to experience isolation. As noted in chapter seven, people do not feel unloved because they are unlovable, but rather they feel unloved because they do not know how to love. Ending isolation can be done individually, through church outreach, or by volunteering in charitable organizations.

By joining a church or a civic organization, a loving individual will inevitably meet like-minded people. A loving person cannot help but feel connected to like-minded people; they will be loved and love in return. In other words, isolation, in many cases, becomes self-imposed. The end of isolation will require people to simply reach out to love other people. Howard Storm learned this lesson during his near-death experience. Prior to his NDE, Storm hated people, mostly because they rejected him. His few associates were equally pessimistic. Storm's isolation was propagated by a cycle of negativity reacting to negativity. During his NDE, Storm experienced love and bliss for the first time in memory. When told he had to return to earth, Storm argued against re-entering a world filled with isolation and despair. His dialogue with Jesus and spiritual beings went as follows:

Storm: "But I saw mostly bad in people and the cruel things they do to each other."

Response: "You will find what you look for in people and in the world. If you are loving, you will find love. If you seek beauty, you will see beauty. If you pursue goodness, you will receive goodness. What you are inside will attract the same from the outside. When you love, love comes to you. When you hate, hate finds you."[9]

Howard Storm's near-death experience radically transformed him. Indeed, Storm did find beauty, goodness, and love after he returned because he learned to love others. Learning to love others requires action. Good or bad, change can be very slow and difficult. It will take a lifetime, and then some, to reach our final goal. A good way to start our mission of love is to reach out to other people, particularly to people who feel isolated.

I would like to share a few other pointers as to how to reduce isolation in one's own life. First, focus on authentic relationships. Don't waste too much time on superficial people. Second, place less emphasis on pleasures and more weight on gratifications. That means curbing television use and other passive activities. Finally, always know that you are never alone, even when you feel alone. God, and other spiritual beings, will always be with you. Spiritual beings, in fact, have a number of related responsibilities to help people through difficult times. In fact, their activities are vitally important to our growth. Accordingly, the role of spiritual beings in our lives will be the topic of the next two chapters.

CHAPTER TEN

SPIRITUAL BEINGS

A lthough religions disagree on many issues, most agree that the spiritual world is filled with benign and malign spirits. The belief in spirits may reach back to the very origins of religion itself. Ancient and modern animistic beliefs included the incorporation of spirits into physical objects, such as trees, rocks, sky, and the underworld. In the Navajo spiritual belief system, for example, earth is populated with many harmful and accommodating spirits. The Navajos practice over 60 rituals to restore harmony and appease spirits when taboos are broken.[1] The presence of angels and demons are accepted in the major world religions, such as Christianity, Islam, Judaism, and Mormonism. Hindus also believe in angels and demons, but often relegate spirits into a pantheon of demigods. What is the purpose of these opposing spirits? Is there an epic spiritual battle raging in the material and spiritual world? Not only do religions believe that spiritual warfare exists, but these spirits can have daily influence on human lives.

I remember walking through the Chicago Museum of Art at age twelve, marveling at all the great renaissance paintings. Many of the early masters, like Giotto, Botticelli, and Michelangelo, depicted various Christian themes in paintings, as dictated by the religious expectations of the era. Some of their paintings included angels watching over mortals from the clouds above. Others depicted grimacing goat horned demons torturing lost souls in hell. I found it curious that the angels were always depicted as ordinary humans, except that they sprouted enormous eagle-like wings. Even as a pre-adolescent, I quickly concluded that these wings were not aerodynamically sound. More ludicrous seemed to be chubby baby cherubs serenely hovering above pastoral landscapes. Partly due to these cultural experiences, I developed a strong skepticism about the larger role of angels and demons. Raised a Christian, I accepted the biblical accounts that angels were divine messengers speaking on behalf of God. Their rare occurrence in antiquity, however, seemed to have little relevance to the modern Western world, or me. Thus, I never gave the proposition of interacting with angels much credence. There didn't seem to be any evidence for their daily existence on earth. Although my belief in spiritual beings has recently expanded, I still reject the traditional renaissance understanding of wing-bearing angels. My expanded belief in spiritual beings may come as a surprise to those who know my materialist roots. My filter of understanding has changed after reading many NDEs from people who have learned a great deal about spiritual beings. This chapter will explore the role of spiritual beings in heaven and the impact they have on those crossing over during near-death experiences.

Spiritual Beings Encountered

Jody Long researched the identity and frequency of spiritual beings encountered during near-death experiences. From this data, categorical percentages were calculated.[2] Out of the 302 NDEs sampled, 212 (70.1%) reported encountering spiritual beings during their NDE. I suspect that the percentage would have even been higher if only complex, lengthy, near-death experiences had been sampled. Of that number, 53% encountered familiar beings whereas 47% encountered unfamiliar beings. This result may be surprising because popular NDE accounts typically depict familiar beings, often deceased family members. Still, familiar and unfamiliar beings were commonly sensed or observed. The highest percentage of familiar beings were blood relatives (25.9%) followed by religious figures (22.9%). As expected, grandmothers and grandfathers were the most common blood relatives encountered, as they are the mostly likely to be deceased at the time of the NDE. In rank order, deceased grandparents are followed by a deceased father, mother, son, daughter, brother, and aunt. Jody Long's research noted many other known beings were encountered that were not blood relatives.

The frequency of each specific non-blood relative group is below three percent; a diverse classification of in-laws, significant romantic relationships, miscellaneous loved ones, pets, and so on.

Interestingly, Jody Long discovered a positive correlation between people over the age of 41 years of age encountering blood relatives during their near-death experience. One might speculate that some NDErs, especially younger people, need life guidance from spiritual authorities, like Jesus. Older individuals, who have already lived the majority of their life, may have a greater need to be comforted by deceased family members. Every venue serves as an appropriate experience tailored to the individual's spiritual needs.

Religious figures have a key role in the interaction with people who experience a near-death experience. In terms of frequency, Jesus tops the list at 12.7%. Encounters with God occurred with a frequency of 5.4%. Encounters with angels occur slightly less, with a measured frequency at 4.8%. The relatively high number of encounters with Jesus and God suggest that status has little relevance to the NDE. Both God and Jesus seem to be accessible to every human, regardless of their social position or mistakes made on earth. Christians may feel validation that Jesus is the most frequently encountered spiritual being. However, one must be very cautious interpreting these results. Most NDERF submissions come from Western sources where Christianity predominates (U.S., Canada, Europe, Australia, and Latin America).

We have explored the nature of the soul in previous chapters. Specifically, we have discovered that spiritual beings are made of energy interconnected with God and the universe. Subsequently, we discussed the expanded abilities of spiritual beings, including their intelligence, loving nature, and benevolent intent. The question arises, how are these expanded abilities applied in the spiritual and material realms? NDErs add significant knowledge to our thin understanding of spiritual beings, although much still remains a mystery. One NDEr wrote broadly:

> I knew the gathering (of spiritual beings) to be a meeting of many groups representing a wide variety of interests and responsibilities pertaining not only directly to earth and physical universe energies but to dimensions and issues beyond. (NDERF #3006)

Based on this NDE submission, it appears that spiritual beings are involved with operating almost everything in the universe. Omnipotent in all things, God could manage and operate the universe alone.

Yet, God chooses to co-create with every being. In the spiritual realm, spiritual beings have important assignments within the constraints of divine rules. In other words, spiritual beings are not spending eternity lounging around on clouds. They have plenty of creative work to accomplish. Howard Storm wrote about the general creative function of spiritual beings. He writes, "There are different kinds of angels with different responsibilities."[3] He further writes, "There is a great deal of intelligence and will bringing the world into being. It is ongoing every moment."[3] Storm appears to be saying that the collective creative intelligence of spiritual beings run a very complex, amazing universe.

Some characteristics of spiritual beings are blocked when the NDEr returns. Perhaps information is withheld based on human spiritual development and personal factors. Furthermore, spiritual interactions appear individualized based on unique intricacies and the dynamics between the NDEr and spiritual beings. Each contributes their unique threads to an enormously complex, eternal tapestry. Considering there are probably well over trillions of spiritual beings, the entire heavenly operation must be quite complex. This should not be surprising. After all, one might expect God's universe(s) to be rich and complex at every level.

Despite the lack of any definitive rules, there appears to be broad commonalities between the experiences of spiritual beings. Based on reading numerous accounts, relationships with spiritual beings loosely fall into two categories. First, the NDEr often receives a homecoming greeting by one or more deceased relatives. Second, the NDEr learns spiritual knowledge through transcendent teaching by one or two spiritual guides. Again, these are not inseparable categories. One NDEr may experience a blending of the two categories or experience something altogether different. Nevertheless, it may be useful to look at each category to better understand the general role of spiritual beings.

The Homecoming

When people die and return home to heaven, they are frequently greeted by one or more deceased family members. The newly deceased are usually expected upon arrival. After all, spiritual beings have a good sense of the future. The reunion setting varies, but often it takes place in a serene landscape. Spiritual beings usually choose to manifest in a familiar way for the benefit of the NDEr. Specifically, they often appear in their human form somewhere in their twenties or thirties. Their appearance differs from human life in that they shine brightly with energy.

The newly deceased are warmly greeted. Everyone is filled with rejoicing, love, and happiness. Spiritual reunions appear to be a common function for the spiritual being. It is their task, as well as their joy, to welcome loved ones home. This welcoming serves several purposes. Reunions not only introduce the deceased to the unconditional love of heaven, but it provides them with a point of familiarity of a forgotten existence. Deceased loved ones provide a line of continuity and comfort for the transitioning soul, especially for those who become confused shortly after death. The scene is usually held in a familiar landscape for the same reason. In all aspects, spiritual beings diligently help the newly deceased move forward into life after death, or in the case of the NDEr, back to physical life. One NDEr described a reunion with his deceased father on a serene ocean-side beach:

> He looked perfect and beautiful. He was consumed with peace, joy and overflowing with understanding and love. I could go on and on. We visited for what seemed like hours (afterward I discovered that I had been without a heartbeat for one minute and fourteen seconds). We laughed and hugged and cried. (NDERF #2816)

Note the intimate nature between father and son. This NDERF submission demonstrates that our closest relationships run deep. An intimate relationship can be defined as a complex interdependence between two people that withstands the test of time.[4] Interdependence involves *minding* another person, or knowing a person in a selfless way. According to one psychological model, minding involves "actively seeking the other's self-expression or information, rather than pursuing self-expression."[5] For instance, a person actively minding appreciates another's unique self-expression through their opinions, goals, interests, and uniqueness. A type of interpersonal unity eventually develops. Consequently, the relationship becomes bonded as "we" instead of "me."

Spiritual reunions educate the NDEr about the critical importance of the "we." Human relationships that are built on need-free love usually withstand the test of time. I have long noted that many of my close relationships pick-up where they left off. To illustrate, I was recently reunited with a fellow psychology intern and his wife whom I had not seen for over 22 years. We shared humor, exchanged ideas, and explored life experiences. Interestingly, the character of the relationship remained constant after decades, if not deeper. My earthly reunion, similar to the spiritual reunion, served to re-engage and strengthen a previously established close relationship. Perhaps loved ones become a part of us, in a fashion. They become imprinted in our souls for a lifetime and beyond.

Close relationships, especially family ties, last forever. In fact, close relationships may be the only part of human life that continues into the spiritual realm, besides the taking of the self. The human acquisition of money, material possessions, career, and power all come to an abrupt end when people die. Most things people covet, such as physical beauty and health, fade long before death. The spiritual reunion teaches the NDEr that loving relationships matter because they are permanent. Conversely, the reunion also teaches that material reality has very little meaning. One NDEr wrote:

> Things are not important; the most important is interaction and experiences with other people. The most important (priority) is love at all levels, and to help myself and others where I can. (NDERF #3379)

This NDEr realized that forming and strengthening close relationships was central to her mission to love on earth. With this realization, many NDErs make fundamental changes in their lives when they return. Many report changing career paths that include, but are not limited to, ministry, missions, social work, psychology, nursing, and hospice. The following NDEr shared:

> All which led me to sell my re-cycling company that I had started with my young sons after their dad died and then pursue a career as a hospice and grief counselor. Now I tell my story whenever it seems needed for my patients or their family. (NDERF #2995)

Many NDErs change careers after developing a spiritual perspective built on love. Although earthly perspectives may persist, they begin to appreciate an eternal reality and a higher calling. Unfortunately, humans often lack the broader perspective. I have often heard inmates lament about losing their children to neglect, conflict, divorce, and incarceration. Tragically, it is often too late. Most will finish their lives embittered by losing the people they took for granted. Yet, inmates are not the only ones who abandon loved ones. How many people sacrifice their relationships for career, money, and prestige? Unfortunately, too many people devote themselves to meaningless idols over what is meaningful and eternal.

Spiritual relationships follow a continuity established on earth. In the case of the father and son homecoming, the two laughed, hugged, and talked. Perhaps they also experienced more intimacy in the spiritual realm, not only because they missed each other's absence, but because they shared thoughts and emotions telepathically. Thus, their communication was pure and complete. This suggests that their relationship not only started where it left off, but grew into something stronger. Interestingly, strained relationships on earth can be mended in the spiritual realm. In the case of Anita Moorjani, she actually experienced her deceased father in a newfound way. She wrote:

> Even though I hadn't always been close to my father while I was growing up, all I could feel emanating from him was glorious, unconditional love… The cultural pressures he'd put on me during life had all dropped away, because they were only part of physical existence. None of that mattered after death; those values didn't carry through in the afterlife.[6]

As indicated by this submission, a purification process occurs when souls fully transition into the spiritual world. Human cultural values, especially those inconsistent with the divine, drop away because they are cultural inventions that impede unconditional love. Although spiritual beings maintain the core of their identity and personality, they have been changed by their interconnection with the divine. Their purification only makes the reunion all the sweeter.

Hopefully, mourners can grasp the spiritual reunion as a source of comfort. Nevertheless, some people, even of faith, become grief stricken following the death of a loved one. This is particularly true when unresolved interpersonal issues impede healing. Treating complicated grief can be challenging for even the most seasoned psychologist. A non-complicated mourning is difficult enough. That difficulty becomes magnified when loss becomes compounded by unresolved issues and conflicts. For this reason, Dr. Kübler-Ross strongly encourages that loved ones address unresolved issues prior to a person's pending death. Based on her extensive experience, she wrote:

> The dying patient's problems come to an end, but the family's problems go on. Many of these problems can be decreased by discussing them before the death of a family member. The tendency is, unfortunately,

to hide the feelings from the patient, to attempt to keep a smiling face and a front of make-believe cheerfulness which has to break down sooner or later.[7]

Unfortunately, resolution usually does not occur in the hospital, hospice, or other deathbed setting because family members resist distressing the dying person with emotional burdens. But there is a heavy cost to avoidance. If confrontation is evaded, then forgiveness and resolution will never take place, at least on earth. The survivor may be left with unresolved feelings of guilt, regret, and anger for the rest of his or her life. If this resonates with any reader's own past experience, then take hope. The near-death experience demonstrates that mourners will meet deceased loved ones again. And in the next life, deceased loved ones will be perfectly equipped to address unresolved issues left over from earth. Specifically, they will be purified by their interconnection with divine love; liberated from negative cultural and material weights. Furthermore, the deceased will take responsibility for any pain they inflicted. No one can hide from the truth in heaven. Accordingly, purification means that there will be opportunity for reconciliation in the spiritual realm.

Communication with Spiritual Beings

Spiritual beings are bound to certain rules separating the physical and spiritual realms. With few exceptions, spiritual beings are not allowed to directly communicate with people on earth. However, indirect communications may occur more often than humans realize, as will be discussed in the next chapter. For this reason, the near-death experience appears to be a rare opportunity for spiritual beings to communicate directly with the NDEr. This opportunity allows them to give messages to loved ones still living on earth. The following includes a submission by a Hispanic female recalling a joyous homecoming with her grandmother:

My grandmother invited me to sit and have coffee like we used to all the time at her house. Her table and chairs were there. She looked like she did when she was in her 30s. She had on a purple dress she had with flowers on it, except that the flowers seemed to glow a florescent yellow. I tell her that we, the family, think of her every day. She stated that she knew... My grandmother told me, "You have to go; you can't stay here. It's not your time." I then felt terrible and started to cry. I told her, "But grandma, I want to stay here." It felt so wonderful I did not want to leave. I remember begging her in Spanish, "Please I want to stay with you, I never want to leave here." She said, "You will be back here when it's your time, don't worry." Then she said, "Tell everyone I love them and think of them all the time." (NDERF #654)

Several important messages were communicated by the participants during this near-death experience. First, a message of love was expressed between the grandmother and granddaughter. Second, the grandmother communicated a general message of love for the people she adored. Third, the grandmother issued a specific directive to the granddaughter. Specifically, she told the granddaughter that she could not stay with her in heaven, that it was not her time. The grandmother knew that the granddaughter would struggle with going back. Thus, she also communicated a promise of a final reunion at the right time.

The exchange between granddaughter and grandmother reflects an NDE trend. Most NDErs are informed that they cannot stay in heaven. They are instructed that they must return to earth in various ways: "It is not your time"; "You have more work to do"; "You have more to learn"; "You have something important to contribute." Continuing with the father-son submission, the son received a similar message by the ocean-side. The son wrote:

And then he hopped down off his post and turned on the ocean floor and started to walk away. I jumped up and said, "Dad...hey...wait a minute." I began to follow him and it was at that moment he stopped, turned around, smiled this huge heartwarming, indescribable smile, and said, "No son. You gotta go back. They're fixing you. It's not your time." (NDERF #2816)

Spiritual beings are charged with smoothing out life and death transitions. The soul could simply be returned to the body without warning. Fortunately, a more loving approach is usually chosen. Deceased loved ones often serve as mediators between the NDErs desire to stay and the divine plan for return. In other words, they provide explanation and a little processing time to soften the blow. Sometimes the NDEr is given a choice to stay, although this level of freedom typically appears to be offered by God, Jesus, or some other high authority.

The NDEr usually resists returning to physical existence. The degree of resistance depends on the traveler's personality and life circumstances. For instance, those who were suffering emotional or physical pain usually put up a strong argument to stay. It usually takes some coaxing to convince them to return to an aging, pain-ridden body. NDErs usually concede after they comprehend how their personal mission impacts their family.

Liberation of Being

It seems ironic that people vigorously resist death on earth whereas they later vigorously fight to remain "dead" in heaven. Why the discrepancy? Perhaps the ongoing human struggle against death can be explained by several factors: a natural survival instinct, fear of non-existence, a lack of faith in a loving God. Regardless of the causes, most NDErs experience a complete reversal in attitude once they arrive in the spiritual realm. They are quickly won over by feelings of bliss, the unconditional love of encountered spiritual beings, and the magnificence of everything spiritual. Fundamentally, the NDEr completely understands that death is actually a birth into a greater existence.

The vast majority of human beings, even very religious individuals, do not fully understand that death actually represents a birth into a greater existence. Granted, they may accept the belief from an intellectual point of view. Yet, they still may feel traumatized by the prospect of death as a function of lingering doubt, lack of experiential reference, and general fear of the unknown. Consequently, lives become emotionally twisted when loved ones are lost or when the individual becomes faced with terminal illness. Grief and loss include a multi-staged process that can only be worked through over time. The late Dr. Kübler-Ross, the field-accepted expert on death and dying, can be credited with listing five stages of grief in her groundbreaking book, *On Death and Dying*.[7] Normally, these five stages are experienced in order, but people can skip or return to stages based on their immediate frame of mind. The stages are as follows:

1. Denial: Most dying patients will deny "bad news" by saying, "It can't really be me!" They will often doctor-shop hoping to find another opinion. Denial actually serves as a temporary defense, usually to buffer shocking news before other coping mechanisms

can be mobilized. Although denial may re-occur from time to time, it is usually replaced by partial acceptance.

2. Anger: With partial acceptance, the question becomes, "Why me?!" The terminal illness appears very unfair, and the dying patient rails against the perceived injustice. Unfortunately, the dying person has no one to blame the disease on, other than a seemingly silent God, so he or she will lash out on doctors, family, medical staff, and others.

3. Bargaining: As a child may bargain for a reward for good behavior, likewise, the terminally ill patient may secretly bargain with God to postpone death as a reward for being a better person.

4. Depression: When anger and bargaining do not work, the dying person may succumb to profound feelings of loss and become depressed.

5. Acceptance: If the dying person has had enough time to work through denial, anger, and depression, then he or she may accept his or her inevitable fate. Dr. Kübler-Ross notes that acceptance should not be mistaken for happiness. Rather, the dying person may not feel much of anything, just an acceptance of the coming end.

The human response to death is entirely unnecessary. People returning from death see the truth that death only represents liberation from what one NDEr called the "human meat jacket." Might an NDEr experience the five stages of grief? Several studies concur that people who have near-death experiences report a significant reduction in their fear of death. Most say that they don't fear death at all.[8] This has also been my observation after reading thousands of NDERF submissions. Rather than fearing death, many report eager anticipation when returning home to reconnect with the divine. An atheist NDEr wrote:

I died an atheist and God gave me knowledge that changed the way I live this life. I do not fear death anymore. I used to obsess over dying. Now I welcome it. (NDERF #3392)

Perhaps such claims are not so absolute. What a person self-perceives may differ from his or her actual response. Unfortunately, there has not been any NDE research on the subject. Anecdotally, I recall a church friend who died of cancer. Because he had a previous NDE, he never seemed to fear death to the amazement of the congregation.

Specifically, he did not appear to work through the five stages. Is his response universal? As mentioned at the beginning of the book, Dr. Kubler Ross asserted that *none* of her patients in the hospital, after experiencing an NDE, feared death. But to be human is to be fallible. I would hazard a guess that some NDErs experience difficulties due to the instinctive fear of death. Yet, even in these cases, the five stages are probably short and mild compared to those who have not had a near-death experience. In any case, most NDErs self-report that they have learned to face death fearlessly. Moreover, they have also learned to live life with less fear.

Living Fearlessly as Spiritual Beings

Fear is a primitive emotion shared by reptiles and humans alike. Although primitive, fear exerts a strong influence on human thinking, motivation, and behavior. As a survival mechanism, fear adaptively keeps people away from real danger. But fear also produces detrimental by-products, both emotional and behavioral. Humans are symbolic beings. With language, people are able to displace time to foresee future dangers. Planning for danger certainly has adaptive advantages for the individual and the species, except when anticipation becomes unrealistic and irrational. Such errors naturally happen because the future is always unclear. Psychologists call the fear of the unknown "anxiety." Unfortunately, strong irrational-based anxiety can be crippling. Like anger, fear can overpower any other positive emotion, including love.

Anita Moorjani's life was paralyzed by fear and anxiety of just about everything and everyone. She learned that her terminal cancer was a consequence of fearing death. During her NDE, she learned that there was nothing to fear; her true essence was a magnificent spiritual being. Her self-discovery of magnificence and the feeling of unconditional love became a catalyst for self-acceptance, authenticity, and fearlessness. Namely, she learned that her life was designed for an eternal purpose. Nothing could ever hurt her. No one wanted to fundamentally change her. She wrote, "My experience gave me a glimpse into what it feels like to be set free from the need for both physical and psychological certainty. In other words, it was possible for me to feel perfection even amidst ambiguity."[6]

Anita Moorjani understood that events in her life, although unknown, were unfolding according to a larger plan. She could now accept an unknown future knowing that all that is not well will be well.

After all, spiritual magnificence cannot be knocked down on the tough schoolyard of earth. Consequently, Moorjani decided to live fearlessly despite any temporary ambiguity. In this manner, Moorjani's life was fundamentally changed. Her career aspirations changed and relationships improved with confidence. She wrote:

> I just had to be myself fearlessly! In that way, I'd be allowing myself to be an instrument of love. I understood that this was the best thing that any of us could possibly do or be, for both the planet and ourselves. Since I realized this, problems just didn't seem that big anymore. I felt that people were taking life too seriously – which I used to do.[6]

Anita Moorjani shared her message of living fearlessly with millions of readers in her book *Dying to Be Me*. I have noticed that God seems to work quietly through people like Moorjani, preferring quiet testimonials to spectacular displays of power. In this manner, God gives people a choice to embrace the divine from a position of faith. In the absence of irrefutable proof, ambiguity will always exist. The belief in spiritual beings, for instance, will be based on faith for those who have not had an NDE. Obviously, many people will not believe. But for Moorjani, and many others, they believe. They believe in spiritual certainty despite the ambiguity.

Transcendent Teaching

Some people receive an extraordinary amount of transcendent spiritual teaching during their near-death experience. It is unclear why relatively few individuals are privileged. For people like Eben Alexander, Howard Storm, and Anita Moorjani, rich experiences produced deep insights into the spiritual realm. Consequently, their experiences have been shared with millions. Perhaps they were blessed in order to facilitate a broader spiritual awakening on earth. In other words, they were the right people at the right time. Like everything else about the NDE, transcendent teaching is quite individualized. Yet, central themes seem to repeat. It has been my aim to discuss these themes throughout this book. Given its breadth and complexity, it is beyond the scope of this section to rehash or prematurely introduce much transcendent teaching. Rather, this section will focus on how spiritual beings teach in the spiritual realm.

Spiritual knowledge may be taught to the NDEr by any spiritual being. Although deceased family members can certainly teach through
their homecoming greetings and brief interactions, fundamental education responsibilities are often delegated to spiritual beings of higher
authority. From Jody Long's research, it is no accident that the most
frequent religious figures encountered are Jesus, God, and angels, in
that order. These are the beings who teach the most. Clearly Jesus and
God have widely accepted spiritual authority in Christendom. What
about angels? Who are they and what do they have to do with us?

Angels, in the context of the near-death experience, usually refer to advanced spiritual beings that serve as messengers and teachers from God. I suspect that they have many other functions, as well.
From reading a varied assortment of NDERF submissions, the term
angel may refer to an assortment of advanced spiritual beings that have
progressed over the eons. According to several NDE accounts, there
appears to be a hierarchy of spiritual beings that are afforded different levels of responsibilities dependent on their progression toward
the divine. Loved unconditionally, each individual spiritual being has
equal inherent value in the spiritual realm. However, spiritual beings
vary greatly in ability, authority, and assignment of duty. Thus, each
spiritual being completes assigned tasks in accordance with individual spiritual development. Howard Storm writes, "There are different
kinds of angels with different responsibilities. One angel may accompany a child, another has the responsibility of a city, another a nation,
another a world, another a universe"[3]

Although humans are quick to demean "lowly jobs" while admiring
"prestigious careers," spiritual beings do not appear to view separation
of labor with the same divisiveness. Consistent with the divine, they
do not become jealous or angry. Positions of higher authority do not
correlate with earthly attributes of power. Absent are the trappings of
arrogance, pretention, entitlement, dominance, acquisition, and coercion. Every being is working toward the same goals in accordance with
God's will. Moreover, every spiritual being understands that they are
progressing, albeit some faster than others, toward the Source. Spiritual
beings have all the time in the universe to develop. It would be interesting to know if there is an eventual equaling as beings progress toward the divine. If so, this would likely occur in the far distant future.
But in the present epoch in time, spiritual beings have a wide range of
individual assignments of duties. One NDEr described her assigned
guides as "Elders." She wrote:

I could feel how the "Elders," as I will call them (these are those who are helpers on the other side who have mastered themselves in many or all ways, and help work with us), see us and find so much humor in the way we do things. (Humor is so valued there!!) It might seem brutally annoying to consider when we are in the midst of a great argument or drama that is playing out in our lives, that the Elders view these things very much like when a mother sees her two year old scream and cry and bop another child on the head with a stuffed animal. The mother doesn't want her child to fall apart, become hysterical and cry. She feels for her child, but at the same time, she sees a little bit of comedy in how seriously the child takes what is usually a trivial drama. She continues to love her child and thinks the world of it, hoping it will go on enjoying the day, living and learning. (NDERF #2386)

Similarly, this NDEr wrote this segment about "old souls":

These people (spiritual beings) were ancient. I don't know how I knew that, but I knew that they were "old souls" who watched over my group. We all had "sprung" from them, like children, each going their way yet connected to the Source. I felt nothing like judgment of our actions from them. If anything, I felt a kind of amused benevolence from them, like parents watching their children playing. Even at the really bad things we did in our lives, there was no judgment. (NDERF #577)

These two NDERF submissions capture the dynamic between advanced spiritual beings and humans. Both compare immature human behavior with the temper tantrums of young children. Perhaps these metaphors only begin to capture the wide gulf between humans and advanced spiritual beings. Moreover, these differences may teach us to look at differences from a developmental perspective. Children mature through brain maturation and experience. Some aspects of development may be continuous, others may be stepwise. On earth, it is the responsibility of a parent or teacher to determine what activities are developmentally appropriate for any particular child. Likewise, it is the responsibility of angels to determine what missions are developmentally appropriate for any particular soul. In this manner, missions are assigned to meet the soul's developmental needs. Despite differences in maturity, there is no chasm separating the love between spiritual beings and human beings. Advanced spiritual beings understand our condition, for they also once endured school earth, or some other tough schoolyard in the universe. There is no shame in being young spiritually. Everyone is loved the same, unconditionally.

Perhaps Eben Alexander received most of his transcendent teaching from God. Prior to his meeting with the Source, he learned the most fundamental aspects about spiritual existence from his spiritual guide, a girl. She gave him a simple three part message, "You are loved and cherished, dearly, forever. You have nothing to fear. There is nothing you can do wrong."[9]

These three statements should seem familiar, as they constitute the central messages of this book. For the purposes of this section, however, note that the girl's message was communicated purely. Dr. Alexander wrote, "Without using any words, she spoke to me. The message went through me like a wind, and I instantly understood that it was true."[9]

Dr. Alexander also experienced pure love and acceptance directly from the girl. Her emotional intent was not interpreted, but directly perceived. Direct emotional communication transcends any love experienced in the material world. He wrote:

> She looked at me with a look that, if you saw it for a few moments, would make your whole life up to that point worth living, no matter what had happened in it so far. It was not a romantic look. It was not a look of friendship. It was a look that was somehow beyond all these – beyond all the different types of love we have down on earth. It was something higher, holding all those other kinds of love within itself while at the same time being more genuine and pure than all the others.[9]

Lastly, Dr. Alexander explains that the girl's communication was augmented by the surrounding environment. Specifically, he witnessed the love of the spiritual world while flying over an idyllic landscape. Given that all the beings were interconnected, he experienced a Whole that was love. He wrote:

> Below me there was countryside. It was green, lush, and earthlike. It was earth, but at the same time it wasn't. I was flying, passing over trees and fields, streams and waterfalls, and here and there, people. There were children, too, laughing and playing. The people sang and danced around in circles, as full of joy and sometimes I would see a dog, running and jumping among them, as full of joy as the people were.[9]

With the synthesis of three different teaching modalities, the authenticity of the teaching was never in doubt. Everything was clear, honest, and soul felt. The girl was to be trusted. For our benefit, Dr. Alexander took that teaching back with him to earth. I suspect he found the spiritual communication in the spiritual realm refreshing. Moreover, I suspect that he found interactions to be deeper and more genuine. Perhaps it is no accident that NDErs frequently describe the spiritual realm to be more real than the physical realm.

Manifestation of Reality

We have explored so many amazing abilities exhibited by spiritual beings in previous chapters: perceiving everything; instant travel; full comprehension; access to universal knowledge. There is another important ability yet to be discussed, namely the manifestation of reality. Manifestation simply refers to reality being created by thought. However, the process is anything but simple. The spiritual realm clearly operates on different principles than the material realm we observe, measure, and manipulate. Perhaps manifestation works on the basis of advanced quantum physics and other unknown principles that govern reality. Such principles are likely to be too complex for humans to describe mathematically at this time. Lacking a common reference, many may have difficulty relating to manifestation. After all, we only know the physical universe. Yet, a great number of NDErs report manifestation in their near-death experiences.

It is not surprising that Dr. Alexander experienced a lush, rural countryside during his near-death experience. Residing in the lush North Carolina piedmont, the pastoral setting provided him with a sense of familiarity and home. Many NDErs also experience a pastoral landscape, likewise finding these familiar, serene landscapes comforting. These landscapes may also be formed to meet people's religious expectations. From the Christian and Jewish perspective, a pastoral landscape harkens back to Psalm 23:2, "He makes me to lie down in green pastures. He leads me by still waters." Although pastoral scenes are common, many NDErs experience many other settings: gardens, glorious cities, ocean sides, libraries of knowledge, universal choirs, courtrooms, cathedrals, and deserts. Although the possibilities are endless, each setting can serve as a learning tool used by teachers in the spiritual realm. Numerous NDERF accounts support this position. For instance, the manifested courtroom setting taught one NDEr divine justice based on unconditional love. Vast libraries, as experienced by George Ritchie, have been manifested to demonstrate the accumulation and/or access to universal knowledge. Manifested choir and tapestry images have been used to demonstrate interconnection. Cathedral halls and monks have been created to demonstrate the proper practice of religion. Manifested walls and doors have been erected to represent barriers that the NDEr cannot cross until final death. The list goes on.

Are these grand scenes real or illusionary? At first glance, they may seem illusionary. The lush countryside vanished when Dr. Alexander approached God. Likewise, his guide changed from a girl back to an orb of energy at one point. Despite the indefiniteness of objects, NDErs state that these heavenly landscapes felt as real to them as any place on earth. Maybe definitions about spiritual reality cannot be based on material existence. The spiritual world has its own reality, not driven by three-dimensional laws, but a reality operating on laws driven by conscious thought. Very little is known about how manifestation works, but it seems unlikely that spiritual beings manifest their own personal realities at the same time and in the same place. Such a "free-for-all" would seemingly lead to anarchy of created objects. Thus, there must be coordination and rules governing the practice. Interestingly, the ability appears shared by all spiritual beings, as each can manifest reality for the benefit of the NDEr. Several NDErs witnessed manifestation directly. One wrote about the immediate creation of a landscape:

> This was energy personified and as its form took on a more solid shape, all that was behind it did as well. It was as if the entire canvas of white I had come to at the end of the tunnel was now alive and I was part of it. Other figures appeared in front and behind the being and myself. Soon there was activity all about, above and below, on every side, more beings, each of different brightness, sizes, and hues. Structures and landscapes sprung from everywhere all in a crystalline state. (NDERF #737)

Similarly, another being described the manifestation of spiritual beings:

> I was surrounded by light. Misty shapes began to form as I looked around. At first they were just moving swirls of light, but they soon took the shape of human forms. There were a lot of them around me.

I heard soft whispering coming from them, like a crowd murmuring and talking among themselves. From this crowd, three shapes came forward and approached me. As they drew near, I could make them out better, like they were slightly out of focus and my eyes were adjusting. They were tall and slender, wearing what looked like flowing robes. One of them was wearing a beard. They all had long, shoulder-length hair. One of them spoke to me. (NDERF #577)

Reality can only be manifested through the access of divine knowledge. According to the compilation of NDE reports, spiritual beings can instantly know everything, know everyone, be anywhere, and build anything. These abilities can be applied as teaching tools during the NDErs brief visit. These abilities can also be combined into one more teaching tool, the heavenly grand tour.

The Grand Tour

NDErs often visit one or two locations in the spiritual realm, such as exiting a tunnel into a beautiful garden. A select few NDErs visit multiple locations in a kind of heavenly tour. The NDEr excursion is hosted by God, Jesus, or unfamiliar spiritual guides. Aside from wondrous, lessons can be taught during the tour. Often, the purpose behind the tour is to demonstrate God's magnificent creation. The itinerary usually includes both the physical and spiritual universe. What is observed? Although tours are individualized, usually the outings take the NDEr somewhere grand: distant galaxies, other dimensions, forward and backward observation of events, habitable planets (although alien civilizations are rarely observed directly), and different spiritual levels of existence. A guide offered one NDEr a tour. She wrote:

It didn't speak to me but it transmitted to me a "want to come with me?" message. I am very adventurous, so I said yes, and together we travelled at the speed of light into a galaxy of bright lights. I knew that all of them were souls or spirits and that each one was a point of light that was another being...I then thought about music and I was instantly in an enormous concert hall. I was like an air particle in this beautiful theater and my (dead) Uncle Sydney was playing the piano with Arthur Rubenstein and Leonard Bernstein. My uncle looked up at me and smiled and winked. He looked SO happy and content and

I was really happy to see him playing, because that is what he always loved to do the most. (NDERF #2922)

An interesting dichotomy is presented here. The NDEr first observed a large spiritual community from a very macroscopic point of reference. The initial experience was contrasted by her later interacting with an individual spiritual being, namely a deceased uncle living out a life fantasy. Her experience suggests that souls are not lost in an infinite universe. Heaven is both infinite and personal.

The NDE experience is customized, in part, to reflect the needs and personality of the individual. When NDErs ask a question, they usually receive an answer. The following experience was submitted by a curious woman who wanted to know everything. She wrote:

"What about aliens? And parallel universes? And life on other planets? And UFOs? And... and..." That's when I perceived a great yet quiet chuckle of amusement. And like a pat on the head, I was given the Source (of creation) into the top of my head. It was like a giant stream and when my head was stuck inside of it I could see from the beginning of the beginning of everything and nothing. I saw the entirety of the universe from its big bang to big stop to big bang and to big stop; I had the memory of the universe. I understood cosmology, biology, spiritualism, consciousness, being, non-being, physics, mathematics, basically I knew everything there is to know and un-know. (NDERF #1654)

This NDEr received a tour of time and creation in response to her question. Furthermore, she received knowledge outlining the entire universe as a part of her soul birthright. Universal knowledge is not the birthright of the human being, however. It is important to note that she knew everything there is to know and *un-know*. NDErs lose a large proportion of the knowledge gained in the spiritual world. As previously discussed, the miniscule human brain cannot begin to process, comprehend, and store the knowledge of everything. Despite losing knowledge, the NDEr remembers the most important information from their journey. Specifically, they learn that they are deeply loved.

Humans are Deeply Loved by Spiritual Beings

Humans, despite their many frailties, are deeply loved by spiritual beings. Perhaps this revelation serves as the greatest gift provided by the near-death experience. Expressions of love are usually communicated by deceased loved ones we once knew on earth. However, sometimes love is also communicated by a host of other beings, both familiar and unfamiliar. Apparently, there are more spiritual beings that deeply care about us than we know or remember. Through acts of love, spiritual beings likely rejoice when we learn and make good decisions and grieve when we make selfish, hurtful decisions. Spiritual beings deeply desire for us to choose the love of God and succeed in our mission to learn on earth.

As we have explored in this chapter, many NDErs have encountered spiritual beings who expressed divine love during homecoming. Their profound unconditional love motivates the NDEr to share that love with other people after their return to earth. Many NDErs become other-centered in various ways: increasing personal authenticity, becoming more tolerant, giving of time and wealth, and selection of career goals. Many NDErs also become more self-aware of their magnificent divine nature through experience and transcendent teaching. With self-esteem and confidence, they learn to fearlessly live in accordance to their individualized mission to love. Finally, spiritual beings teach people about God's magnificent creation through the grand tour. The grand tour informs people that creation is not just reserved for God and angels, but is a birthright for all spiritual beings. Every spiritual being, every human being, is integral to creation. Specifically, humans are fully integrated with spiritual beings who deeply want to see each of us succeed on earth. Despite this integration, the vast majority of people on earth are unaware of the presence of spiritual beings. Yet, NDErs report that spiritual beings work closely to help us throughout our lives, just as they eagerly welcome us home and help us after death. How do they help us during this life? We will explore the purpose of spiritual helpers in the next chapter.

CHAPTER ELEVEN
THE BETTER ANGELS
OF OUR NATURE

Can science and spirituality be both true? Some scientists would say "no." They would point out that knowledge can only be derived through the scientific method. The scientific method involves the reproduction of empirical findings by measurement. What cannot be measured is unverifiable. Clearly, spiritual beings are not a subject of scientific investigation because they cannot be empirically measured, defined, or reproduced. Purely scientific-minded people are at a loss as to why the majority of people don't reject such "superstitious beliefs" in a scientific age. All technology, ranging from biochemistry to space-faring rockets, were created by science, not spiritual inspiration. Yet, according to a recent Gallup Poll, 92% of Americans believe in God, defying apparent scientific logic.[1] Furthermore, this trend has remained relatively constant over the last 65 years despite so many new gadgets created by science.

The human species clearly has a religious core, whether a consequence of biology or reality. However, the spiritual core does not negate the impact science has on religious beliefs in Western culture. For many, miracles have been relegated to rare events or historical artifacts. Demon possession and spiritual communication are now explained by mental illness, such as schizophrenia and other psychotic disorders. Consequently, the average person is faced with opposing influences: the human hunger for religious meaning and the competing marvels produced by science. What is a religious person to believe in a scientific age? Many people in Western cultures mitigate these two opposing belief systems by walking a middle ground. In other words, they dilute their spiritual beliefs in order to decrease the dissonance they feel in a modern world. Spiritual beings become relegated as existing somewhere "out there" in some type of mysterious, spiritual place called heaven. Beings may be viewed to breach the physical realm as messengers on rare occasion, like when they announced the birth of Jesus to Mary. Otherwise, they stay separated from modern "educated" people. The proposition that spiritual beings comingle with humans seems preposterous in a scientific age, even among many religious individuals who believe in angels and devils. There are some who beg to differ. The idea of a guardian angel has gained popularity in the New Age movement, but continues to have little traction in Western mainstream religious culture. Not wanting to defend accusations of superstition, it is simpler for religious people to compartmentalize spiritual beings into a non-defendable niche shrouded by mystery.

In the scientific age, it is easier to believe that spiritual beings exist as abstract entities rather than as tangible beings with specific purpose. With abstraction, accusations of superstition can be more easily defended. It is easier to assert, "I believe that grandfather is in a better place" more than "I believe that my dead grandfather is standing with me giving me direction and peace." The first quote reflects a widely shared belief whereas the latter may suggest, to many, signs of craziness. Why? The more specific a religious belief becomes, the more vulnerable it becomes to scientific attack. People can hide behind the ambiguity of "I believe in something but I can't tell you what it is" rather than risk appearing deviant by "rational-minded" people.

Alternatively, some may acknowledge spiritual beings during certain events, such as funerals. Let's say someone's mother passed away. A funeral attendee might provide comfort by verbalizing, "Your mom is in a better place. She will always be part of you. She will forever love you and live inside your heart." What does "living in your heart" signify? Does mom reside inside your chest muscle? Obviously, this phrase is only a metaphor. Although some believe mom to be just an active memory, others believe that mom is actually with loved ones, to comfort and guide during their life journeys. Why do people acknowledge spiritual beings during times of loss? Perhaps people are more in tune to spiritual realities during life transitions; spiritual beings become more real. Months after the burial, however, mourners are less likely to talk this way, perhaps to avoid the "crazy" label.

According to the NDE experience, spiritual beings are quite entwined with people's daily lives. Spiritual beings are not hanging around for their amusement, even when human behavior becomes amusing. They have assigned work to accomplish. Specifically, their collective mission is to assist our mission in succeeding during our challenging journey through life. They become angels of our better nature. It is the purpose of this chapter to describe how spiritual beings assist people in life.

Symbiosis and Synergy of Being

Thomas Hobbes wrote in his classic book, *Leviathan*, that typical human life is solitary, poor, nasty, brutish, and short.[2] Indeed, life does appear painful, ignoble, and inconsequential compared with the blissful spiritual existence in heaven. Some reflect on the inane course of life and ask, "What's the point of it all?" The NDEr would probably respond, "Spiritual growth is the point." As discussed in chapter six, humans have been given the freedom of choice. Freedom necessarily entails the interplay of good and evil in the material realm. Faced with this interplay, humans learn by experiencing the consequences of every decision between darkness and light. God understands the challenges that spiritual beings face by surviving the tough schoolyard of earth. Thus, God assigns a host of spiritual beings to mentor people through the tougher lessons in life.

Through revelation in heaven, the NDEr learns that spiritual beings are always loving and helping them during their life journey. Howard Storm was provided an unusual amount of revelation about spiritual beings because of the many questions he asked during his near-death experience. Because of his unusual depth of understanding, I reference him frequently in this section.

Howard Storm wrote that there were countless types of angels. Furthermore, he reported that the total number of spiritual beings exceeded the number of stars in the universe.[3] He wrote, "Angels are with us constantly and they are everywhere. We are never apart from them."[3] There are approximately 100,000,000,000,000,000,000,000 stars in the known universe, according to recent astronomical estimates.[4] If Storm is meant to be taken literally, as I suspect to be the case, an unfathomable number of spiritual beings populate the universe. NDErs consistently report that the universe teams with life on other planets. Their reports are consistent with recent scientific estimates based on recent exoplanet findings by Kepler and other measuring orbiters. For instance, astronomers at the Royal Astronomical Society estimate there are over 100 billion habitable planets in the Milky Way galaxy alone.[5] Multiply that number by billions of galaxies, and you have a very large number. Thus, a significant percentage of these spiritual beings may populate vast numbers of unknown biological centers. If this is indeed the norm, then it is not farfetched that spiritual beings are seemingly "everywhere" on populated planets like earth. Their prolific co-existence cannot be by accident. Their individual and collective purpose in the material realm serves a greater divine plan. Although the grand plan remains elusive to us, one might speculate that a heavily populated universe was designed to create a limitless diversity of sentient experience.

Here on earth, spiritual beings are assigned many mentoring tasks tied to our mission to grow toward the Source. At the same time, spiritual beings also grow toward the Source by mentoring us. Not every soul is ready, or suited, to mentor. Tasks are assigned based on the soul's interests, talents, and spiritual maturity. Howard Storm wrote:

> Some people have left behind loved ones that need their protection and guidance. They can live as guardian angels for a while as part of their spiritual development. Some apprentice themselves to great angels to learn lessons they missed in this life. Anything good is possible.[3]

Note that Howard Storm, consistent with other NDE accounts, states that spiritual beings protect and guide loved ones left behind. Who is being helped by these spiritual beings? According to NDE reports, we all are. The following individual became sensitive to seeing spiritual beings after her near-death experience. She described an incredible moment of divine revelation:

> When I was able to tear myself away from the spirit, I glanced slowly at the vista around me and everywhere I looked every single person in my view had beautiful, loving spirits attending them. People walking nonchalantly down the sidewalk were accompanied by spirits. From within cars, unfettered by physical barriers, I could see the glow and form of beings around the occupants. I saw joggers with flutters of

light streaking behind them as their spirit kept pace. As people entered and left buildings, light beings followed...

The lights, a connection to the humans, which were glinting off the beings were so bright and expansive, they interconnected, forming a sort of light grid. I remembered reports in books on the near-death experience of people seeing grids on the other side that they didn't know how to explain... I realized the connection of human beings to the Beings of Light was through love and that the love itself was connected through this grid. (NDERF, #1011)

According to this NDERF account, spiritual mentors accompany every person everywhere throughout their earthly lives. Interestingly, all these billions of spiritual beings are interconnected to each other and to the Source. Collectively, they form a vast energy grid; an integration of love, information, common purpose, and combined will.

One might hypothesize that spiritual mentors have less influence on charges motivated by ego. The self-absorbed person rarely focuses on the needs of others, much less guidance from ethereal beings. In other words, they are living off-grid. Spiritual beings can't help the spiritually deaf and blind very much.

If we really are accompanied by spiritual beings, the question begs, "Who are they?" According to many NDE accounts, spiritual mentors are generally deceased family members. The ramifications are important. Spiritual beings and human beings grow toward the Source in symbiosis, or inter-reliance. Relationships and spiritual growth are tied together in love. Referring back to the tapestry metaphor, humans progress together with a group of other spiritual beings in life and in heaven. Some groups involve family members, whereas others represent different relationships. Some NDErs refer to grouped beings as soulmates. Over eons, we have become bonded to soulmates typically more than other beings. Bonded relationships help us ward off isolation while living in the physical realm. Jody Long, in her book *Soul to Soulmate*, wrote:

We are fragmented from God when we are born to earth, and trying to regain that lost love is a core motivator and part of the collective human consciousness. We are trying to be reunited and reconnected with the love from whence we came...The NDErs describe incomprehensible love that we can only glimpse here on earth. Soulmates describe that same intense love and connection. This love is unlike anything else that we know on earth, yet brings us the closest to reconnecting with God.[6]

One might speculate that spiritual families grow when people marry and have children, forever adding to the complexity of soulmate relationships. Unfortunately, not all earthly family relationships are built on love. Some are even abusive. I venture to guess that spiritual relationship dynamics are individualized in heaven as they are on earth. Again, anything good is possible within God's plan. The converse may also be true; anything bad is impossible.

There is another ramification for soulmates growing in symbiosis. Namely, spiritual beings work hard to help each group member living on earth. Moreover, they do so with deep concern and compassion. Spiritual beings know, from their own prior life experience, that loved ones struggle with daily physical challenges and severance with the divine realm. For these reasons, spiritual beings are very concerned about the progression of loved ones under their vigilant charge. Howard Storm wrote, "Angels can experience what we think and feel. When this is consistent with God's will, they are joyful. When we are opposed to God's will, they suffer emotionally."[3]

Spiritual guides are so concerned about our growth that they never leave us. If fact, they are *with us* throughout our entire lives. It may be helpful to define the concept, *with us*. As previously explored, spiritual beings know our thoughts and emotions by direct, shared experience. Although they may use human language, more often they communicate using images, emotions, and telepathically-induced ideas. They also experience our emotions through interconnection. Given their capacity for pure empathy, it is not surprising that they feel great joy or suffering when we succeed and fail in our mission. When spiritual beings are with us, a synergy of being is shared. Thus, when a person tells you at a funeral, "grandmother will always be *with you*," what this actually means is that she will be with you in a much more intimate and complete way in death than she was while living.

After realizing that spiritual beings interact with me intimately, my first thought was, "Wow! The world I live in is not what it seems!" Previously, my world view was based on a perspective of relative isolation and self-containment; my thoughts and emotions were private. According to the NDEr, all of our intimate thoughts and emotions are shared with spiritual guides. Nothing is kept confidential, be it a silly thought, sexual fantasy, selfish intent, envious emotion, or violent impulse. Thus, spiritual guides know the real us in our raw, base form. This may seem a bit disconcerting, especially for those who are ashamed of their psychological lives. I have often told therapy clients that their thoughts can do little harm because they are private. Alas, negative thoughts are really not so private after all. Yet, people can take comfort that spiritual beings understand and accept us. Howard Storm shared an awkward moment discovering that spiritual beings knew everything:

> I could hear their individual voices in my mind as they addressed me. I thought, "What if I say something I don't want you to hear?" And no sooner had I thought that than I thought the word "breast." They all laughed and told me that they knew everything I had ever thought and that I couldn't surprise them. I was both embarrassed and relieved.[3]

Although embarrassed, Howard Storm was relieved that he was not judged. Indeed, spiritual beings are not assigned to judge people, even during particularly raw life moments. Neither do they sneer at us, laugh maliciously, or hold grudges. Spiritual beings only want to help. The following NDEr wrote:

> They were not there to criticize, scold, or to punish. They were there to give me strength, comfort, and guidance. The angels were there to show me God's love. They were there to bring me God's comfort, understanding, and love. (NDERF #566)

How do spiritual beings provide strength, comfort, guidance, and love when people do not even perceive them? To avoid violating human self-determination, spiritual beings are relegated to working in relative secrecy. Thus, they tend use very subtle tactics in order to maintain a "low profile" on earth.

Gentle Nudging from the Beyond

Spiritual beings and humans are not equal in knowledge, power, or status. They fully know us whereas we hardly know them. They have the power to do just about anything we cannot. They realize their status as magnificent spiritual beings whereas we can't even agree on who we are. Although spiritual beings are greater in all aspects, their power is curtailed by divine decree. This is done for good reason. Destiny changes whenever spiritual beings overtly intercede. Imagine how your faith decisions would change if a deceased family member suddenly materialized in front of you. To preserve the rule of human self-determination, spiritual beings *typically* are not allowed to announce themselves or interfere with human choice. The divine maxim is that people need to learn from their own mistakes. Spiritual beings are tasked to assist their charges in completing mission, not to dominate the very mission they are assigned to protect. Although spiritual beings faithfully adhere to divine rules, adherence can be distressful when serving lost loved ones under their care. Howard Storm wrote, "They told me that they always want to intervene in our lives but sometimes God restrains them. God wants us to experience the consequences of our actions."[3]

If spiritual beings are typically not allowed to overtly interfere with human free will, then how do they help us? On very rare occasions, spiritual beings are allowed to act overtly. Most often, however, they are limited to guiding us in subtle and often imperceptible ways. Howard Storm likens this influence of spiritual beings to gardening:

> The function of the angels in relation to the evolution of the earth is a lot like gardening, with a gentle touch. You plant the seed, you water it, you prune the plant, you tend it, but it has a life of its own. Anyone who gardens knows that the more in tune you are in allowing the thing to be what it can become, rather than forcing it, the more effective you are in helping it develop to its full potential.[3]

Spiritual beings serve as catalysts for growth, but they do not force growth. Neither do they stop our reckless behavior. When all is said and done, human beings are responsible for their own choices. At a more profound level, every individual is responsible for the self and what that self becomes. However, spiritual beings are allowed to gently nudge people in a positive direction toward the Source: provide an alternative thought; pang us with a corrective feeling; send messages through lucid dreams; nudge another person to help. They typically do these activities with great stealth. In fact, the vast majority of their work remains unobserved. During a life review, an NDEr learned that she had been nudged to talk to a lost student in grade school. The following conversation ensued:

> "Yes, I see her." I answered in my mind. "I have never seen her at school before. She must be new here." I believed that I was speaking back to

my own thoughts, my own voice. "She looks funny." I remembered wondering if she was sick. She had black circles under her eyes. The angel continued, speaking to my mind sounding like my own voice. "Why don't you go and talk to her? She looks so afraid and lonely, doesn't she?"

"Talk to her, why? She is not in my class. I am afraid. I don't like taking to people I don't know. I don't know what to say." I continued what I thought was a conversation with myself. Children can be fearful and cruel and I was no different. But the angel persisted. (NDERF #566)

How much of our shining behavior is influenced by spiritual guides? Is our nagging conscience always our own, or can it be the voice of a spiritual being? My guess, there is probably quite a bit of influence. I also speculate that people who seek positive growth may be more influenced than people who are indifferent. In the study of attribution, psychologists examine how people attribute causes to their behavior, from the self or the environment. There are many thinking errors related in assigning attribution. According to research, people tend to overrate their personal control over good outcomes. Conversely, people tend to underrate their role in causing bad outcomes.[7] If spiritual beings are covertly inspiring people towards acting better, then people may be overrating personal control even more than the research numbers suggest.

The fact that humans need so much help speaks to the deficient biological nature of human beings. According to Howard Storm, many wars have been avoided by spiritual beings nudging world leaders to seek peaceful solutions to conflict.[3] Unfortunately, some leaders still choose war because they so strongly desire aggression and power. The same may be said about other individual and group conflicts on a smaller scale. Despite the sobering view of humanity, our struggling species may be due a little credit. Namely, humans are given the final choice between darkness and light. Many people really do listen to that quiet voice and sometimes choose the better option. After all, the system would not be set in place if it didn't work. It would work better, of course, if more people were *mindful* of their thoughts and feelings. Let's return to the NDEr who was encouraged to help a new, troubled student in grade school. She concluded:

Angels are sent to each and every person born on this planet to deliver the message that God is with us. Angels speak to us and try to help us complete our purpose in this life. We need to learn to listen, and to be able to do that we need to find silence within ourselves. (NDERF #566)

Spiritual guides feel more effective when their charges listen to them. Spiritual guides become empowered in the same way teachers are empowered when students focus on lectures and complete daily assignments. The most brilliant educator in the world cannot teach a truant pupil. Likewise, the most powerful spiritual being cannot guide a truant person stumbling through school earth.

How are people expected to listen if they are not even aware of spiritual beings? Complete awareness is not a necessary condition to learning. Many psychologists, from various theoretical orientations, agree that learning does not always involve full awareness. Open, loving people naturally listen to the quiet voice of change, regardless of the source. Conversely, a self-absorbed person becomes deaf to the quiet voice of spiritual inspiration. The more we ignore our spiritual guides the more we shut them down.

Even when they are ignored, our spiritual guides remain by our side throughout life. Unlike people who quickly abandon each other, they are steadfast in their loyalty. Our angels are always with us, helping, even when we go deaf and astray. They take their mission seriously because they love us more than we will ever realize in our lifetime.

Grieving and the Unconcealed Spiritual Intervention

Although spiritual beings typically work subtly and covertly, exceptions are allowed based on individual circumstances. Whereas many human systems are rigid and bureaucratic, divine organization is flexible and individualized. God fully recognizes that what is best for one individual is not appropriate for another. Appreciating this complexity, spiritual beings may directly intervene to meet an overriding need. When spiritual beings meet and/or communicate directly with people on earth, this is called an *after death communication*.

Hundreds of people have recorded their personal after death communication accounts on a website called the After Death Communication Research Foundation (ADCRF), created and maintained by Jody and Jeffrey Long. Although the frequency of direct communications is unknown, there are likely fewer people who receive after death communications than don't.

After death communications are most often directed toward the grieving shortly after a family member has died. Submissions from the ADCRF website will be frequently used throughout the remainder of this chapter. It should be noted that after death communications are technically not near-death experiences. However, all spiritual communications are an extension of a larger transcendent reality consistent with the NDE information provided throughout this book.

Spiritual beings are most often allowed to communicate with living family members who are paralyzed by overwhelming grief. In many instances, the mourner cannot move forward in life without direct spiritual intervention. The inability to move forward often jeopardizes the mourner's own spiritual mission due to their unresolved loss. In some cases, fulfillment of mission appears to be more important than maintaining a strict rule of non-interference. One woman shared:

> One night in October, I had just gotten in bed when I saw a ball of softly glowing mist slowly descend upon my bed from the corner of the ceiling. I was speechless as I saw it slowly coming towards me. Somehow I knew it was my mother, even though I couldn't discern a body or a shape. The mist enveloped me as I lay in bed and filled me with feelings of love and calm...
>
> My mother communicated telepathically with me by repeating my name over and over, saying, "Eve, Eve, Eve, I love you so much. I love you so much. Don't worry about me. Where I am, there's complete freedom, freedom, freedom! Tell your brothers and sisters I love them and I will always be with you all."
>
> I realized that I had just been visited by my mother! I felt an overwhelming sense of appreciation and renewed self-worth. It gave me the strength to overcome my depression and to live again. (ADC #701)

Most people slowly work through the five stages of grief as defined by Dr. Kübler-Ross: disbelief, anger, bargaining, depression, and acceptance.[8] Although tough, most psychologists view grief work to be healthy, especially in cases where family and friends provide emotional support. In the case presented, the mourner appears to have experienced a *complicated grief reaction*. In a complicated grief reaction, the mourner becomes stuck in a stage of grief that blocks a normal course of healing. The daughter, for whatever reasons, appeared to be trapped in a downward spiral of self-devaluation and depression. Namely, depression increased hopelessness which, in turn, further increased depression. The mother's communication broke the cycle by giving her daughter the strength to overcome and live again. Perhaps love was the most therapeutic agent. Specifically, the mother calmly affirmed the daughter's worth. The mother, by her mere presence, may have also provided the daughter with the strength that comes from certainty. With eternal hope and faith, isolation and the fear of permanent death were alleviated. For these and other reasons, the daughter was able to finally separate her thoughts from the deceased mother and be an individual again. She was able to dislodge herself from grief and proceed with her divine mission; this time with the continued living guidance of her mother who had visited her from the spiritual realm.

The next ADC submission provides another good example of a person stuck in grief:

> I had been spending most of my time in bed, about a month. My family was getting worried that I was giving up on life, and I was. This was my twin, my best friend, and the love of my life. As I sat up in bed crying with my head face down in my pillow, I felt a comfort come over my body. As I pulled my head away from pillow I saw my twin sister Roslee standing in front of me, SOOO beautiful, wearing a white gown, with a beautiful light around her. She smiled at me and said, "I love you very much and you must go on, you are not finished here. There are things that you will need to complete. Then when you pass on from this world, I will be here to take your hand." She then said, "I love you." And she and the light faded away. I believe that she knew that I was giving up and that she needed to let me know she would be back for me. (ADC #695)

As with the previous submission, the surviving twin sister was transformed by love, hope, and faith. Note the spiritual guide's emphasis on mission. Direct spiritual communication was deemed necessary to redirect the mourner to finish her individual mission in life rather than be paralyzed by grief.

Some readers may be asking, "Why didn't I receive an after death communication from my loved one? Am I not good enough for God?" Put another way, why are a few people allowed after death communications whereas the majority of people are not? There are no sure answers to such divine mysteries, but one can make educated guesses. Contributing factors may include the severity of the grief, complications in healing, individual needs of the grieving person, and openness to unusual spiritual experiences. There are undoubtedly many unknown factors, depending on any unique set of circumstances. In reading ADC accounts, I did not sense that the individuals who experienced after death communications were better and more special than anyone else. As discussed throughout the chapter, God loves everyone unconditionally. So, to answer the second question, "being good enough" does not appear to be a relevant concern.

From reading many NDERF and ADCRF submissions, a primary reason why some people experience after death communications has to do with their individualized mission. Each person walks a unique path. Some paths veer to the right whereas other paths lead to the left. Each path yields different spiritual fruits along the wayside. There are as many paths as there are people. Sometimes an individual path may lead to a briar patch of complicated grief where after death communications are allowed. Rarer still are other types of unconcealed spiritual intercessions. One type of overt spiritual involvement includes redirecting people to make different critical life choices.

Messages and the Unconcealed Spiritual Intervention

Humans rely on logic and personal convictions when making decisions. Born in a world of ambiguity and competing ideologies, every person has to make their way by defining the self. Each individual creates a life path established by his or her combined life choices. Good choices produce learning and ultimately spiritual development. Poor choices may also produce learning and ultimately spiritual development. In the case of poor choices, learning and development occur through the natural consequences of adversity and self-reflection. Just because someone is learning through the "school of hard knocks" doesn't diminish their growth experience. In either case, human independence is the primary vehicle for humans to grow in their individual mission. Yet, for whatever reasons, some people are allowed to receive direct guidance during strategic points in their life by spiritual messages. One may speculate that messages may be instigated by a guardian angel, or spiritual being, advocating for intervention on behalf of their charge. For whatever the reasons, these messages are not purposeless.

They all have spiritual growth undertones. Howard Storm wrote, "On special rare occasions God allows angels to help. When we ask God for spiritual gifts of love, faith, and hope, God always allows angels to help us...Angels hear our prayers."[3]

As Storm points out, God allows spiritual guides to help people develop in love, faith, and hope. Although most are guided through the subtle spiritual nudge, spiritual beings are occasionally allowed to overtly help people develop love, faith, and hope. In other words, messages convey the same spiritual purpose regardless of whether spiritual beings are observed or not. Yet, the specific messages vary depending on factors like severity, individual need, and individual growth. Several notable examples will be provided in this section.

The first example of an after-death message was submitted by a woman who recently lost her grandmother, the strong matriarch of the family. The portion begins with a request to the grandmother, Oma, from the granddaughter:

> "Oma, I know we have no money or stomach for a fight now, but you know how much we still love and need this place. If you send me a four-leaf clover to let me know you're still with us, I'll know what we have to do and that everything will be all right. I'll stop at nothing to see that we keep the house in the family."

> It normally took me only a few minutes to find one of the lucky clovers among the lush growth of Oma's yard, but not that day. I searched intensely for at least half an hour among matted ranks of thickly growing clover, but my "sign" was nowhere to be found. Finally, tired and desperate, the thought came that possibly I was going about this the wrong way. I tried something drastic. "Oma, please, send me a four-leaf clover if you think we need to...let go." Without even taking another step, I looked down at the ground to begin my search afresh, and saw a perfect specimen beside my shoe.

> At the time I was crushed, but I obeyed the "omen". I can't say whether it was the right choice, and wish there had been a greater variety of options; it has certainly not made losing the house (which was practically given away to the first comer) any more bearable to date, at least for me. The only thing it unquestionably has done, is prevent untold additional misery and strife in the family had I persisted in taking an adversarial route. (ADC #141)

The granddaughter received a challenging spiritual message that put her treasured beliefs to the test. She was able to put aside her desire for justice to avoid strife. Note how the granddaughter was distressed despite the sign. Spiritual beings do not always tell us what we want to hear. But they do tell us what is right if we are ready to listen.

In the next example, the submitter received a series of thoughts from a deceased friend. The friend's message involved attending a particular church. Similar to the previous example, the message was less about attending a particular church and more about compassion and forgiveness:

A series of "thoughts" started coming into my head. They were not my own thoughts, I knew, because I always think in words, and these had no words even though their meaning was quite clear... I could not remember, even immediately after it was over, what the specific messages had been. But I was left with the distinct and unquestionable conviction that I should stay in this church. It bothered me that I couldn't remember exactly what I had been "told" were the reasons for that decision, but I remembered feeling during the event a sense of "of course, it is perfectly reasonable - how could I have ever thought otherwise!" A few weeks later I did consciously try to remember what the messages were, but I was only able to discern that the general message was about complete forgiveness and compassion, even toward the people at church who had done me wrong in the past. I feel certain this communication came from my friend who had passed away the previous day. (ADC #1272)

The next example involves a recently deceased father who wanted to communicate love, hope, and faith to his daughter. Interestingly, the deceased father lacked these loving qualities in life. The daughter wrote:

My entire family was hurt by this man that we loved. He neglected his family in favor of his friends until the day he died. He said hurtful things to me and all the others, including my own children, until right before he died. This was just the way he was... He appeared in my dream. He did not speak to me, he just patiently taught me how to change the oil in my car. It was his patience that struck me, because he completely lacked that quality in life. I felt loved by him and I felt his compassion toward me.

The content of this dream was very significant to me because one of the cruelest things my father did to me involved this very issue (an oil change or lack thereof). It was like he was trying to handle the event like he wished he would have in life... I was considering buying my aunt's car, but before I did, I asked my dad to look it over to make sure it was okay. My aunt was a widow and probably even more naive than me when it came to cars. My father did look at the car, but as usual, he let me know how much I had put him out by the request. He also didn't really look it over very closely, and told me to buy it. It turned out that the oil was drained from the car (we don't know why), and within a day of driving it the engine exploded. (ADC #992)

As a spiritual being purified by the divine, the deceased father regretted how he treated his daughter during life. He likely realized the pain he caused during a life review. Normally, it would be too late to make amends after death. But in this case, the deceased father was allowed to make amends.

Spiritual Beings as Protectors

Bad things happen to good people. Injury, pain, and death can strike anyone indiscriminately, through illness, accident, war, and random acts of violence. Why does a church bus drive over a cliff and kill two dozen children? From an eternal perspective, souls are only returning home. But for survivors left behind, these young deaths caused trauma to family, church, and community. On rare occasions, people report that spiritual beings protect them from injury and death. Why are a few spared where most are not? This seems to be an area of great mystery. Again, spiritual intervention is likely tied to the path of the individual, what a person is supposed to accomplish or learn on earth. The pertinent question often becomes, "Is it your time yet?" Divine intervention does not appear to have anything to do with individual worthiness or a measurement of God's love. Although the reasons are not clear, a number of people do report direct, overt spiritual protection. The first example involves a woman who was saved from intolerable pain by her grandmother and mother in-law. She writes:

Fifteen minutes before I was taken to the operating theater, I was lying in my hospital bed feeling overwhelmed with pain. Suddenly my awareness changed and the room became filled with a bright light. And there before me were my late grandmother and late mother-in-law, floating toward me! They came to rest on either side of my bed – my grandmother, to the left of me, and my mother-in-law to my right. Only my mother-in-law spoke. She said it wasn't my time to come with them, but that they were here to help me with my pain. (ADC #3151)

Some mistakenly believe God inflicts pain on mortal subjects, either to punish, smite, or put their morality to the test. In the Jewish/Christian tradition, these themes can be read in the book of Job, one of the early books in the Hebrew bible. Personally, I have difficulty believing that a completely loving God intentionally inflicts pain in order to punish or test people. All aspects of the near-death experience demonstrate that adversity is not about rewards and punishments from God. Pain is the natural consequence of physical existence, the mechanical firing of neural pain receptors. Any organism needs pain to successfully adapt and survive a dangerous natural environment. Yet pain can benefit the human beyond the physical. From the angle of growth, pain can sometimes be useful in teaching endurance in the face of relentless adversity. Pain can also teach empathy for others who similarly suffer. Other times, pain is just pain. In the previous vignette, two spiritual beings were allowed to help ease this woman's severe pain as a consequence of her surgery. Her pain would not have been alleviated if it were inflicted as a punishment from God. Such assistance appears to be allowed only on rare occasions. In most instances, we are left to endure suffering as a natural state of the human condition. Yet, this is only a temporary condition while living on school earth. Pain and suffering do not exist in the spiritual realm, our true home. Do we learn from the pain we experience on earth? That is up to each one of us and the path we choose.

Sometimes spiritual beings protect a person from serious injury or death. In the next example, a woman experienced a dream where her deceased aunt protected her from physical injury from an oncoming train. She writes:

She told me she had received permission to see me, but that we would probably not see each other again until I die. She told me that she had come to warn me to be very, very careful on the following day. She warned me that I would be in danger, and I would need to be very "in tune" and aware of my surroundings. She didn't explain what would happen, only that I would need to pay attention and be very careful. Then she left...

I looked out the driver's side window to see the lights of a train coming toward us very quickly. I realized then that we were on railroad tracks. I quickly reversed the car off the tracks, narrowly avoiding the train, and we watched as the train sped past. In that moment I realized this must have been what my aunt was trying to warn me about. (ADC #1293)

Note that the aunt did not explain any information about the future danger. Ambiguity seems to be the rule when warnings are provided by spiritual beings. Nonspecific warning signs leave interpretation up to the receiver. Namely, it is the recipient's responsibility to accept the message as authentic in faith whilst processing the meaning of the message and choosing to make corrective action. It would have been simpler, and perhaps safer, for the aunt to have provided all the details. In doing so, however, the rules for self-determination would have been violated. The niece could have either ignored the dream as a figment of her subconscious or trust the warning. In accordance to flexible rules guiding individual free will, the niece was still responsible for accepting the message as authentic and choosing to take a path to avoid danger.

Divine intervention can sometimes occur during dangerous and traumatic situations, even during atrocities. A coworker, I will rename Mary, was attending Columbine High school in Littleton, Colorado when two students, Dylan Klebold and Eric Harris, opened fire on classmates with semi-automatic weapons. The tragedy made national headlines after the two killed 12 fellow students and injured 23 others.

Listening to the loud popping of gunfire and screams, Mary understood that her life was in grave danger. She decided to bolt out of the main doors of the Columbine school building. Running across the front property, Mary suddenly heard a loud, distinct, command burst in her mind. The message simply said, "DUCK!" She immediately fell to the floor as a bullet whizzed over her head. Mary believes that God rescued her life by issuing that one saving word. After the incident, many students shared their harrowing experiences with counselors and with each other. Mary noted that many other students reported similar accounts of being saved through divine intervention.

From Mary's current standpoint, the Columbine shootings embodied a greater spiritual battle between good and evil. Although the shooters were allowed to act in accordance with their own will to accomplish evil,

God interceded. In other words, God did everything that could be done to save lives without violating human free will. According to Mary, "God ultimately has power over evil, and was not going to let those two win."

Mary struggled emotionally after the incident. With help, love, and fortitude, she prevailed. Working in both psychology and law enforcement, Mary was recently able to help during the Arapahoe High School shooting. Specifically, she was able to help process female students exiting the school following the shooting. Her sensitivity and understanding surely benefited many traumatized students. Mary believes that her life journey reflects divine intercession over the years. Indeed, she has risen above the tragedy and opened spiritual doors to allow God's love to shine into her life and the lives of others. After all, anything good is possible with God.

Anything Good is Possible with God

People are not alone in this world, even though it may feel that way sometimes. Some individuals despair that they have been abandoned in their suffering. Despair exists in this world, in part, because self-understanding becomes twisted by conventional belief. A human does not first become a spiritual being after death. Rather, it is the spiritual being that becomes human after they are born on earth. Thus, each person has a strong support system the moment he or she is born. During our short brutish stay on earth, we are surrounded by our other spiritual beings, usually deceased family members, who love and guide us. They love us so much that they always are with us. Even when we do not listen, they never give up. In this chapter, we have explored how spiritual beings work with each human being through the gentle nudge. We have also explored how they may occasionally interact with the individual in overt, unconcealed intervention. They do so by comforting us during grief, redirecting us toward mission, and protecting us from harm. Whatever the venue and whatever the method, they are ready to guide and comfort us through the briar bushes of life.

Coming up in the next couple of chapters, two case vignettes will be presented showing how spiritual beings interact with people. In the first chapter, titled Ray, a man discovers hope by receiving messages from his recently deceased mother. In the second chapter, titled Teresa, deceased family members help a woman become un-snared from some of the very worst briar bushes of life.

CHAPTER TWELVE

RAY

(TESTIMONY NO. 2)

Sometimes spiritual beings are afforded the rare opportunity to deliver multiple messages to loved ones. As the complexity and number of messages increase, so does their impact. Multiple messages can even enrich a person's life mission by opening new spiritual doors. A small number of people in the world are afforded one overt message, and even fewer are afforded multiple messages. In this chapter, we will examine an exceptional account where a person received divine information at several levels. Like most spiritual communications, the story involves love and personal growth. But in this unusual case, the story involves a son who became spiritually transformed by the cooperative work of a dying mother and a caring friend. The special friend, who I will call Marie, helped a dying mother reach her son through spiritual communication. Specifically, the friend cooperated in a combined effort to facilitate emotional and spiritual healing.

Marie acquired the ability to communicate with spiritual beings approximately one month after she had a near-death experience. Like the majority of brief NDEs, hers primarily consisted of an out-of-body experience. Marie died after her car was squarely hit by a drunk driver. She first remembers floating above her motionless body lying in the back of an ambulance. She wondered, "Why am I looking down on myself?" Marie watched an EMT provide emergency medical assistance while yelling, "Get her there! We are losing her." She recognized him as her brother-in-law's brother. Marie was subsequently saved by medical resuscitation efforts, but not before she had died for a period of 33 seconds.

After about one month of physical recovery, Marie began to notice shadows shift around in the dark of night. "How can I be seeing dark forms in the dark," she asked herself, worried that she might be losing her mind. One can only imagine her fear and confusion. Marie frantically searched for a rational explanation to dispel her fears. Perhaps she was seeing an animal scurrying about, or worse, an intruder. But a search in the light demonstrated that there was no one in the house. Now she began to panic.

Marie's fear piqued when a spirit materialized and came by her side. Her fear quickly subsided, however, when she recognized that the spirit was a deceased friend who she dearly missed. The friend told her not to be afraid, that the dark shapes were other spirits who would not hurt her. The friend reframed the frightful scene as a divine gift; she was able to see into and communicate with the spiritual realm. Over time, Marie learned that she could learn to use her gift to help people.

As a result of her out-of-body experience, Marie reconnected with the spiritual realm. Through this connection, she frequently sensed, and later began to communicate with, spiritual beings. Although mystical perception is common with people who have had near-death experiences, the degree of spiritual connection varies between people. For Marie, communication was strengthened if she had once touched the deceased when they were alive. There were several occasions when Marie used her gift to comfort friends in need. Concerned about being overwhelmed, she called on her gift sparingly to avoid multitudes of people in spiritual want. She also was concerned that her gift might be misused, so she was careful to "weed-out" irresponsible seekers. Marie pointed out that she does not use her ability for financial gain. She believes that her gift was endowed by God. Applying spiritual powers to boost ego, in her view, would only corrupt the gift.

The present chapter centers on an occasion when Marie helped a mutual friend, Ray, in a momentous way. The account was first relayed to me by Ray, who later introduced me to Marie. Their story begins with Ray anticipating the imminent death of his beloved mother, Joann, who was dying of organ failure due to advanced age. The death of a parent is difficult in ordinary circumstances, but in this case Ray's sorrow had become complicated by other emotions. In the forefront of his mind, Ray felt conflicted about accepting a career promotion in another state. Although a great professional opportunity, the thousand-mile separation from his mother weighed on him. Ray had always been very close to his mother and helped her whenever possible. She was the pillar of strength and the white flower in his heart. Now, due to logistical reasons, he was unable to provide in-person support during her final days dying in a nursing home. Although her needs were well attended to by other family members, Ray wanted to be there during her last hours. His heart was darkening, shadowed by the billowing storm clouds of guilt and doubt.

Mixed in with his guilt, Ray was experiencing a spiritual crisis. Ray had long questioned the existence of the Judeo-Christian God, who seemed to be smiting the unfaithful in one section of the Bible and loving people in the next. In other words, it was difficult for him to accept the "hell and brimstone" portrayal of God; he could not accept that a loving God inflicted pain and suffering as punishment. Ray was caught up in a perfect storm. He had recently lost three brothers to illness and now faced the death of his beloved mother. It was difficult enough to deal with normal emotions associated with losing a parent. But those emotions were magnified by spiritual doubt. Ray did not know what was to happen to his mother after she died. Would she, like his brothers, cease to exist? One by one, would he be left alone as people continued to die and fall into oblivion? Would he soon share that same, final, empty fate? In his questioning, Ray feared the connective loss of everyone he knew and loved. He also faced disconnection to his own existence. Not having the answers, Ray faced confusion and despair during his grieving.

Ray traveled to visit his mother, Joann, at the nursing home as his work responsibilities permitted. These visits increased as his mother's condition worsened and she was placed on hospice care at the nursing home. There comes a point in the cycle of life where everyone is faced with the inevitable death of a loved one. Some months ago, Ray visited his mother knowing it was for the last time. Ray met with family and friends who came to pay their final respects to a woman who was much loved and respected in life. One of those individuals was Marie, a friend of Ray and his wife. Marie primarily had come to offer support to the family and to visit Joann. Sometime in the evening, Marie looked down on an elderly woman, thinned and drained, who was alive but unconscious. She looked so different than a year ago, when she had held her hand in a casino. It was at that time when Marie no-ticed a spiritual presence to her side. She turned toward the welcom-ing presence of a translucent, young, vibrant woman. As the ethereal presence moved forward and gained definition, Marie recognized the woman as Joann.

Joann smiled and conveyed the following message, "Don't let them cry for me. I am fine. I am not in any pain." She then disappeared.

Joann visited Marie again the next morning in her bedroom, around 10:00 a.m., just moments after her death. She simply said, "I'm so happy!"

Joann appeared a third time the next morning at 4:00 a.m. She hov-ered for a moment. Marie then asked her, "Are you okay?"

"I am doing very well," she answered. "I want you to please tell Ray it was not his fault for moving to his new job. I am very proud of him. I have never been so proud in my life."

Marie approached Ray to tell him the good news she received from his mother. She found him standing dejected and forlorn. She had nev-er seen him look so down. Ray listened to Marie's messages with rapt attention. As she continued explaining what had happened, Ray's de-meanor brightened. When she conveyed that his mother was proud of him, Ray beamed with a big pumpkin-faced grin. Marie also asked him, "Do you feel something touching your shoulder?"

Shocked, Ray replied after a long pause, "Yes, but I didn't know what that was."

"That is your mother greeting you," Marie explained.

When I interviewed Ray, he agreed with Marie's account. He added, "That conversation really helped me at that time. I guess when you are in that state, you are willing to grab onto anything hopeful." As insin-uated by his response, the rational side of Ray began to question Ma-rie's fantastic claims. Yet, Joann would continue communicating to Ray through Marie. Moreover, she would communicate information that only Ray would know; idiosyncratic facts that could not be dismissed. In fact, she challenged his long held views about life after death.

Marie witnessed additional spiritual incidents just prior to and after Joann's death. First, Marie saw a medium-sized, brown dog lay next to Joann in her hospice bed hours before her final breath. The dog's color was faded, however, due to the soothing glow of a white hue. The dog was resting its snout against her arm, as if to say "I am with you and I love you." Ray confirmed that the family owned a friendly, medium-sized, brown dog many years ago. Prior to its passing, the dog would place its snout on Joann's arm, exactly as Marie observed.

On a personal note, I find it comforting that animals appear to have an ongoing spiritual existence. Animals sometimes are discussed in both NDERF and ADCRF accounts. Some Christians believe that animals do not have souls, despite the Bible saying that the lion will peacefully lay down with the lamb in heaven. Personally, I eagerly look forward to being reunited with beloved, deceased pets. There is another important point regarding the existence of animals in the spiritual realm. Namely, all intelligent life is sacred, even the lives of our junior animal cousins.

Marie witnessed something truly grand shortly after Joann passed away. Namely, Marie experienced a vision of Joann overlooking a beautiful meadow filled with hundreds of lovely flowers popping with vibrant colors. The entire scene was filled with radiant pigments, similar to an impressionist painting. The meadow was mixed with every flower imaginable, except for a patch of bluebonnets carpeting an area next to a small bridge. The bridge, no longer than ten feet, was made of pretty white wood and spanned a meandering creek. Marie intuitively knew that the bridge represented a final barrier between earthly existence and spiritual life.

Marie could see Joann standing quietly in the meadow next to the bridge. She was focused on her deceased youngest son standing on the other side of the stream with his hand outstretched. It was his task, apparently, to ease Joann's crossing by providing a familiar, loving presence. Furthermore, it was his job to escort Joann toward her late husband who was also standing beyond the stream far in the background.

Despite the splendor of her new existence, Joann was reluctant to initiate her crossing. She was too worried about Ray. No matter how strongly heaven beckoned, she first wanted to resolve Ray's emotional turmoil. Resolution came when Marie conveyed Joann's message of hope to Ray at the hospital. With Ray comforted, Joann eagerly moved forward to join her family in the realm of God. When Joann finally crossed over, Marie could hear Joann's youngest son yell out, "Here comes mamma! Here comes mamma!" Marie then had a final vision of Joann fishing on a lake with her deceased husband and three deceased sons. The family living in the spiritual realm had been reunited with mamma at last.

Marie was faced with a difficult decision in how much to share with Ray. She was well aware that he struggled in faith. Marie decided to open all her experiences to Ray and his wife, despite risking their angry skepticism during a sensitive, personal time. To her reckoning, it was more important to help Ray find peace and healing. Surprisingly, Ray responded openly to Marie's mystical visions. He realized that Marie could not be making-up these wild stories from her imagination. She simply knew too much. First, it seemed unlikely that Marie would have known that his mother loved flowers. She probably would not have known that his youngest brother was the joker in the family. Lastly, she probably would not have known that the family loved to fish. Ray also reflected back on our conversations about the spiritual realm and this book. Marie's mystical experiences appeared remarkably consistent with my descriptions of the spiritual realm. Ray's belief in Marie would continue to solidify, however, as she continued to have more visions. The second set of visions revolved around Joann's funeral.

Joann appeared before Marie with two additional messages to convey to Ray just prior to the funeral. She instructed Marie to ensure that her body was dressed in pink, her favorite color, and placed in a white coffin; not the off-colored coffin that a relative had picked. She also instructed Marie to look for her near a hanky lying on the left-front pew. These things would come to pass during the funeral. Joann was sitting on an orange recliner, next to her husband in a blue recliner, just beyond the hanky. They both appeared young and attractive, presenting as they once did in their middle twenties. Joann and her husband sat throughout the ceremony to "watch the show." Ray later confirmed that the chairs were a perfect description of his mother and father's favorite recliners when they were younger. Curious, I wonder how many of my own deceased relatives and friends have watched their own funerals. I'm sure their emotions were different than that of the mourners.

Ray cherished all the messages sent by his mother. Ray understood that his mother delayed her own spiritual crossing because she loved him so much. Arriving back home, Ray shared with me that he felt a real, lasting peace associated with his mother's death. Gone were his overwhelming feelings of loneliness and other tumultuous emotions. Ray's fundamental shift in perspective can be attributed to the powerful messages sent to him by his mother through Marie. First, much of his guilt had been eased through his mother's love and absolution. Second, his fear that his mother suffered during the dying process had been alleviated. Finally, Ray had developed a greater faith in God and eternal life. He no longer had to dismiss God as a jealous, vengeful deity. God unconditionally loved him and his family. His soul felt liberated knowing that he would never be alone.

Joann now looks down on Ray with all her love from heaven. Her love makes an impression on Ray every day through interconnected ripples between realms. Marie was given a final message by Joann to impart to Ray. Joann said that she would kiss Ray every night before he went to sleep. Her kiss, she described, would feel like a feather on his cheek. She also informed Ray that he would sense her presence whenever he saw a cardinal bird or whenever the wind stirred. I remember the day when Ray shared this touching part of his story. He just finished when a strong gust whipped-up outside. I thought to myself, "Here comes mamma!"

CHAPTER THIRTEEN

TERESA

(TESTIMONY NO. 3)

S ome people think of spirits as ghosts. Yet, spiritual beings represent deceased loved ones, guides, and protectors. They love us with deep compassion and patience. Spiritual beings understand the dynamics of human conflict, discern every mistake, and intensely feel our pain. Although they would like to intervene in our life struggles, their enthusiasm is explicitly restrained by God. But when allowed, they enthusiastically assist those under their care. Most interventions are isolated experiences; recipients are lucky to experience one in a lifetime. Yet, everything good is possible with God. There are rare circumstances when spiritual beings are allowed ongoing, direct communication with a person who has special spiritual needs.

Psychics claim that they communicate with the dead. Because they receive the most media attention, some misperceive that only psychics are afforded opportunities for spiritual communication. Indeed, many psychics only call on spirits for a fee. It is not my place to judge the industry. I will only say that spiritual communications discussed in this book are highly personal and private events. Most importantly, they are directly tied to the special needs of the individual. For example, the recipient may have an unusual life mission requiring spiritual guidance. This may occur when extraordinary life challenges compromise spiritual goals. God understands that some weights are just too heavy to carry. To avoid a spiral of self-destruction, spiritual beings may be allowed to intervene to achieve a greater good. In this chapter, a case will be presented that embodies the best and worst in human nature. The account involves a woman who faced severe ongoing challenges and even horrific events. She endured and conquered many challenges through the assistance of God working through her spiritual guides.

Let us begin by sketching the woman behind the story, who I re-named Teresa. Teresa is a middle-aged, Caucasian woman, who can be noticed by her broad smile and her genuine eagerness to please. Her social energy can be described as infectious. She usually finds a spark of goodness in each person, no matter how battered. Teresa works for modest wages in the service sector. She presents humbly; her greatest desire is to help other people in need. Her professional guests adore her. They would never guess at the past she endured, nor the dark winding path she trod over the years.

Seeking neither recognition recognition nor compensation, Teresa graciously agreed to share her life story anonymously. This is no small feat. Teresa fears ridicule and rejection. Yet, she has set her fears aside, with God's help, in order to fulfill her mission to serve as a beacon of light for people who live in spiritual darkness. Given her personal ex-perience, Teresa believes that she is best suited to serve the demoral-ized, mainly because she experienced what it feels like to be trapped in a deep well of darkness; waiting for the final, fatal tumble. Teresa survived because she peered up to discover a ray of light streaming into the pit. The light was God. Stumbling and fumbling, Teresa slowly climbed over the lip. She now shares her story hoping to give courage to others fumbling to find the light.

THE DARK PIT

Teresa was born to a household torn apart by rage. Namely, she was exposed to ongoing violence between her father and mother. Shoving and hitting were common, sometimes escalating into brutal attacks in-volving knives, baseball bats, and other homemade weapons. Whereas most children enter a relatively warm and secure world, Teresa entered a life as cold and hard as winter stone. Psychologists have learned that traumatized children, especially younger victims, sustain psychological damage beyond their ability to cope or comprehend. Imagine beginning life far from the youthful norm: playful romps, birthday parties, hugs at night, and adoring parents. Teresa missed these and other childhood fundamentals. Her childhood focus was primarily one of survival. Unfortunately, Teresa could not even find sanctuary from the threat of her protectors. Her fear was not an ordinary childhood fear, but rather a primal terror existing somewhere between survival and death. Trust and love were only luxuries reserved for other children. Teresa could see the dark pit even at a young age. Looking down, she knew that a fall might be fatal. Isolated, Teresa coped by silently pushing the terror into the emotional corners of her mind. Consequently, she became like a fiery volcano capped by a thinning plug.

Anger festers for a lifetime if left unresolved. Teresa suppressed her anger, and other negative emotions, to avoid provoking others to violence. Rather, she turned her anger inward. This psychological impact was profound and sustained. Teresa engaged in various mental and physical acts of self-scourging, eventually leading to self-injury and a plummet in self-esteem. Moreover, Teresa's constant fear led to another unhealthy emotional byproduct: chronic anxiety. Like other traumatized children, Teresa fantasized that she could stop the hate and the violence, if only she were good enough. Yet, Teresa lacked the power to stop her parents. Consequently, Teresa became paralyzed, especially at night when the abuse would crescendo. This is when her spiritual beings began to intervene.

Despite the emotional chaos, Teresa experienced love emanating from Jesus and her spiritual guides. God was orchestrating lines of assistance to help Teresa cope with the violence. Primarily, it was her deceased grandparents who were assigned to intervene. These spiritual beings provided Teresa a coating of protective peace during her thickest fears, especially when her parents became most violent. They also distracted Teresa with playful dreams and supported her fragility with complimentary messages. They even soothed her anxiety by saying, "There is nothing sacred here between your mom and dad. You can bend, but you can't break." Teresa interpreted their messages to mean, 'Do not accept that this abusive behavior is normal. You are not responsible. Your family will not be torn apart if you remain faithful to God and do not yield.'

By her account, God gave Teresa the ability to have out-of-body experiences (OBEs) to cope with the abuse. With an OBE, Teresa's spirit would exit her body at will, rise above her bed, and travel throughout the house. The out of body experience served two important purposes.

One, the OBE helped Teresa witness the violence. Most consider a young child witnessing violence to be highly detrimental. Yet, from Teresa's point of view, witnessing the violence helped her validate her fears. Knowing was better than guessing. She didn't want to be lied to. Second, the OBE allowed Teresa to check on her parents to see if things were truly peaceful and quiet in the house. Only when she discovered that her parents were not fighting could she fall asleep.

Teresa's parents were not evil people. Their violent behavior can only be attributed to inadequate relationship skills, not intentional cruelty. Perhaps it would be more accurate to say they were spiritually adrift. Rather than embracing all the aspects of unconditional love, Teresa's parents were motivated by ego and pride. They constantly competed to be right and exert control. If the last word was not enough to win a battle of wills, then they would use more extreme, violent measures. Their hatred and violence eroded whatever love remained in the household. After all, love and hatred cannot be expressed at the same time. In its wake, interpersonal interactions between the parents usually involved the battle over the "me." Teresa, and the other children, became collateral damage to the self-absorbed behaviors of their parents. Over time, their actions deprived everyone in the household of compassion and personal validation. Consequently, Teresa did not receive the necessary foundation to mature into a confident young adult.

Despite living through extremely difficult circumstances, Teresa's future was not lost. She had several "angels" in her corner. First, she had a living angel in a grandmother who provided her love and guidance. Second, she had spiritual angel in a deceased grandfather who was later joined by a deceased grandmother. All these loving beings, in either realm, were helping her in both subtle and direct ways. Teresa was never alone, even during her most dark and terrifying moments. In fact, her angels would later save her life.

THE MISSION

The violence escalated throughout the years, even to the point where Teresa felt that someone in the family was going to be killed. The edge of the abyss was creeping ever closer. Teresa turned to her primary loving support. At the age of twelve, she desperately prayed during a church service. In her prayer she offered God a bargain: "God, if you keep my family alive, I will serve you for the rest of my life." Teresa immediately felt a supernatural force push her down on to the pew as a boy stood up. Teresa heard God's voice proclaim, "He will serve Me. You will serve your family." In that captivating moment, Teresa understood that her mission was to serve her family. As a young adolescent, her task would be monumental. Most children would seek any opportunity to escape from an abusive family. Yet, Teresa embraced God's message and took it to heart. From that point forward, Teresa served her family in many unexpected ways.

Spiritual connections are a two-way street. Spiritual beings served Teresa in unexpected ways as she served her family in unexpected ways. After hearing God's voice in church, Teresa began to perceive her spiritual beings in a more direct, communicative manner. Specifically, she could hear her grandfather and grandmother's voice in her mind, both while awake and in dream. She could also sense the presence of Jesus, at times, especially during the most terrifying moments. These beings were continuously with Teresa, serving as an anchor in the storms of life. Then, in a twist of events, Teresa's parents divorced.

Children often cope poorly with divorce. Divorce can spin a family into emotional crisis. In Teresa's case, her parent's divorce lifted the crisis as the lesser of two bad situations. Foremost, the violence stopped, so day-to-day survival no longer became a pressing concern. Although her immediate fear lifted, Teresa's home-life hardly promoted healthy childhood development. The father moved to a new residence while the mother became a non-functional parent. Namely, she was neither able to maintain steady employment or effectively parent the children. The job of parenting was thereby delegated to Teresa, the oldest daughter, by default. Not only did Teresa help parent her siblings, but she also nurtured her mother and father in a "parent-like" role. Within this reversed family dynamic, Teresa cared for her parents' individual and emotional needs. For instance, she served as a mediator by defusing a steady volley of grudges and insults.

Family systems theory explains various family dynamics. Individual behavior is interpreted within the context of a larger unit, or system. In a family system, each member plays out his or her prescribed roles in accordance with unspoken rules. In Teresa's case, she served the role of parent to both her siblings and parents. Any ethical family systems therapist would be alarmed. Adolescents are not developmentally prepared to assume such a difficult adult role, much less within an unhealthy, volatile system. Failure, if not catastrophe, seemed assured. More importantly, the stress could break Teresa's defuse identity and fragile self-esteem. A systems therapist would also be concerned about Teresa's long-term future. Specifically, Teresa would be deprived of the life experiences that adolescents need for healthy development into adulthood: guidance in discernment, peer relational development, dating, and defining a personal identity. Although Teresa was safe from violence, her psychological and emotional development was now in jeopardy.

All good things are possible with God. Looking back at this transitional period, Teresa currently views her parental role differently than a family systems therapist would. Somewhat surprisingly, she believed that she was ready to assume the parental role as part of her mission from God. If she didn't serve her family, who would? In other words, she perceived herself to be the glue that held the domestic pieces together. Although her role was far from ideal, it was preferable to the family imploding. Teresa explains that her emotional support at that time was healing for everyone. For example, her parents benefited from having an outlet to vent their frustrations and grudges. Additionally, the role of mediator helped Teresa understand the reasons behind her parent's violence. With this new understanding, she no longer felt as much need to blame herself. Perhaps more importantly, Teresa was not acting alone. Spiritual beings guided her in her new responsibilities by giving her patience and proper direction. This was certainly true regarding her father and mother.

Teresa continued to live with her father and siblings after her parents' divorce. She cooked family meals, cleaned house, offered supportive advice, and assumed most of the non-sexual roles of a wife. Appropriate father-daughter boundaries were soon to be further crossed. One day, Teresa's spiritual beings told her that her father would come downstairs on three occasions to watch her dress. She was also informed not to be alarmed because his wrong would create positive change. Indeed, Teresa states that her father violated her privacy three times, although he did not pursue any sexual contact. Teresa confronted him on the third occasion. Surprising to her, not only did the father admit to the inappropriate behavior, but he also began to take responsibility for many poor choices in his life. The first steps for any radical change first involves insight followed by taking responsibility. Teresa's father took both of these reforming steps. He gradually became a more mindful, accountable, and compassionate individual. He also took the responsibility of being a father more seriously. With this odd twist of events, Teresa's relationship with her father actually improved following the violation. Teresa viewed this series of events as a blessing because it moved her forward in one aspect of her mission, namely to forgive her family in order to teach them love.

Teresa constructed a unique strategy to meet the mission objectives to serve her family. She recognized that her family desperately needed to learn the type of love she received from Jesus and her spiritual guides. The best strategy to soften their hearts, she reasoned, was to teach them forgiveness. Accordingly, Teresa set out to teach forgiveness in both conventional and unconventional ways. Using a common strategy, Teresa taught people forgiveness by forgiving them of their transgressions, no matter the wrongs. Applying a more unusual strategy, she also would create opportunities for people to forgive her through engaging in reckless behavior. The reader may view this as a bizarre strategy, as any outcome would appear self-defeating. Yet, the two strategies were oddly connected. Teresa believed that she could only forgive others because she needed forgiveness. Basically, she was serving as a martyr for the entire family and others; forgiving and suffering so that others didn't have to. Teresa would be the first to agree that her strategy, in retrospect, was personally unhealthy. Yet, she would also argue that she ended up serving both family and God in a roundabout way. Indeed, martyrs can inspire others to act under the right circumstances. Surprisingly, later events would bear this out. Perhaps the best example of Teresa's reckless service was her heavy consumption of alcohol.

THE DESCENT

Teresa was drinking on a regular basis by the age of fifteen. Even at that early age, she knew that her drinking would degenerate into severe alcoholism. Yet, she also knew that she would serve as an alcoholic for a larger good. Although she did not know the details, Teresa believed that her alcoholism would unite her family in a way that they could cooperate and forgive each other. Teresa also had a premonition of "hitting rock bottom" before she could help herself and others. Her premonition became especially clear after a family member committed suicide. One of her spiritual beings informed her that she did not have to die because her family member had died in her place. Teresa understood the message to signify that she would become suicidal at different times during her life. The underlying purpose was clear to her. By remembering her family member's suicide, Teresa could draw on the strength to live with despair. More pointedly, she understood her spiritual guides to be saying, "Don't go there. We will help you." Indeed, that is exactly what happened as Teresa entered adulthood.

Early adulthood was an unremitting "hell" for Teresa. Alcoholism never solves tough problems; it only exacerbates pain and a cycle of self-destructive behavior. Teresa's judgment became so impaired that she was unable to make sound choices. She began to develop destructive relationships and risky career decisions. Her general lifestyle placed her at risk of general exploitation and violence. Her life became a self-perpetuating vortex of pain, avoidance, and self-defeating behavior. Specifically, painful memories and guilt were self-medicated through alcohol. Alcohol only paved the way for more self-defeating behaviors. When she tried to be sober, Teresa was left with acute feelings of guilt, anger, and despair. Painful memories would soon return, and so the entire cycle would repeat. As Teresa spiraled down into her well of despair, she began to exhibit thoughts of suicide. These thoughts persisted throughout her twenties. Teresa started to tumble into the pit.

Teresa became trapped midway down the pit. Her world was dark save a thin ray of light streaming from above. Because people are afforded self-determination, Teresa's spiritual beings could only go so far in providing assistance. They helped however they could, mostly by guiding her toward positive people to ensure her safety. They would simply communicate, "Go with this person" or "Do not go with that person." Teresa's spiritual beings also eased her pain through personal affirmations communicating, "Keep going. You have worth." When Teresa wanted to give up, her grandmother repeated, "Little girl, please keep on dancing." Although her spiritual guides could not stop the cycle of personal deterioration, their efforts probably saved her life. Teresa was now clinging to cliffs deep in the well. But she was determined not to give up. Even during the depths of her despair, a part of Teresa knew that she was loved by her spiritual guides, Jesus, and God. Furthermore, she believed that she was serving a divine purpose through her pain.

Teresa kept slipping into the well of darkness. Slippage accelerated after she began abusing drugs, mixed with alcohol, during two brief, turbulent marriages. After the second divorce, Teresa could not maintain employment. She obtained two DUIs and served time in county jail. At worst, she legally lost her daughter and residence. Teresa quickly found herself wandering the most dangerous and impoverished big city streets, alone. In all, Teresa had slipped and collided with the rocky bottom. She was homeless.

Teresa landed in a place seemingly without hope. Teresa wandered the inner city streets as a young, attractive, impressionable woman. Alone and penniless, she wandered around shadowy corners that teamed with a sordid assortment of predators. Not only did she worry about food and the elements, but also various forms of exploitation, including rape and sexual trafficking. Even in the worst tragedies there is always the hope of deliverance, for all good things are possible with God. After all, Teresa was never really alone. Her diligent and faithful spiritual guides were right by her side. For instance, Teresa's spiritual guides told her to shave her head and wear baggy pants to ward off sexual predators. They also guided her to various street angels, usually homeless people who taught her the "where, how, and what" of street survival. Through their loving guidance, Teresa learned where to find food, shelter, and sanctuary. Blessed with spiritual and human guides, Teresa survived.

CRACK IN THE SADNESS

Despite having lost everything, Teresa experienced a break in the sadness where light filtered through. Teresa looked up at the shining over the lip of the well. She considered tackling the precarious climb, but was discouraged by the daunting distance. Still, there were encouraging developments as Teresa reverted back to survival mode. Perhaps most importantly, God gave Teresa the strength to curb her alcoholism and drug abuse to avoid being exploited by street predators. Teresa learned that she did not have the power to stop drinking on her own. She needed God. Survival also taught her confidence. For the first time in her life, she had the fortitude to establish some boundaries and fight for her life. After months of slow and gradual healing, a miracle occurred. Teresa's parents came together to bring Teresa out of a state of homelessness.

Teresa's estranged parents contacted each other after a decade of mutual avoidance. Out of desperation, they cooperated to bring Teresa home and arrange for her to attend an inpatient alcohol treatment center. Their love for Teresa somehow transcended their own hatred for each other. By working toward a common goal, Teresa's parents gradually recognized a degree of good in each other. A mutual respect gradually developed that had been previously absent. The development of respect, and later friendship, did not materialize out of a vacuum. The groundwork was laid by God working in their individual lives for the last decade. As Teresa explained, her parents were previously incapable of love due to their "me-centered" competitive state of relating with each other. At some point, God primed them to develop a more "other-centered" state of cooperating with one another. Teresa elaborated, "They each thought they knew best. They were stubborn in keeping control until they had no more fight. They finally surrendered." At long last, the engine of change was primed. However, the engine needed an ignition. That ignition was Teresa.

Teresa's premonition was right all along. Her reckless, self-destructive behavior saved her family. Despite years of hate and horrific abuse, Teresa's parents reconciled. The other children soon followed suit, eventually leading to a cohesive family unit. The reader may choose to disassociate God with Teresa's alcoholism. That is to say, the reader may believe that family reconciliation was just coincidental. Does God use suffering for a greater good? This is a difficult question to answer. It is my personal belief that God does not cause suffering. God did not cause Teresa to start drinking in order to save her parents. I do believe, however, that God uses what is available to create a greater good. God knew that Teresa was going to choose a self-destructive path through alcoholism. Although there was no rejoicing in her suffering, God used Teresa to create life opportunities for learning, personal growth, and reconciliation. Teresa never blamed God for the consequences of her poor choices. On the contrary, she credits God for saving her family through her suffering. Her mission had been partly accomplished. In doing so, Teresa started climbing out of the well of darkness towards the distant opening. For the first time in years, life seemed to develop in a positive way. First, she was no longer homeless. Secondly, her family was in the process of reconciling. Lastly, her family backed her decision to attend a 30-day treatment center. Teresa was given a promising second start. Unfortunately, humans tend to sabotage themselves when they are not spiritually ready for change. This was the case with Teresa as she slipped back down into the abyss just as she began to climb.

A FEARSOME FALL

Teresa attended alcohol treatment in a far-away state. Teresa did not achieve a full-length sobriety. Many alcoholics will quickly relapse if the underlying symptoms behind the addiction are not addressed. For Teresa, her treatment program did not address childhood trauma. Although the binge drinker may abuse alcohol for rebellion or excitement, the chronic alcoholic becomes powerless over alcohol for deeper psychological reasons. In Teresa's case, she was paving over her pain with inebriation. She needed to blot out her horrendous past: the stabbing hurt, the rage, the shame. Another reason treatment failed is due to the overwhelming power of addiction. From Teresa's experience, addiction to alcohol can only be conquered through the power of God. For both these reasons, Teresa believes that she could not have stopped drinking even with the best manmade treatment.

Incompleteness in the treatment was not the only obstacle Teresa faced during this time. Teresa also had to cope alone with her psychological pain given that her family lived thousands of miles away. Moreover, Teresa had to face the skeletons of her past; they were tumbling out of her closeted subconscious during brief periods of abstinence. For all these reasons, Teresa dived into a deep depression. Her depression spiraled out of control with the remembrance of deep hurts sustained by family, friends, and strangers. Having been abused and rarely loved, Teresa began to distrust everyone, thereby becoming increasingly isolated. Suspicions developed into irrational paranoia, even to the point of shunning her supportive spiritual guides. Feeling isolated and suicidal, Teresa had fallen again to the bottom of the well. This state made her very vulnerable to outside spiritual attack.

According to Teresa, the darkness pervading her mind attracted demonic beings that hovered at the edge of her psyche. Sensitive to spiritual beings yet rejecting her own guides, Teresa could feel their evil presence waiting and growing in the shadows. Teresa challenged these dark beings, stating, "I will meet you anytime, anyplace! I'm not afraid of you because I have God." One demonic being met her challenge and attacked. Teresa fell to the ground and felt her eyes roll in her sockets. A feeling of evil possessed her mind as it felt like it was going to explode. Teresa described the demonic being to be made of just pure meanness. She then said, "Jesus pushed it off, just like that" while making a quick sweeping motion with her hand. The demonic beings would never attack her again. Teresa later heard Jesus proclaim in her mind, "They do not want you. They want me." Teresa believed Jesus' message to mean that the demonic beings wanted to curb God's divine power by consuming her soul. Most psychiatrists/psychologists would likely diagnose Teresa with a mental illness, probably a brief psychotic reaction due to stress. Scientists, and many others, believe that demonic possession is nothing more than an archaic superstition. Yet, Teresa's account cannot be explained by any rational, scientific explanation, because the apex of her experience only lasted seconds. A brief psychotic reaction typically lasts much longer and tends to repeat for weeks or months if not medicated. Moreover, Teresa recalls that demonic possession was the central turning point in her life.

MISSION REVITALIZED

Teresa redirected her attention to God after her frightening incident. With God in the forefront, Teresa welcomed her diligent spiritual protectors back with open arms. Never having left her side, they answered her call with active enthusiasm. Teresa understood that she had rejected her spiritual beings, not the other way around. She also understood why they could not have helped her out of the pit. She described her former self in this way, "As much as I wanted help, I could not ask for it. There was not enough of me to work with." Now Teresa was finally ready, emotionally and spiritually, to make lasting changes. With her newfound receptiveness, Teresa's spiritual beings set out to gradually guide her out of the pit, one upward grinding pull at a time. First, they helped Teresa process her anger. She described the process as, "Getting real down and dirty where I could get my resentments out." Second, her spiritual guides conveyed numerous positive affirmations, as they had before, by telling Teresa that she had inherent value to God and others. Finally, they guided Teresa on a life course of loving others. Namely, they taught Teresa to harness the love she received and give it back to people in need. It was natural for Teresa to respond to their call. She generalized her love for family to serve a bigger family. With everything in its rightful place, real transformation was beginning to take a lasting hold.

Love is the most transforming power in the universe. Through the giving and receiving of love, Teresa became a changed person. Empowered by spiritual support and a newfound confidence, Teresa found what it truly meant to be an alcoholic freed from intoxication. Healthy friendships developed as a product of her genuine love, thereby decreasing her sense of isolation. Feeling accepted by family and others, Teresa dared to believe in a bright future and even allowed herself some happiness. Consequently, Teresa's debilitating depression lifted.

She eventually reunited with her family in a healthier way. She even reestablished a relationship with her daughter.

Teresa was able to recover from the debilitating disease of alcoholism only through the grace of God. Her arduous journey would have otherwise failed. People naturally respond to adversity with avoidance or escape. Indeed, tough life struggles can bring a person to their knees, but if a person searches for guidance and growth, there can be healing through the worst adversity. By turning to God, shadows can turn into light. Although her transformation was remarkable, Teresa would agree that her life struggles have not disappeared. Like every fallible human being, Teresa continues to face difficult challenges inherent to life. She continues to struggle with self-doubt and periods of sadness. Yet, her life is now qualitatively better. Moreover, she now has the resiliency to tackle new obstacles. Consequently, her spiritual guides have tapered off their supportive communications. Their original divine task was to keep Teresa alive so that she could complete her mission. With success, they have retreated so that Teresa can be more independent. Teresa is very excited about the next stage in her life. Namely, she guides and supports people struggling with alcoholism, homelessness, and spiritual alienation. Teresa seems well suited for the job due to personal experience and connection with the divine. In order to immerse herself in new mission, however, Teresa will need to put closure to the past. Teresa is still tethered to the well; so many years of alcoholism, pain, and trauma cannot immediately be undone. But this is part of her life journey. Provided she follows her current course, Teresa will walk steadily toward the good and continue to find healing.

I asked Teresa to share some of her learned life lessons. Motivated to help others, Teresa shared several personal insights. Foremost, Teresa learned that every person shares a general mission to love, forgive, and heal. Learning our general mission can sometimes be very painful, however, especially if one does not take direction from God. Teresa asserts that both good and bad experiences have taught her God's truth, which all served the good in the end. In learning about herself, Teresa discovered that she no longer fears judgment. Judgment, from her current perspective, only keeps people from healing. Rather, Teresa believes in the power of forgiveness, both for others and for herself. She states, "I take full responsibility for all I have done. I am not proud of the choices in my life, but they have helped me heal. Despite all I have done, I do not have a punishing God." Nor does she focus on punishing herself. Teresa no longer needs to act the role of a martyr.

Although martyrdom once served a larger purpose, Teresa knows that sacrificing herself lacks value in her new life. She shared this insight, "I learned that I can't save evil with love. Evil and various cruel works block me from God. My goal is to love as many people as possible who will benefit from my love." Indeed, she is on the path of meeting this goal. Teresa is ready to move forward in her life mission, armed with the spiritual lessons of the past.

THE TESTIMONY

Teresa's remarkable story was included in this book for a number of reasons. The most obvious, Teresa's spiritual beings saved her and her family. God desires everyone to ultimately succeed in achieving their individual missions on school earth. To maximize success, God assigns spiritual tutors to each person. Perhaps they help us best when we are open to their guidance. Although few encounter them as clearly and frequently as Teresa, spiritual beings relentlessly dedicate themselves to prod us toward the good, even if our chosen path becomes long and winding. They never give up on their assignments, nor are there limits to their creativity. They quietly influence us through dreams, images, insights, feelings, self-talk, and interactions with other people. They generally are more active during times of stress and grief, particularly when one's mission becomes compromised. Although helpful, they will not solve every nagging life problem. Just as a student is responsible for studying for a test, every person is responsible for making difficult life choices. Not unlike the overwhelmed student, however, tutors are available to help with the most challenging curriculum, especially if one asks for the fruits of the spirit: wisdom, patience, kindness, faithfulness, peace, and self-control.

How does one ask for fruits of the spirit? One asks God, the Will and the Source. Spiritual beings do not act without divine approval. The reader may think, 'I am not like Teresa. I have never seen a spiritual being and I likely never will.' That was my thinking, until recently. Then I began to communicate in faith, look within, and look without. Sure enough, they were there beside me, within my circle of faith. They are also beside you.

Teresa's story was remarkable as a testament of hope. When life becomes seemingly unbearable, the easiest human response is to lose hope and give up. By giving up, a person chooses to cut off God's efforts to work through the pain. Spiritual beings have difficulty penetrating through a cloud of doubt and despair. The struggling individual needs to allow them to work in patience. Words of hope may ring hollow coming from anyone who may have not experienced great pain. This is why Teresa's chapter has great importance. She has "gone through it." Suffering chronic abuse and raging alcoholism, Teresa lost everyone and everything because she had no self-control over her alcoholism. Yet, Teresa found hope in God. God helped her, partly, through the direct assistance of her spiritual beings. By maintaining hope and purpose, she eventually made the necessary life transformations to transcend despair. Through transformation, she could properly attend to life mission objectives and made possible what seemed impossible. Some readers are struggling much in life, as Teresa did. Take comfort in the following news. God placed you on earth for an important purpose. God would not have put you on earth if you were doomed to failure. One answer is to seek help through prayer and guidance. God may answer by providing assistance from family, friends, clergy, mental health professionals, addiction counselors, etc. Teresa received answers to prayer from her spiritual guides. She also received help from family, drug addiction meetings, and digging deep within. Only by becoming humble and by giving her addiction to God was she able to heal. In this manner, her faith, resilience, and hope became a testimony to others.

CHAPTER FOURTEEN

LOST SOULS

Hell. The word is potent. According to the Association of Religion Data Archives, approximately 73% of the American public believes in the existence of hell.[1] For them, hell conjures up fear associated with eternal pain, suffering, and punishment. Even many people who dismiss hell as superstitious probably feel some emotional stir, perhaps a primal twinge of fear or intrigue. Perhaps these elicited emotions explain why people celebrate Halloween or watch horror movies; to taunt their primal fear of hell and its host of demonic beings. Because hell resides deep in our human psyche, possibly in the collective unconscious, the belief in hell goes back to the recesses of human civilization. The roots of hell echo four thousand years ago with the Sumerian and Egyptian underground realms of the dead.[2] The Christian understanding of hell can be traced back to the Persian religion of Zoroastrianism.[2] In both religions, hell is a dark realm ruled by an evil god and populated by demonic tormenters. Over the millennia, all the major religions in the world integrated hell into their theology (Hinduism, Buddhism, Judaism, Christianity, Islam). In several instances, the concept of hell developed independently in isolated communities. Thus, the concept of hell is practically universal.

The worldwide belief in hell suggests a universal psychological process underlying its construct. Namely, there appears to be a deep-seeded human need to punish the wicked, if not in this life, then the next. Hell serves as a vehicle leading toward non-escapable justice for the wicked. Although the wicked may escape human accountability through power and loopholes in law, they will be punished someday by a higher, righteous power. What goes around comes around, sooner or later.

For many, heaven and hell are two opposites; there is no gray in between a singular right and wrong. The righteous will have everlasting peace whereas the wicked will be severely punished by means of physical and mental torture. Not only will the wicked be tortured, but God will avenge the righteous by torturing them eternally. For the immoral, there is no possibility for redemption, forgiveness, or growth. Religious authority seeking control has added the infidel to be condemned for their unforgivable unbelief. Could it be that humanity displaces human justice on God? Alice Turner, in the book *The History of Hell*, cites a related concept called *abominable fancy*, which means "that part of the joy of the saved lay in contemplating the tortures of the damned."[2] The human psychological need for hell may bring in question its very existence. What does the near-death experience say about hell? What is the fate of the wicked and the non-believer?

Thousands of NDE submissions highlight the differences between divine justice and human justice. With divine justice, people are loved unconditionally by God. The overwhelming majority of NDErs did not experience external judgment during their life review or any time in heaven. Some NDErs, in fact, interpreted divine love to be inconsistent with the existence of hell. They assert that hell does not exist. Other NDErs, however, recount glimpses of hell during their brief stay in heaven. More fearsome, a very small number of NDErs reported firsthand hellish experiences. It is the purpose of this chapter to explore God's arrangement with evil, NDE inconsistencies, the nature of good and evil, the soul's manifestation of hell, and the spiritual development toward the good.

The Patient Sculptor

The path to hell is not wide, as some might suggest. In reading NDERF accounts, I have come across about ten hellish experiences out of roughly 3300 positive submissions (0.33%). The actual rate may be much higher, however, simply because people may be more likely to report positive experiences than hellish experiences because those who return from them may feel ashamed. Furthermore, it is possible that souls who experience hell are rarely allowed to return to physical life to fulfill mission. A number of NDErs observe lost souls traveling toward hell from their vantage point in heaven. What do they see? Most see lost souls that have become encapsulated by their own dark nature and are unable to see God. The following NDEr reported their progression toward the darkness:

> I could see many other spirits, beings who were also leaving their bodies and moving away from the earth. However, many of them in their spiritual bodies seemed to not be able to see the light and love above. They had almost like clouds above their heads, like clouds blocking out the sun. It's still there but they can't see it. The more negative ones also seemed to be looking down, not even up. I could experience their feelings of anger, etc., and wanted them to look up and see the love and come to the Light. But I couldn't get my message to them. (NDERF #2366)

Why is the path to hell narrow? The narrow path supports the unconditional love of God. God does not want anyone to be lost and disconnected. Salvation does not depend on the amount of growth a person makes within a lifetime. Rather, salvation depends on a person's journey toward the Source. It is an issue of trajectory. The vast majority of NDErs agree that God does not judge anyone, much less send them to eternal torment. Then how does hell exist? Lost souls reject God rather than the other way around. Lost souls, in other words, choose to exist in a hell of their own making. Hell is a series of past choices consistent with the maxim of self-determination, as discussed throughout this book. Although the body dies, the soul remains. The soul takes its earthly essence into the spiritual realm, good or bad, in accordance with the path forged on earth. The author of the last submission continues:

> The love and light [of God] didn't want them to experience that, and was doing all it could to let them come to it. But they could not, or would not, accept it or see it. It was obvious they were creating this experience, not a separate devil or god punishing them. (NDERF #2366)

God does not turn away from any being at any time. In fact, great spiritual efforts are made to rescue anyone who pleads for salvation, even in hell. It is never too late to be saved. Rob Bell explains why God does not send people to an eternal hell. God's love is unconditional. It is against God's perfect, loving nature to torture people for eternity. In his book, *Love Wins*, Bell wrote:

> The belief that untold masses of people are suffering forever doesn't bring God glory. Restoration brings God glory; eternal torment doesn't. Reconciliation brings God glory; endless anguish doesn't. Renewal and return cause God's greatness to shine through the universe; never-ending punishment doesn't.[3]

Howard Storm serves as an example of God's reconciliation and restoration. Having lived a life defined by anger, hatred, and self-centeredness, Storm entered hell. He was soon taunted and then assaulted by a platoon of lost souls. He prayed for deliverance and was immediately saved by Jesus. Moved toward heaven, he was quickly accompanied by a host of other spiritual beings. Who are these spiritual beings? One NDEr wrote the following:

> But above them were also a legion of beings, waiting. Whenever someone looked up and asked God for help they were whisked away to another place; a place more peaceful and tuned to God and God's love. But many seemed lost in this place, never looking up and never asking for help. (NDERF #2932)

God can only save those who desire deliverance; those who choose to be associated with the light. This truth was revealed to George Ritchie while touring hell under the protection of Jesus. Dr. Ritchie was impressed by the degree of empathy that Jesus exhibited for hell's inhabitants. He wrote, "No condemnation came from the Presence at my side, only a compassion for these unhappy creatures that were breaking His heart. Clearly it was not His will that any one of them should be in this place."[4]

It is a tragedy that lost souls *refuse* to turn to God despite their ongoing suffering. This appears to be the case on earth as well. I have been perplexed how very criminally-minded inmates refuse all opportunities for self-improvement in prison. Most understand, at least intellectually, the value of an education. They understand the purpose of the rules governing behavior. They understand that they hurt other people by their actions. They refuse to adhere to sensible action because they simply don't care. Rather, they prefer to languish in confinement while becoming involved in every negative, self-defeating activity. Similarly, lost souls choose to languish in the spiritual darkness by their own free will. Howard Storm, based on his first-hand experience, explains why this may be the case:

> Why would anyone choose hell? Why do people reject God? Why do people hate one another? The answer is, because we can. God gave us the godlike ability to create and destroy. God has given us godlike capacity to become saints or demons. God has equipped us to become whatever we choose. My heavenly teachers stated that we cannot say we don't know the difference. Every person has sufficient spiritual insight to know the difference...Heaven is a gift from God we don't deserve, except for God's love for us. Hell is what we desire when we reject God.[5]

The fallible human being can be thankful that the road to hell is narrow. Everyone can choose God at any time, despite making a myriad of life mistakes. Perhaps God can be likened to a patient sculptor and people are the marble to be sculpted. Through living on school earth, and other teaching venues, imperfections are chiseled away and thrown out over time. As the final form begins to take shape, finer tools may be used to chisel individual lines and curves as the final form becomes perfected. In the Christian belief system, people are saved by grace; dirty rags become white as snow through the sacrifice of Jesus. In this manner, God can look at sinners with perfect acceptance and love. The near-death experience also speaks of a similar purification process. Recall Moorjani's example of her father being transformed after death. The father's sexist attitude in life was transformed into an attitude of tolerance in the spiritual world. Thus, his growth developed in both the material and spiritual realms. But what if there is not enough material to be sculpted and the process never begins? This is the situation of the lost soul. To understand the lost soul better, it becomes important to define good and evil.

The Nature of Good and Evil

People can be defined in shades of gray; everyone has a mixture of strengths and weaknesses. Following this logic, different cultural beliefs may be viewed as variations within the human continuum of existence. In an age of relativism, it may be tempting to assert that evil does not exist. There are a few NDErs who have come to that conclusion after their near-death experience because they have been accepted rather than judged. Furthermore, the NDEr experiences a beautiful unity with all of God's spiritual beings, including the spiritually immature, through divine interconnection. Anita Moorjani was once asked if everyone went to heaven. The dialogue went as follows:

> Q: Are you saying that a criminal - say, a murderer - would go to the same place and feel the same non-judgment as a saint?

> A: Yes, that's what I'm saying. In that state, we understand that everything we've done-no matter how seemingly negative - has actually come from fear, pain, and limited experiences. A lot of what we do and feel is because we know no other way. Once we're in the other realm, however, our physical limitations become clear to us, so we're able to understand why we did things and why we feel only compassion.

> It felt as though those whom we label "perpetrators" are also victims of their own limitations, pain, and fear. When we realize this, we feel only connected with everyone and everything. I understood that in the other realm, we're all One. We are all the same.[6]

There are very few discrepancies between NDE reports. The existence of evil and hell are two such discrepancies. It is my position that evil and hell do exist. It is not my aim to discredit Anita Moorjani or others with a similar egalitarian point of view. Perhaps there is a broader understanding that can explain both positions. Discrepancies derive not from errors in the near-death experience itself, but from the complexity of truth. When an NDEr returns to their physical body, their understanding of the experience is limited by the finite human brain, as previously discussed. Thus, people only remember facets of the truth. Moorjani makes a cogent observation that people act badly out of ignorance, not maliciousness. Once enlightened, they are transformed into beings of compassion in the spiritual realm. I believe that this is the case for everyone entering the divine spiritual realm, which includes the vast majority of people who complete school earth. People do not have to worry about being "good enough" to go to heaven. If one cares enough to seriously reflect and worry about their own salvation, then that person will probably not go to hell. Yet, Moorjani's experience is only one facet of the truth. Her revelation does not explain a sizable number of hellish experiences or revelations about hell. Working in prison, I have learned that some people welcome evil, not out of ignorance, but with full relish and understanding. They embrace evil as a choice of being. Let's take a look at what this means.

Can a murderer receive the same level of non-judgment and compassion as a saint? I would say, absolutely. A murderer will not be judged by God for his crime, per se. However, the murderer may certainly have much more to learn about love. The murder's long term future may require a significant amount of remediation in both the physical and spiritual realms. Might a murderer, or a person from any walk of life, *not* receive the same level of non-judgment and compassion as a saint? This is a rare but distinct possibility.

Love is the cornerstone of God and everyone connected to God. Selfishness is the cornerstone of evil. A lost soul completely rejects the path toward love, and thereby God. Take, for example, the most criminally-minded individual, the psychopath. These are the worst type of criminals usually found in high security prisons. These are the people who sadistically exploit and hurt everyone under their power. Whenever I have asked an incarcerated psychopath to define love, they can never answer the question. Some will simply say, "I don't know." Others will say love is feeling that only weak people claim to experience. Yet, they will dismiss the experience as a lie or a stupid delusion. Unknown to the psychopath, it is him or her who has become deluded. There are many attributes of love, as discussed in chapter seven. Some of the attributes explored include compassion, respect, tolerance, altruism, forgiveness, and sacrifice. The psychopath becomes self-deceived because they are *incapable* of experiencing love. If an individual categorically rejects love, how can they participate in a divine realm created by the very fabric of love? They cannot. It is a matter of inconsistency. One cannot mix water and oil. Likewise, good and evil are separated in the spiritual realm. If there is no material available to be sculpted, then there is no opportunity for remediation or growth. Specifically, the very presence of a psychopath would corrupt God's realm.

To understand why a psychopath would corrupt God's realm, one only needs to contrast good and evil. Good and evil are sometimes seen as mystical spiritual states. In the field of psychology, however, general concepts are much more useful if they are defined in terms of specific behavior. At the most simplistic level, good is everything that evil is not. The following is a brief "top twenty" list of opposite behavioral differences between good and evil as presented by the psychopath:

1. Caring about people *versus* exploiting people at all costs.
2. Respecting people out of admiration *versus* respecting power out of fear.
3. Freely giving away time and possessions *versus* exploiting and stealing at every opportunity.
4. Sacrificing one's self interest for the benefit of others *versus* sacrificing others best interests for selfish desires.
5. Having compassion toward the helpless *versus* despising the weak.
6. Rejoicing in other people's blessings *versus* undermining other's success in fits of jealousy.
7. Caring about people's suffering *versus* sadistically reveling in people's pain.
8. Forgiving people's transgressions *versus* retaliating against the most minor of insults.
9. Seeking peace through prayer and silent reflection *versus* seeking excitement through danger and reckless behavior.
10. Humbly serving others *versus* dominating people to make them serve one's self.
11. Being curious by seeking out knowledge *versus* dropping out of school due to mental laziness.
12. Being responsible to authority (i.e. work and government) *versus* working against all institutions of authority.
13. Nurturing the growth of a family *versus* neglecting all parental responsibilities.
14. Seeking and speaking truth *versus* intentionally being deceitful for personal gain.
15. Learning from past mistakes *versus* behavioral, emotional, and spiritual stagnation.
16. Relying on a greater power *versus* relying on the sole power of ego.
17. Focusing on spiritual growth *versus* focusing on sensual pleasures of the body.
18. Planning for personal growth *versus* living in the moment.
19. Constructing a better world *versus* acting on destructive impulses.
20. Adhering to spiritual rules to create order *versus* intentionally breaking rules to create chaos.

This list reflects my experience while working with psychopaths. It is by no means an exhaustive list. I knew a patient who said he was a self-proclaimed Satanist. He explained that the cornerstone of the Satanic Bible, written by Anton LaVey, was not based on any particular demonic acts, such as animal sacrifice and the like. Rather, the Satanic Bible was built on the concept of hedonism. Hedonism basically means, "Think of your own needs first and do whatever feels good." Although I have not read, and will not read, the Satanic Bible, I will take this man's word for its content. I have, however, read the Bhagavad Gita, a Hindu text, which spoke similarly about the wicked in hell. The Bhagavad Gita is a short book involving the spiritual conversation between God, called Krishna, and a spiritual warrior named Arjuna. Consistent with the Satanic Bible, the Bhagavad Gita defines evil in terms of hedonism. Krishna reportedly teaches Arjuna:

> Firm is the belief, these men of dead souls, of truly little intelligence, undertake their work of evil: they are the enemies of this fair world, working for its destruction. They torture their soul with insatiable desires and full of deceit, insolence, and pride, they hold fast their dark ideas, and they carry on their impure work. Thus they are beset with innumerable cares which last long, all their life, until death. Their highest aim is sensual enjoyment, and they firmly think that this is all...Led astray by many wrong thoughts, entangled in the net of delusion, enchained to the pleasures of their cravings, they fall down into a foul hell.[7]

I appreciate the active verb *fall* in the context of hell. This text is consistent with the NDE notion that evil people are not thrown into hell by God. Rather, they *fall* into hell when they trip over their own thoughts and entanglements.

Evil works for the destruction of good. For this reason alone, good and evil are incompatible. Let's take a look at evil within the divine realm from a perspective of logic. If evil is truly irrelevant, as some may suggest, then what would stop anyone from accepting evil as an acceptable spiritual path? In a universe where evil could not be contrasted with good, every form of existence would have equal merit in heaven. Thus, moral relativism would be the norm in the afterlife and good and evil would mix in the spiritual world as they do on earth. Yet, this is clearly not the case. Not a single NDEr, that I have read, reported evil co-existing with good in God's realm. In fact, many say there are rules separating the two realms, perhaps the only true boundary in the universe. One writes on the boundary separating darkness and light:

Below me, in the expanse of darkness, I could hear human beings in distress. I could tell they were suffering. It sounded something like a busy emergency room, but the suffering was palpable. Somehow I knew if they would just turn to that Light, their suffering would end, but they were stubborn and would not turn to the Light... I saw that there are no limits to the universe, there were no boundaries except the one between the universe and the darkness. (NDERF #2555)

What demarks the boundary between the universe and the realm of darkness? Most simply, the universe is demarked by God's creation permeated by Light. The darkness, conversely, is where God's Light is absent. Consequently, lost souls are afforded the right to create their own existence with the absence of God. As we will explore shortly, their nightmare creations are extensions of their worst attributes.

Not only are the two spiritual realms separated by a boundary, they also follow a different set of rules. The following NDEr reported that he almost made a poor and dangerous decision because he did not know the rules between realms. He writes:

I sensed beings in the darkness surrounding the tunnel. They were crying out to me in anguish. I recognized two of them. They were begging me to help them. I felt so powerful, invincible, that I moved toward them to grab their hands and bring them out of the dark and into the tunnel. A voice told me sternly not to do that. He said (yes, it was a "he") that there were rules, and I didn't know them. I could not take people out of the darkness, but they could drag me into it. He said to keep going straight ahead and that I knew nothing about anything, and shouldn't presume that I did or I could get into trouble. (NDERF #2965)

This NDEr's spiritual guide sternly warned him that good can be dragged down and corrupted by evil. This concept may generalize to most interactions between good and evil. Evil strives to destroy any good thing or person, even in the spiritual world. Consequently, such destructive forces are not allowed to be interconnected with the Source. Again, there are very few that intentionally reject all that is good. Most destructive human behavior is ignorant, not evil. Evil is a state of being, and evil beings choose a dark path absent from God. Who are these few who reject all that is good? Most of them are psychopaths. Let's review the psychopathic character in more depth.

Mental States of the Psychopath

The United States Constitution holds that it is self-evident that all people are created equal. Perhaps people were created equal, but they do not stay that way. The psychopath does not think, feel, or act like the average man or woman. Working as a prison psychologist, people sometimes ask me about the nature of criminals, usually with an expression of outraged bewilderment. They may ask, for example, how a person can rape, molest, and kill a child and still look at himself in the mirror. Such a question underlies a faulty assumption that the criminal thinks and feels as they do. I answer that the perpetrator looks in the mirror and smiles. I usually get an incredulous scowl followed by a series of 'how can this happen' questions: "Have these unfortunate individuals suffered childhood trauma?" "Might psychopathic behavior be determined by genetics?" "Could mental illness explain these seemingly inexplicable behaviors?" "Could neglectful or otherwise ineffective parenting explain heinous crimes?" My answer to all these questions is, "No. Psychopaths are not victims." Although evidence suggests that genetics may have a *small* role in psychopathy, there are no conclusive, sufficient causal reasons explaining why psychopaths engage in heinous crime. Psychologist and criminal expert Stanton Samenow writes about the futile blame game in the effort to explain psychopathy:

> No factor or set of factors - sociological, psychological, or biological - has proved sufficient to explain why a person becomes a criminal. So far, the search to pin down causation has been futile. But this does not stop people from coming up with ever more explanations, some seemingly plausible, others just plain kooky.[8]

The need to "do something" has led society to create various intervention strategies, such as incarceration, education, religious indoctrination, and therapy programs. A few efforts, such as cognitive therapy, have been successful in reducing antisocial behavior in criminals with low to moderate levels of psychopathy. Such individuals might have a criminal history, for instance, consistent with drug dealing or theft. However, no amount of remediation efforts, even the best psychotherapy, has been shown to rehabilitate the pure psychopath. Quite the opposite, psychotherapy actually becomes counterproductive. Psychopaths only see people as objects to be manipulated. Imagine a silk worm producing silk for a factory worker. Once the worm stops spinning the desired silk, it becomes discarded or destroyed. That is how a psychopath views you, me, or anyone – like a silk worm. Perhaps a real life example might be helpful. I remember when a chaplain and I informed a psychopath that his mother had died. He looked up at us with an unconcerned stare and demanded extra phone privileges. In other words, the psychopath was using his mother's death to exploit the system, perhaps to engage in further criminal activity. As a psychologist, I was just another object to be manipulated. Therapy is only a vehicle to obtain social security benefits, or for some other secondary gain, by faking mental illness. J. Reid Meloy, another expert in the field of criminality, writes, "Psychopathically disturbed patients may hate goodness itself and through their envy and oral rage destroy all that the clinician offers."[9]

Hating goodness is not an attribute consistent with the orderly running of society, much less heaven. Remediation efforts are ineffective because the psychopath does not think like everyone else. According to criminal psychologist Glenn D. Walters,[10] the criminal mind engages in a number of thinking errors. Collectively, thinking errors allow the psychopath to create pain and havoc in society without any internal deterrents. These criminal thinking errors include:

MOLLIFICATION: A psychopath will play down the seriousness of his misconduct and conflicts by blaming problems on outside circumstances or others. Rather than taking responsibility, he or she makes excuses for misbehavior, pointing out the unfairness of the world, and belittling their victims.

ENTITLEMENT: A psychopath believes that he or she is entitled to violate the laws of society and the rights of others. Their entitlement is often expressed by an attitude of ownership, privilege, or by labeling wants as needs.

CUTOFF: The psychopath cuts off normal feelings in order to engage in hurtful behavior. Specifically, they may stop fear, anxiety, guilt or other deterrents for criminal activity. Full blown psychopaths do this automatically. Criminals with lower levels of psychopathy may cut off feelings by abusing drugs and alcohol.

POWER ORIENTATION: The psychopath exerts power and coercion to control/exploit others.

SUPER-OPTIMISM: Experience has taught the psychopath that they get away with most of their criminal activities. This leads to a growing sense of overconfidence. They soon come to believe they are unbeatable. Ironically, this belief eventually leads to their demise.

SENTIMENTALITY: The average criminal wants to be viewed as a "nice guy." Consequently, they may perform a few "good deeds" with the intent of cultivating a "Robin Hood" image. Unfortunately, these modern Robin Hoods only end up "robbing the hood." One psychopath I knew claimed he helped an elderly man by assaulting and robbing him. He stated, "I didn't kill him. What doesn't kill you makes you stronger. I did him a favor my making him stronger."

COGNITIVE INDOLENCE: Lazy in both thought and behavior, psychopaths take every shortcut possible. Most never finish high school and fewer seek employment.

DISCONTINUITY: Criminals have difficulty maintaining focus over time because of being easily influenced by events and situations occurring around them. As a result, they have difficulty following through on initially good intentions. This more frequently occurs in criminals with moderate levels of psychopathy. The true psychopath does not have any good intentions.

The psychopath will declare that all people think just like they do. They will try to list, with an air of ingenuous disbelief, the faults of individuals, groups, and government agencies. True, even normal people engage in criminal thinking and behavior. Driving five miles per hour over the speed limit may be an example of minor criminality shared by most people. However, there are fundamental differences between a psychopath and the average person. The average person makes daily mistakes, ideally accompanied with feelings of guilt and ideas for self-correction. The psychopath, however, revels in every moment as a habitual offender because it is ingrained in his or her character. The psychopath does not act out of ignorance or fallibility. Rather, the psychopath acts from his or her very state of being. The psychopath is incapable of correcting thinking or behavior because he or she lacks concern, compassion, or remorse. People frequently ask me, "What makes a person want to hurt other people?" The question should be phrased differently. People should instead ask, "What does a psychopath lack within?" The answer, unfortunately, is that the psychopath lacks all the better qualities of humanity.

I knew a psychopathic inmate who eviscerated himself from crotch to sternum. He did this heinous act solely to punish staff for not giving in to his ridiculous demands. He had little concern that he lived in a body cast for nine months. He was incapable of feeling joy or happiness anyway, so it did not matter to him whether he was in a cast or not. He only cared to "win" by punishing his caretakers for taking away his power to control. The next time he became frustrated (after he was released from his body cast), he eviscerated himself again. How can someone do this? It is easy for a person who is incapable of feeling empathy, compassion, respect, or remorse for self or others. If a person has no ethical or moral standards, what is to keep them from engaging in crime? Criminal behavior becomes a natural course for a person who is filled with envy, rage, sadism, contempt, and a need for control.

The psychopathic brain has been compared with the reptilian brain. According to J. Reid Meloy, both the psychopath and reptilian brain are focused on "home site selection, establishment and defense of territories, hunting, feeding, mating, competition, dominance, aggression, and imitation."[9] Working with prisoners, my gaze has been met by the reptilian stare of a psychopath. I feel my skin tingle while staring into their cold, empty, calculating, and predatory orbs. A psychopath is even incapable of feeling depression. Think about what causes depression: guilt, sadness, grief, loneliness, personal failure. The psychopath is incapable of experiencing depression because they cannot experience any associated feeling states. J. Reid Meloy writes, "The conscious experience of depression as an affect within the psychopathic process probably does not exist."[9] Interestingly, psychopaths may claim to feel depressed. But the depression most people experience is quite a different emotion than the depression a psychopath experiences; a state Reid Meloy refers to as "zero state depression." Zero state depression is where, basically, the psychopath feels "bad" because they are bored. I have frequently observed zero state depression when psychopaths are placed in single cells for the protection of others. In a typical example, I had an inmate tell me that he was depressed because he was sanctioned from recreation due to numerous infractions. Instead, he had to stay in his single cell for the day. The inmate ended up screaming, ripping-up his cell, taking off his clothes, masturbating, smearing feces, and throwing urine. The inmate was not mentally ill, as one might expect. He knew exactly what he was doing, understood it was wrong, and he seemingly enjoyed every minute of the mayhem.

How does a psychologist correct destructive behaviors when a person lacks the fundamental ability to change? Neither the professional therapist nor loving chaplain can make the change. Psychopaths generally do not change. The following woman had an NDE after her sadistic boyfriend tried to kill her without reason or provocation. She writes:

> I was also amazed at how stupid and evil my boyfriend was. This was the second time he had presumably been to hell and had never changed his path or bad behavior. He once told me, after many drinks, that he had died and seen Hell after being dead for almost 30 minutes...
>
> What he said was that he went into the light and was sort of in a space with a wonderful presence full of light and love, but he was aware of a shadow lurking "in the corner", although there was no corner, of course. The light expressed infinite love and acceptance but said he had to measure out how much good and evil he had done in his life. He said his life was sort of a liquid light that was poured into a beautiful vessel of some sort on a scale. The scale measured his good vs. bad actions on earth. It obviously tipped toward bad, because the beautiful being told him that although he always loved him, he had to go with the dark shadow. Then the dark shadow grew huge and covered him, making him terrified. He screamed, "I'm young; I'll change" and begged to go back. Suddenly he was back in his body and his friends were doing CPR on him. My first question was, "Well, did you change?" He said no, and that's when I knew I had to get rid of him. Of course, I never dreamed he would lay hands on me, let alone try to kill me. (NDERF #2834)

Manifestation of Hell

A psychology coworker, and friend, described the horrible natural death of an inmate who had exploited and killed people throughout his life. Lying on a medical table, the inmate became terrified as death approached. He began screaming, "They're coming to get me! They're coming to get me!" With the last scream he died. The inmate appeared to be on the first leg of manifesting a new evil existence in hell. What may have happened next? The following NDEr reported her brief experience in Hell prior to being saved. She reported having only contempt for God during life. She wrote:

> I immediately descended as if in a speeding elevator car. My only sensation was that of being taken downward in total darkness, total silence. When the descent ended I was in the deepest, darkest void I had ever experienced. Suddenly everything became clear to me. I WAS DEAD. I HAD BEEN CREATED BY GOD. GOD WAS A REALITY BUT I WAS NOT WITH HIM. As it turned out, he was with me but I did not know that yet. I tried to see but could not. I began to hear noise and what I heard was extremely distressing and eventually unbearable. As the noise grew in intensity, I realized it was voices, the countless voices of many, many souls, saying nothing, only weeping and wailing... I heard my own voice echoing on and on, GOD, HELP ME. The next thing that happened was a gigantic hand came down and moved under me and lifted me out of that abyss. (NDERF #1734)

There are a multitude of parameters that define the human physical existence. Human behavior is limited by physical design, brain capacity, health, culture, socio-economic status, societal laws, and so on. Thus, behavior becomes confined, in part, by external factors. Although the psychopath works to circumnavigate societal constraints, ultimately society places limits on their mayhem through forced deterrents, such as incarceration. In other words, society sets limits to behavior for its own protection. In the spiritual realm, however, lost souls are freed from external constraints that might deter destructive behavior. As the adage goes, "Absolute power corrupts absolutely." With the complete absence of God, moral order ceases. Lost souls run a disorganized spectacle of horrors in hell. Hell is a realm where the limits of evil are only defined by the creative depravity of the beings that exist there. Just as goodness becomes accentuated in the heavenly spiritual realm, evil becomes accentuated in the hellish realm.

Some people may dismiss NDE reports of hell due to the seemingly absurd nature of its occupants. Lost souls often present like a group of haunted-house ghouls preying on each other. Some may be seen as zombie-like creatures, vampires, demons, grim reapers, and other creatures from human mythology. Do these mythological creatures really exist in hell? Not in pure form. Spiritual beings, including lost souls, exist as beings of energy. Yet, as previously discussed, energy beings can manifest reality by thought. In the case of lost souls, they instinctually manifest themselves into ghoulish creatures set to intimidate or destroy.

Many inmates tattoo ghoulish creatures all over their bodies, particularly psychopaths living in high security institutions. These images depict grimacing skulls, zombie creatures, laughing jokers with wicked teeth, devils, and other demonic beings. Why do psychopaths ink cruel mythological creatures from head to toe? For the psychopath, gruesome tattoos represent the evil that burns inside. In other words, their character becomes expressed symbolically through permanent visual depictions on their skin. What can be a more telling canvas of self than the human body? Lost souls also permanently display evil in the spiritual realm. Specifically, they incorporate evil mythological symbols from earth into their own appearance and identity. In a sense, they actually become these mythological beings through their manifestation of reality.

In fairness, people tattoo ghoulish characters on their body for a variety of reasons. Perhaps some people just want to sport a tough, cool image. A ghoulish tattoo, in and of itself, does not necessarily indicate that a person is evil. Yet, for the psychopath, ghoulish tattoos mirror what lurks on the inside – a desire to inflict pain and create destruction.

Howard Storm's near-death experience included a vivid and traumatic experience that included relentless assault. He writes about Hell's occupants:

> These creatures were once human beings. The best way I can describe them is to think of the worst imaginable person stripped of every impulse of compassion. Some of them seemed to be able to tell others what to do, but I had no sense of there being any organization to the mayhem. They didn't appear to be controlled or directed by anyone. Simply, they were a mob of beings totally driven by unbridled cruelty.[5]

Imagine a mob rioting on city streets after the loss of a major sporting event. The mob has no purpose other than to vent their frustration through hatred, destruction, and violence. Moreover, the mob follows no rules or leadership. Interestingly, NDErs who have Hellish experiences rarely mention Satan. In fact, far more NDErs assert that Satan does not exist than those who claim otherwise. The existence of Satan would suggest leadership and organization. That does not appear to be the case. Storm adds that lost souls have relatively little intelligence or ability, especially in contrast with spiritual beings existing in the heavenly realm. Rather than organizing or creating, lost souls are too busy preying on each other in a repetitive, compulsive fashion. The following NDEr made the following observation from heaven:

> Those negative beings seemed to come from the earth and go down away from the light. I was aware of them going to a void of darkness and suffering – their behaviors went round and round in circles based on their experiences like a negative record player of habits, thoughts, and feelings. (NDERF #2366)

One might anticipate that lost souls would eventually become tired of their relentless, circular behaviors. That does not appear to happen. For without guiding rules of God, relentless compulsions lead to an unending cycle of suffering. Specifically, lost souls are unable to break free from the cycle of evil due to the absence of will and the habitual nature of their actions. George Ritchie, during his brief tour of hell, observed the following habitual nature of evil behaviors:

> Here were no solid objects of people to enthrall the soul. These creatures seemed locked into habits of mind and emotion, into hatred, lust, destructive thought-patterns. Even more hideous than the bites and kicks they exchanged, were the sexual abuses many were performing in feverish pantomime.[4]

The suffering of lost souls can serve as a warning to people on earth, especially regarding the relentless pull of addiction. The human being can be addicted to anything that makes them feel good: food, sex, shopping, eating, substances, and so forth. The addiction takes power away from the will. Over time, the person becomes enslaved to a pattern of self-destructive behaviors. At some point in the process, the addiction becomes more powerful than the individual's ability to reason soundly or make choices. Consequently, people will completely destroy their lives just to feed the addiction. The only useful fortune cookie I ever read said this, "First we make our habits and then our habits make us." How true. This quote is even more apt in the spiritual world. Habits have transformed lost souls into compulsive addicts of evil. Unfortunately, these souls are too lost to turn to God. They do not have the will to save themselves.

Suicide and Remediation

Psychopaths are not the only type of people who are lost. Some people have lost their purpose in life because they become spiritually adrift. In the case of suicide, the afflicted are drowning in so much pain and hopelessness that they choose to take their own life. Some believe that many NDErs who kill themselves are doomed to hell. I have not found this to be the case after reading numerous suicide related NDERF and ADC submissions. Although suicides represent a disconnection from the divine, they do not always represent malice toward the divine. Rather, suicide stems from a person's immersion in intolerable pain. People who kill themselves are not typically evil, they just become hopeless due to difficult life circumstances, spiritual dryness, or poor coping skills.

There are many reasons for suicide. For some people, especially the elderly in chronic pain, suicide represents an end to needless suffering. In other cases, suicides represent a discontinuation of mission. Human lives are not randomly selected. Missions are carefully assigned according to the spiritual needs of the individual. Although God does not punish anyone, some people who kill themselves may continue facing the same struggles toward growth after they die; suicide does not alleviate the responsibility to accomplish mission. Consequently, God provides remediation efforts in the spiritual realm to help those adrift find anchor. Specifically, souls that have killed themselves may have a rest period where they are mentored by more spiritually-developed beings. Interestingly, remediation is not only reserved for actual suicides, but anyone who has flagrantly disregarded the sanctity of their own life. In the next NDE submission, a woman observes a room full of people who have lived and died recklessly. Searching for answers, she finally met a man with answers. She wrote:

> At a certain interval, I noticed a man move into the room. I sensed something about him. He felt safe and balanced to me... He told me that he was not a perfect man, but that he had mastered humility. He explained that he had come to help teach the importance of humility to this group of people because they had been in some ways self-absorbed in their lives to the degree where this had blocked their own vision and progression. They hadn't been able to learn vital lessons and had aborted their own lives, unwittingly for all I knew. He seemed to be telling me that in one way or another, these people had committed suicide, but without that exact terminology. (NDERF #2386)

The woman soon learned that most of the people in the room had not actually killed themselves. Still, their reckless behavior was viewed as a suicide in the spiritual realm. She continued:

> The teacher continued to offer more information. He explained how in aborting their own lives, these people would have a rest period, but that learning what they needed to learn would be needed and the process would not be easy. I came to understand that as much as they were taught and infused with good and helpful information there, and even if they agreed wholeheartedly with what they needed to learn, that learning without a body is like learning to get over an addiction to drugs with no opportunity to do the drugs!... He shook his head, smiling slightly, and implied that there was still very little he could help them with, without their bodies. His service was to help instill more of a passion for what he had to teach, strong enough that it would leave a seed of Light that might stay with them through their sojourn. (NDERF #2386)

According to this submission, the reckless souls were adrift from their mission. Unfortunately, adrift souls generally progress little in the spiritual realm. Although spiritual beings may learn, some through their rest period, real change comes from learning through life choice and experience. This NDE submission conveys a critical message for all humanity. It is vitally important for each person to take human life seriously. One cannot become an outstanding doctor by flunking medical school. Likewise, it is almost impossible to master oneself spiritually by flunking earth school.

Triumph of Good over Evil

Some claimed there is a spiritual war between good and evil. Although this may be true, I prefer to think of spiritual opposition as a type of evolution occurring toward the good. One NDEr asked God about the existence of evil. She wrote:

> I knew that He had the answers to all questions. So, I began to ask Him things I had wondered about the most, like "Why is there evil?" His reply, "Because there is good." (NDERF #2965)

One cannot chose good without the existence of evil. Thus, evil is necessary for sentient beings to have spiritual self-determination. Yet, there was never any doubt about which of the two is stronger. In the grand scheme of eternity, good will ultimately gain ground over evil as beings move toward God. Even the evil beings in hell, with enough time, will turn toward God and be saved. The following NDEr learned this about the progression of souls from the vantage point of heaven:

> The prevailing feeling that I had whilst observing these souls was one of deep compassion and a learning to comfort them. I wanted so much to see them relieved of their horrible suffering. But, alas, as painful as this scene was, I was reassured that these souls were here only temporarily and that they, too, would heal and move back in a forward direction and ultimately return to the Light. All souls, without exception, eventually return to the Light, according to what was revealed to me. (NDERF #364)

Evil has very little power over good in the spiritual realm. Lost souls lack the power, organization, discipline, or intelligence to create any threat to the divine. The only real power in the universe is God. Not only is good more powerful, it is more predominant. During his tour of the universe, Dr. Alexander learned about the abundance of good over evil. He writes:

> Small particles of evil were scattered throughout the universe, but the sum total of all that evil was a grain of sand on a vast beach compared to the goodness, abundance, hope, and unconditional love in which the universe was literally awash...Even on earth there is much more good than evil, but earth is a place where evil is allowed to gain influence... allowed by the Creator as a necessary consequence of giving the gift of free will to beings like us.[11]

Dr. Alexander's lesson about good and evil has fundamental relevance to all humanity. He brings back a message of hope. Many people live in dire, hopeless situations. Large segments of the world live in crushing poverty, especially within the war-torn, third world. Even in industrialized nations like the United States, too many people are subject to repeated violence and mental abuse. For those living in dark places, the "might make right" philosophy may seem the norm. In an environment defined by oppression, one may choose to be an aggressor.

Such a person may believe, for instance, that it is okay that the strong survive whereas the weak perish. Yet, Dr. Alexander learned that evil will never triumph over good through time, even in dark places where evil now predominates. Those who choose evil have no long-term future, as all power ultimately comes from God and divine organization based on love. Even though people suffer on earth, souls will eternally participate in a love-filled universe freely shared by God. The existence of the lost soul is tragic. Despite this uncomfortable reality, the divine will always serve as a beacon of hope.

CHAPTER FIFTEEN

GUIDED BY GOD'S DIVERSITY

In the television science fiction series, *Star Trek, The Next Generation*, humankind moved beyond warring against each other. Nationalism and money have also became obsolete. Although these possibilities bolster a fine ideal, they appear overly optimistic. Although human technology continues to evolve, human psychology appears largely stuck in the hunter-gatherer period. Yet, it no longer benefits any local human tribe to destroying competitors. World wars not only destroy millions of families, but they also create economic havoc on entire nations. Entire ecological systems become collateral damage when human weapons generate global mass destruction. Although aggression no longer serves a functional purpose, many people instinctually respond to the "other stranger" with a desire to coerce or destroy. The "other" seems to have no definable limits, be it different skin color, religion, ideas, economic status, political party, or any other differences. For the human animal, just being different can lead to divisive conflict.

Human differences produce social inequalities, prejudices, hate crimes, and war. Fortunately, human beings do not need to be entirely enslaved by their biology. After all, human biology coexists with the soul. The soul is continuously unified with the spiritual world, and therefore interconnected with an unconditionally-loving God. The power of love can transcend the human drive to survive through domination. People can, and do, proclaim that prejudice and violence are wrong. It is the purpose of this chapter to explore God's view of prejudicial hatred. The chapter continues by deciphering moral relativism, God's diversity throughout the universe, and human religious diversity.

God Does Not Hate

Some atheist groups have blamed religion for starting wars and group violence throughout world history. Religious orthodoxy, however, does not generally advocate acts of hatred. In Christianity, for instance, the faithful are encouraged to dislike the sin but love the sinner. Yet, people have historically used religion to justify almost any act of hatred regardless of pacifist religious teaching. These actions reflect a misuse of religion, either intentionally or out of ignorance. Hatred in the name of God is an abomination to God. There is no basis to harm each other if every man, woman, or child has been created by God. The question should become, did God just create people like me in His image, or every living being? Most spiritual people would agree that God designed and created every living thing. NDErs return back to earth from heaven with an additional understanding that there is a unity that binds all of God's creation, infused with love. If love binds all creation, then hatred and prejudice have no place in the divine mission. Howard Storm, who disregarded others prior to his NDE, learned about the divisions he created on earth while visiting heaven. He came to understand the following:

> The egocentric view of God is often projected into a tribal view of God's love. God is not confined to individuals, tribes, nations, religions, or any other institutions. Our cultural bias is collective egocentric pride. Since we are finite creatures raised in specific cultures, we are shaped by our culture. To know God, we have to surrender our individual and collective pride/ego if we are ever to know God's love.[1]

Hatred is often rationalized without good justification. What is truly behind justifying violent attacks against people on the grounds of religion, rigid morality, or culture wars? Are these attacks really motivated by divine decree or by self-righteous human ideology? One must be careful not to substitute human ideology with God's ideology. After all, perfect truth and justification only comes from God. Unfortunately, God's truth may conflict with cultural beliefs or religious dogma. Just because unknown parts of God's creation seem strange to us, they are not unfamiliar to God. I remember when a college professor posed this question: "If this blackboard represented all knowledge in the universe, how much of the blackboard represents the knowledge you know?" Most students answered "just a dot." If all we know is a mere dot of reality, it seems rather presumptuous to believe any individual or group has cornered universal truth. Similarly, it seems rather presumptuous to hate someone based on differences of opinion, or even worse, to use that prejudice to kill. Perhaps, for these reasons, it befits people to be humble. In fact, learning humbleness would be a worthy school earth lesson, even if it represented an entire life mission.

Unfortunately, pride seems to permeate society, not humbleness. Divisive and hypocritical influences pervade various systems of control, even within religious corners. In the following NDERF submission, the submitter was a "victim" of other people's intolerance and dogmatic beliefs. He had a medical disorder, called Tourette's syndrome, causing various unseemly behaviors outside of his control. He was also homosexual. Because homosexuality contradicted his parent's religious beliefs, he was taught that he was unclean in the sight of God. Thus, the submitter was universally ostracized because he didn't fit the cultural mold. How did he respond? He responded with a quiet anger directed at society and God. His anger was also directed toward himself, culminating with an attempted suicide. His near-death experience, however, taught him that his anger at God, at least, was misplaced. He writes:

> My parents were Protestant Christians, but I thought it was certainly "horse dump." I was a physical and forensic anthropology student. A devout atheist - angry for how my life had been. Surely no God would have let me suffer as I had. Surely no God would have allowed me to be born into a family with such strong issues or be born a homosexual if that was against His will. But I noticed I didn't need my glasses and that I no longer seemed to have Tourette's Syndrome...Being a homosexual had no meaning on the other side - it didn't matter. I mattered. (NDERF #3240)

Note that the submitter, on a fundamental level, mattered. How do God's people respond to social and religious outcasts? How God's people respond to individuals with different sexual orientations? Do we use God's name to create additional struggles in their lives? Or, do we use God's love to help them struggle less? Our response, according to the near-death experience, should involve the ideals of tolerance and unconditional love.

The Truth about Moral Relativism

The life review during some near-death experiences exemplifies acceptance. People are automatically forgiven through God's unconditional love. Although God's model encourages the acceptance of various beliefs, lifestyles, and cultures, it does not encourage a permissive "anything goes" life strategy. In other words, God's unconditional acceptance should not be confused with moral relativism. Moral relativism is a philosophical position that argues that morality is invented by man, as evidenced by discrepant moral codes practiced from culture to culture. Because morality is thought to be invented by man, right or wrong are only fictional inventions. If this position is true, how should people live without morality? The result, it seems, would be anarchy. Most adherents to the moral relativism position recognize the need for order. They solve their created paradox by advocating that every individual is responsible for developing their own moral compass.

God does not want each person to develop an individualized moral compass. Such an attempt would represent a blatant exercise of ego and pride. Despite the wide range of acceptable life experiences, the fabric of the universe is built on what is right and wrong. Specifically, right is built on love and wrong is built on its opposite. Such a definition of morality may appear simplistic at first glance, but it is anything but simple. In chapter seven, we explored the multifaceted nature of love, discussing attributes ranging from respect to sacrifice. The lengthy list discussed in chapter seven is by no means exhaustive. In this chapter alone, we have added humility to the list. The point is that living God's moral code is exceptionally difficult to master. Yet, it is a flexible code. God's moral code is built on living by the fruits of the spirit and not on legalism. Unfortunately, human morality too often exemplifies a dualistic mode of thinking; everybody and everything becomes labeled into neat "good" and "bad" categories. Perhaps some aspects of morality can be more accurately captured by shades of gray. The NDE experience seems to teach this lesson. One NDEr wrote about her shift from a perspective of duality to tolerance. She wrote:

I had never realized the all-encompassing monster of misery that my duality way of thinking was in my life until my NDE. If someone had walked up to me before my NDE and had asked me if my "duality" way of thinking was tiring and miserable for me, I would have been utterly confused and unable to agree with the statement, or even make sense of it. I had never been aware of how my mind had always tried to label, judge or compare in one way or another everything I came across. Even if in ways I thought of as "good," for example; "She's the nicest" or "He's the best guy!" or "That backyard is the prettiest one, etc." It was me judging one thing as better than another. Divisive. (NDERF #2836)

This NDE submission illustrates how natural it is for people to slip into divisive, judgmental thinking. Given the multitude of divisions around the globe, it stands to reason that human systems of morality, whether national or religious, are largely culturally derived. Yet, humans still believe that their cherished moral systems are irrefutable. I suspect these human systems provide order in a disorderly world by supplying clear and simple answers to mystery. Unfortunately, rigid moral systems often lead to divisiveness, intolerance, and ultimately discrimination. Humanity will need to transcend tribal ideology in order to advance toward a greater spiritual awakening and love one another. The first step is for humankind to realize that we are all interconnected with a highly diverse universe.

A Highly Diverse Universe

God designed the universe with diversity in mind. Even the planet Earth is filled with extraordinary variety, ranging from a diversity of animal life to human cultural expression. The following NDEr noted this rich diversity while looking over the Earth:

I was able to move around the planet and feel different continents, countries, races, even certain smaller states, cities, and people! Each held its own kind of personal vibration and energetic pattern. I learned how we are each made up of so many different or various layers of energetic influence. This was fascinating to me! Each race, each country, even a state, each family in a way, is like its own organism. Connected to all, but with an influence of its very own and very important unique purposes. Each is sacred and vital. (NDERF #2386)

The submitter of this near-death experience realized that various layers of reality make up the Whole. To expand a bit further, unity in the universe is made up of complex, harmonious sets of diverse interconnections. The human species is only one small link in an inestimable large chain of sentient experience in the universe. In other words, God created the universe with diversity in mind; enormous variation is integral to the overall plan. Each component is vital to the Whole, much like a heart and lung are both vital to the human body. In regard to human beings, every culture has a vital and sacred role within the Whole. I have personally found that embracing cultural differences has enriched my own life by shaping me into a more rounded and complete individual. On an intellectual level, divergent ideas diversify my own understanding of reality and enhance my own creativity. On an interpersonal level, different cultural customs add to the possibilities of shared human expression and interconnection. On a spiritual level, different religious beliefs can expand my own understanding of the divine. I do not need to fear other cultural and religious beliefs, unless those beliefs genuinely threaten to harm me or others. I also understand that all these differences, although enriching, are partly illusionary. They are illusionary because cultural differences are not pronounced at home in the spiritual realm.

Every human is a spiritual being in true essence. We are all the same regardless of mannerisms, accents, cultural expression, and skin color. Specifically, we are all magnificent beings of energy created by God. The following NDERF submission discusses the unimportance of race in the spiritual realm:

> There is no race, color or creed in Heaven, only here for the test.... And then He infused within my mind the knowledge that we all are of solid light, male and female, each with our own identity and purpose. (NDERF #1369)

When I see an Asian, African American, or anyone racially different from myself, I try to visualize them as a being of energy that looks exactly like me. This helps remind me about the unified spiritual nature of all people. If everyone could visualize each person in similar fashion, perhaps there would be less violence toward our fellow spiritual beings connected to God. Let me provide a personal example for practical application. I grew up fearing African Americans after hearing stories of violence from the White community. Living in North Carolina for a few years, I had the opportunity to work, socialize, and worship with

African Americans. With time, my fears were replaced by understanding and respect.

Human Tribalism and Religion

Human tribalism, the ugly product of our biology, undermines the coexistence of unity and diversity. How will humanity realize that tribalism is antiquated? Science may play a role. Over 99.5% of the human genome does not vary across races.[3] In fact, there are more differences between individuals within a single race than between racial groups.[4] Not only are we the same from a soul perspective, but we are also very similar at a biological level.

Not everyone is persuaded by genetic science or by any other evidence. Old prejudices remain. People ignore differences to thwart threats against the established order. Religion, in particular, creates uniformity through liturgy, belief, and cultural affiliation. With few exceptions, one rarely finds people of ethnic and cultural diversity sitting in the pews. Anita Moorjani profoundly experienced interconnection between differences during her near-death experience. She wrote about unity within the context of religious institutions:

> I'm not saying that I'm against organized religion, but I am skeptical of any message when it leads to all the divisiveness, strife, and killing that go on in this world in the name of religion, when in truth, we're all One-all facets of the same Whole. Human beings are so varied that some fare better with organized religion or spiritual paths, whereas others don't. If we simply live in a way that nurtures us and allows us to express our creativity, letting us see our own magnificence, that's the best we can possibly do. To advocate any option or doctrine as being the one true way would only serve to limit who we are and what we've come to be.[2]

Anita Moorjani's near-death experience taught her to break the stifling bonds of cultural tradition. After her NDE, she became freed to author her own life and realize her own spiritual mission. When people exclude others, by either subtle or coercive means, they are stifling their own creativity. In essence, they limit themselves to the experience and will of their group. In doing so, they are also stifling the creativity and potential in others.

Although spiritual creativity may be stunted on earth, there are no ideological barriers stunting creativity in heaven. That does not mean, however, that cultural differences are not integral to the near-death experience. Each person's near-death experience has been designed to accommodate their own cultural and religious framework when they first cross over. As discussed earlier, NDE experiences are individualized to reduce anxiety and fear during the transition between realms. In this transition, it is the person that matters, not any national or religious system. Many Christians, for instance, report meeting Jesus during their near-death experience. That is usually not the case for non-Christians. The following represents a near-death experience for a Native American who maintained his own religious traditional beliefs:

> During all this I went to a place that was in the stars. At first my friend Kuauhtli reached out and took me by the hand. Kuauhtli is a Peyote Road Man, who does ceremony all over the world. He is also a 20 year Sun Dancer, who has given his flesh for 20 years.

> Kuauhtli led me inside a big yellow school bus. I looked around like where are we going? All Kuauhtli did was smile. There were no words spoken. When we entered the school bus, the interior had transformed to a Peyote Ceremony, and we were in a tepee. There were many Elders sitting around the Sacred Fire. Some looked to be very old. Some I recognized! I was amazed! I had just walked into a school bus, and now I was in a Peyote Ceremony! I went to look out of the windows, and we were in the cosmos!!! I touched the window and something outside touched back! I could feel the pressure, and we were floating in space, having a Peyote Ceremony!!! I was loving it! I had never felt such peace before in my life. There was never any talk of death. Only the Elders singing their songs. Then I was in the ICU. (NDERF #2577)

Some readers may find this peculiar Native American submission difficult to accept. It is natural for some people to view this unorthodox belief as threatening. After all, religious beliefs are held sacred and integral to one's personal identity. Thus, most people are willing to defend their religious traditions from outward attack, including a book about near-death experiences. It is certainly not my goal to negate all the beliefs that people hold sacred. Quite the opposite, I have personally maintained my Christian identity despite developing a more comprehensive view on spirituality. In fact, the near-death experience has only strengthened many of my Christian beliefs. So with some daring, let's take a look at the role of different religious traditions that operate within the Whole.

Diversity in Religion

There is an astounding diversity of religions across the globe. Can only one be right and the rest be wrong? Many people have wrestled with this question over the ages. Not surprisingly, many NDErs have also posed this question to God, or other spiritual beings, during their near-death experience. In combing through NDERF submissions, I have found that the divine response to this question appears remarkably consistent. Specifically, God values religion as a tool for spiritual growth. Yet, God is primarily interested in the spiritual development of individuals rather than the adherence of any specific religious doctrine. Let's take a look at a couple of relevant NDERF submissions. One NDEr wrote:

> I'd also wondered at religion while I was there, and I quickly received the knowing that this wasn't important in the way I imagined it was prior to my NDE. That one's religion, no matter which they joined or didn't join on earth, was what was written in their own heart. It was about who the person was, not what label they wore or who or what they worshipped or believed in. (NDERF #2386)

Real spirituality, it appears, is expressed internally rather than through external religious institutions. Even Howard Storm, an atheist who became a Christian pastor after his NDE, received a similar answer to the same question. He asked Jesus and other spiritual beings, "Which is the best religion?" They answered, "The religion that brings you closest to God."[1] Jesus and other spiritual beings elaborated on Howard Storm's question and he came to learn the following, "There are good people in bad religions and there are bad people in good religion...Religion is only a means to find God. Religion is not the destination. True religion is the love of God in every word, thought, and deed of the person."[1]

True religion is based on love and personal growth toward God. That is not to imply that religion lacks value. Religion can have great importance connecting people to God, especially in a realm where the material is partly separated from the spiritual. Religion provides people with an organized system of looking beyond the mortal and into the eternal. Furthermore, there are many religious practices that promote a closer spiritual connection with God. These include, but are not limited to, teaching love, facilitating community service, and engaging in communal prayer. But to reiterate Howard Storm, religion is not the destination. God is the destination. The primary focus of any religious institution should be to serve the spiritual needs of man rather than man serving religion. Destructive religious ideology enforces strict doctrine by means of fear, guilt, and other methods of coercion. They also teach intolerance toward science, secular philosophy, different religions, and any other competing belief. Again, it is the individual soul that matters, not the doctrine. The following NDEr was presented a poignant image regarding this question of religion. She wrote:

> The first question I asked was, "What is the right religion?" I was told, "They all are. Each religion is a pathway trying to reach the same place." I was shown a mountain, with each religious group trying to reach the top, separated from each other by distance, but each one was trying to get to the same place. I was then told that people choose to be born into whichever religion or group that will help them achieve the lessons they are sent here to learn. (NDERF #2932)

The metaphor of a spiritual mountain top seems particularly pertinent to the present discussion. Each religion has a certain degree of value and truth depending on the needs of the individual. Christianity resonates for me because of Jesus' emphasis on love and grace. Buddhism may resonate more for someone who is passionate about non-violence and introspection through meditation. Native American beliefs may resonate for someone who respects harmony and interconnection with creation. And so on. Many religious beliefs have merit because they are consistent with the concept of God and love. They are all viable paths up the mountain toward God. In other words, the right religion is the religion that brings you closest to God.

Are all religions equal? Every person must evaluate the merits of each religion based on their own spiritual path. How does a spiritual searcher differentiate one religion from the other? Love should be the relevant standard by which such discernments are made. Perhaps the evaluation process should also occur at the congregational level. Ask yourself, does your specific church, mosque, temple, or synagogue facilitate love, or does it enforce intolerance and rigid dogma? The following NDEr tried to answer this question in this way:

> It doesn't matter what religion we are. Prayer as a single person, family, or a community is important. Try to find a church that feels like home. All religions are here for a reason. But any religion or religious person that preaches: fear, hell, fire and damnation; we do not deserve God's grace; He wants us to suffer; disown our family if they do not believe the same as we do; or a certain amount of money will get you into heaven, etc...IS LYING! There are no strings attached to God's love! (NDERF #682)

If there are no strings attached to God love, one could also question whether agnosticism or atheism are viable paths leading up to the mountain of God. This is a complex question to answer. Many agnostics and atheists have positive near-death experiences. God does not condemn people to hell on the basis of disbelief. However, spiritual growth may be more difficult for many agnostics and atheists because of their disbelief. Specifically, the belief in a higher power promotes humble servitude rather than reliance on ego. It is easier to love humanity by both loving God and accepting God's love. Furthermore, love is valued more when relationships are built eternally. On the flip side, it is more likely that unconditional love will become stunted by human ego for those who cannot see beyond a lifetime. Rather, their goal may be to seize the moment and create as much prestige, power, and wealth for themselves before final death. I am not suggesting that all non-believers are egotistical or that all believers are loving servants. I have met agnostics who have chosen a genuine humanitarian path by believing in something greater than the self. I have also met some Christians who present as sanctimonious and callous. Everyone has their own unique path. Still, faith in God does matter.

The Tapestry

Every person, tribe, nation, race, and planetary species is woven together as part of a Whole entity, making up a rich tapestry in God's universe. The human species is at a crossroad in understanding interconnected relationships with each other and the divine. It is no accident that more people are reporting deep near-death experiences. Many are coming back with important messages to share with humanity, including the importance of God's diversity. Humanity faces unique challenges involving overpopulation, disease, environmental change, degradation of resources, and the potential for mass destruction through terrorism and war. With weapons of mass destruction, humans may likely destroy earth if we cannot advance beyond the tribal psychology inherited by our ancestors. The only way humankind will resolve these serious global challenges will be through mutual cooperation. Global cooperation will be necessary to resolve global problems. To accomplish this goal, diversity must be respected. As a species prone to violence, do we listen to our fears? Or, do we elevate our spiritual intelligence to embrace a diverse, greater reality?

There is some room for optimism. The human race has made limited but real progress in battling intolerance. The rapid change in Western Europe may serve as a beacon for hope. Europe's history has been riddled with racism, religious schisms, nationalism, and war. Despite several millennia of violence, a cultural shift of relative tolerance has redefined Europe since World War II. Western and some Eastern Europeans have become economically and politically unified after the creation of the European Union. No longer are kings pitted against queens. No longer are Protestants pitted against Catholics. But will it last? Will Europe continue to walk down the path of tolerance and integration, or will economic and political instabilities reignite old prejudices? This question not only applies to Europe, but to every human tribe, nation, and race in the world. God is fostering a new spiritual awakening. The fate of the world depends on whether the human species, as a whole, will accept or reject God's message by our own free will.

The tapestry of creation is personal, interconnected, and ever changing. Hatred and intolerance strike against God's beautiful, rich tapestry. Suffering exists in the world, in no small measure, due to a disconnection between humankind and God's higher love. Divine love celebrates differences within unity. One of the main reasons spiritual beings live human lives is to learn tolerance. The near-death experience plays a significant role in teaching that you are within me and I am within you. As interconnected spiritual beings, we are all charged with the mission to embrace each other as part of the Whole. Will humankind ever really learn this lesson? Time will tell. Unfortunately, time is not on our side. Time will be the topic of the next chapter.

CHAPTER SIXTEEN

TIME

D o you make good use of your time? This simple question may hold the key to your happiness and the meaning of life. This is quite a bold assertion, certainly. But it is the quality of time that is integrally tied into our divine mission on school earth. From the near-death experience perspective, God thrusts souls into earth time for a special, divine purpose. Time is one of the most valuable gifts bestowed to humanity by God. Consequently, misusing time equates to wasting God's gift of life. In this chapter, we will examine time from several different angles. We will begin by briefly exploring the nature of time and how it works in the spiritual realm. We will finish by exploring how earth time relates to free will. First, let's talk about the views of Albert Einstein, the expert in matters of time.

Touching on Einstein's Theory of Relativity

Almost everyone recognizes the name Albert Einstein. Einstein's fame has become associated with exceptional brilliance. The typical physicist can find irony in that many people revere Einstein without understanding his contributions. Einstein achieved no less than turning Newtonian physics on its head. Namely, Einstein discovered that time is not fixed, but relative based on conditions of space. Thus, concepts of alternative dimensions, time travel, and black holes all have roots with Einstein. Einstein provided humanity with an understanding of reality beyond what we see and conventionally measure. It may not be accidental that revelations about the spiritual realm have coincided with Einstein's theory of relativity. Although near-death experience accounts reach back thousands of years, it has only been within the last century that some organizational aspects of the spiritual realm have been revealed by first-hand experience. Perhaps Einstein created a theoretical foundation for people to understand basic divine truths for the first time in human history.

Isaac Newton believed that time was uniform. In a Newtonian universe, synchronized clocks tick at the same rate everywhere. Newton also believed that time was separate from other properties in physics, such as mass, gravity, or speed. Physicists readily accepted the Newtonian law until it was proved wrong by Albert Einstein. After all, Newton's mathematical explanations coincided with human experience. But as often happens in science, inconsistencies accumulate with measurement and advancements in theory. Tackling these inconsistencies, Albert Einstein discovered that time was actually enmeshed with space. Amazingly, he discovered that space was not uniform. Rather, space is actually curved by wells of gravity. Specifically, he discovered that time speeds up or slows down with changes in gravity and the associated curvature of space. A person who lives on a very massive planet, for instance, would experience time slightly differently than on earth. Such a small time difference could only be measured by an atomic clock. However, time would be quite different near a supermassive object, like a black hole. According to Stephen Hawking, "Each observer would have his own measure of time as recorded by a clock that he carried."[1] In other words, real time is relative.

Explanation for the theory of relativity is beyond the scope of this chapter. I refer the reader to author Brian Greene and his national best-selling book, *The Fabric of the Cosmos*.[2] Greene describes the theory of relativity, and other related topics in physics, in laymen's terms. For our purposes, I will simply mention that Albert Einstein made a number of startling discoveries about time. For instance, the theory of relativity does not discriminate whether time should go forward or backward. Furthermore, it does not differentiate between the past, present, and future. Rather, the theory of relativity suggests that time can be likened to a loaf of bread, fixed and fully observable no matter how it becomes sliced. Interestingly, Einstein was bothered that human beings experience time as a constant forward flow of *now*. There is no clear mathematical explanation explanation for the biological perception of time. Thus, the experience of time may be brain based. Brian Greene poses this related question, "Is science unable to grasp a fundamental quality of time that the human mind embraces as readily as the lungs take in air, or does the human mind impose on time a quality of its own making, one that is artificial and that hence does not show up in the laws of physics?"[2]

Most people do not bother wrestling with this question about time. Why question when the human flow of time seems to work perfectly for everyone? Only a few physicists seem to worry about why humans experience time. That does not mean, however, that physicists are wrong. Perhaps the human brain somehow dictates the experience of time. If so, it may be possible that time constraints are lifted when the soul leaves the body. Indeed, this may be the case in the spiritual realm. The theory of relativity may very well apply to the perception of time during near-death experiences.

Time in Heaven

NDErs often returns to earth awed by their altered perception of time in the spiritual realm. For the first time since human birth, they experience the past, present, and future simultaneously. Why? Spiritual time is experienced as a unified entity rather than a continuous forward flow. Events can willfully become merged, somehow, into a singularity of experience. Interestingly, spiritual time appears more consistent with Einstein's theory of relativity than our human experience of time. How can this possibly work given that the act of thinking seems to require a singular flow of time? Without sequence, how would anyone differentiate between cause and effect? As Einstein stated, "The only reason for time is so that everything doesn't happen at once."[3] Spiritual time has greater complexity than just experiencing "everything happening at once." Indeed, a type of linear time flows forward in heaven so that cause and effect events can be sequenced. In other words, spiritual beings perceive time so that connections between events can be untangled and understood. Although reality can be understood in terms of ordered arrangements, packets of experience do not necessarily follow in chronological order or even at the same pace. Time does flow in heaven, but in a relative way.

Albert Einstein provided a theoretical framework to understand relative time. A framework, however, does not equate to complete understanding of physics. Human beings, limited by biology, cannot explain relative time in the spiritual realm. As Eben Alexander commented, "Cause and effect exists in these higher realms, but outside of our earthly conception of them."[4] Time is one of the many aspects of reality that remains mysterious, perhaps by design. Even the experiential aspects of relative time cannot be understood without a common frame of reference. To know relativity, one must experience relativity. Everyone on earth has been trapped in linear time since birth, with the notable exception of NDErs who witnessed relative time while in heaven. For NDErs, words are inadequate to capture their experience of relative time in the spiritual realm. It would be like explaining color to someone who is colorblind. Nevertheless, NDErs still try to share their experience by using cryptic, human language. One wrote the following:

> I am not sure if the following took place before, after, or simultaneously with what I just shared. For the sake of some level of written chronology, I express as, "next", "after" or, "then". It could be in that order, but know that I am often tempted to say that it was "all at once." (NDERF #2386)

Another NDEr similarly shared bafflement regarding his experience of time:

> Time there does not exist in the way that we understand here. There is something done to time there that nullifies it in some way. I do not know how this works, I only know that it is that way. Events happen but their 'gauge' is not time as such. There is something like time there but it is not anything like what we understand as time. (NDERF #3253)

Consistent with theory of relativity, another NDEr described relative time almost as a fixed entity. He wrote:

> I also experienced "time" as a oneness and not as something that is linear. Time, for lack of a better analogy, was like a block of wood that I could look at, examine, and turn around. (NDERF #3265)

Many NDEs speak about time in the spiritual realm. In numerous NDERF submissions, the perceived altercation of time may depend on the complexity of the near-death experience. NDErs who receive transcendent messages, like life reviews, seem to experience time relativity more profoundly than NDERs who only receive a brief glimpse of the spiritual realm. This discrepancy makes sense, as transcendent experiences involve a broader context of present, past, and future. Not surprisingly, these NDErs often return to earth somewhat confused about the sequence of events during their near-death experience. Anita Moorjani shared her difficulty sequencing events when she returned to linear time on earth, "Although being able to perceive all points of time simultaneously lent to the atmosphere of clarity in that realm, recalling it and writing about it creates confusion. The sequence isn't obvious when there's no linear time, making the retelling sound clumsy."[5]

Moorjani's difficulty in sequencing events is understandable. After all, people consciously experience linear time as a forward flow of *now*. Because *now* involves immediate conscious experience, it is difficult to define or measure. Everything else falls in the past or future, which can only be inferred symbolically. The term "symbolically" simply means that the past and future must be understood in terms of mental symbols. In the case of memory, people symbolically recall parts of the past through mental images and native language. By recalling something that is not actually occurring in the present, one is, in a sense, displacing time. Unfortunately, displacing time is an inexact process. Who can remember everything perfectly or accurately predict the future? Although incomplete and inexact, the ability to symbolically displace time greatly enhances human intelligence. With this ability to abstract, humans can learn from the past and plan for the future. Humans can even symbolically anticipate their own death. The symbolic displacement of time is what separates us from non-verbal animals. A dog, for instance, will never be able to comprehend its own limited life span.

The qualitative separation between humans and animals can be likened to the qualitative separation between spiritual beings and humans. Human memory, filled with consolidation errors and decay, is severely flawed. The human grasp of the future is even more woefully incomplete. Anticipating future events consists of crude guesswork based on a few known variables. Spiritual beings, on the other hand, have the ability to *know* all facets of time. The complete experience of *knowing* the past is qualitatively superior than the partial remembering of the past. Likewise, knowing the future is superior to making educated guesses about the future. Turning time, like a block of wood, is a powerful tool with profound ramifications. Knowing time allows spiritual beings to know everything. When NDErs report having access to universal knowledge, they are, in essence, saying that they have access to a fixed entity called time. Everything ever done, everything that will ever be done, is written in the timeline since creation. In other words, if the past is known, all variables are known. If all variables are known, then all future consequences or possibilities are also known. By knowing past and future together, decisions can be made by spiritual beings in accordance to divine will. There are no mistakes made in heaven.

Why are spiritual beings given the keys to time and knowledge whereas humans are not? The experience of time boils down to having different spiritual missions. Spiritual beings directly serve God within the context of eternity. Spiritual beings can serve God best by knowing the future, past, and present. God cannot allow for mistakes in heaven because all tasks are completed in accordance with the divine plan. For instance, a spiritual guide cannot be allowed to lead a human charge astray. The same applies to every assigned mission, no matter the function. Spiritual beings experience the totality of time because they are interconnected with God, the Source of all time. This arrangement does not occur on earth, where the direct interconnection with God has been largely severed. Through free-will, humans are given the choice to serve God. Without divine interconnection, mistakes will be made on earth, repeatedly, whether people choose to serve God or not. Human life is a messy existence. Consequently, time serves an entirely different purpose on school earth.

Time on Earth

Time on earth can be easily taken for granted. People feel the flow of time so naturally unwavering, that few ponder its complexity. Rather, most people approach time in regard to utility. Humans schedule and plan by the calendar and the clock. For major life achievements, like attending college, great swaths of time are required in order to meet long term objectives. Time sets the parameters for what can be accomplished and what cannot. In this regard, there is no greater parameter than certain, impending death. No matter the measure, everything becomes possible, or impossible, through the medium of time. As you read this chapter you are carving out time. Hopefully, there is nothing better for you to do, as you will not get these moments back. In other words, time is free but priceless. Renowned psychologist, Philip Zimbardo, wrote the following aspects about time in his book, The *Time Paradox*:

> Most things that can be possessed - diamonds, gold, hundred dollar bills- can be replenished. New diamond and gold deposits are discovered, and new bills are printed. Such is not the case with time. Nothing that any of us does in this life will allow us to accrue a moment's more time, and nothing will allow us to regain time misspent... Our scarcest resource, time, is actually much more valuable than money.[6]

Time has more value than money because it is a necessary, limited resource. People set goals very early in life to beat with the cadence of time. Parents send children to school in order to prepare for work as adults. Young adults date and marry in order to prepare for family and the propagation of the species. New work goals are set in order for the individual to promote toward greater levels of responsibility. Many working adults also save money to prepare for retirement. Finally, people retire in order to accomplish new goals and rest before physical death. These life phases generally repeat across cultures. But do they have meaning?

If life is truly finite, and God a product of superstition, then everything lacks meaning. Even the continuation of the species ultimately serves no purpose. After all, humans seem to be slowly killing the planet with their unrestrained reproduction and pollution. Without God, Philip Zimbardo's premise, "time is more valuable than money," is just an illusion. Why not just fritter the hours away or seek immediate pleasure if life flickers momentarily. But if there is a God, and time serves a larger purpose, then our short lives become invaluable. The value of life extends far beyond the propagation of the species. Rather, time on earth relates to our eternal mission of growing toward God. Growing in divine purpose does not necessarily hinge on the major life phases, as described. Instead, purpose becomes fulfilled during our moment to moment dance with the flow of linear time - during the *now*. It is within these moments that people define who and what they are. That is the meaning of life.

For the human being, linear time is experienced with the conscious forward flow of the present. Although difficult to quantify, the *now* is a long series of moments of soul awareness. Dr. Zimbardo wrote, "Where can you find purpose? Like success and happiness, our purpose exists in the present, and we constantly strive toward the future to maintain it."[6] God created the human perception of a unidirectional time flow for a special purpose. In the material realm, time maximizes both learning and choice. If people fully knew the future and past, as they do in the spiritual realm, they would consistently make all the right decisions. Mistakes would be avoided because the best future would be clearly understood within the context of a perfectly known past. In other words, decisions would be externally determined by perfect knowledge in relative time. However, there is a cost associated with determinism. People would miss out on the experiential lessons of existence. They would not experience the joys of making good decisions or the pain of making poor decisions. Nor would they experience the thrill of new discovery and accomplishments of personal growth. Constrained by linear time, people are free to create their own destinies. Earth is a realm of choice where good and evil mix. Do we serve ourselves or others? Do we choose to love or hate? Whatever our choices, time will be the medium as to how every individual chooses to be and become.

The primary life choice boils down to this question, "Do we choose to move toward God or rebel against God?" Finite existence forces the choice. We cannot be all people and all things in life. Time narrows human existence, forcing everyone to *prioritize* choices based on personal motivation and values. Some routes refine human nature and bring people closer to the divine. Other paths stagnate or even corrupt. How we choose to fill time in this short life will define who we become in the next life. As previously discussed, we bring ourselves into the spiritual realm after we die. It is for this reason that our brief stay on earth has such monumental importance.

People tend to interpret every personal thought and behavior in isolation. In reality, human behavior is embedded within the tapestry of time. Individual choice ripples across the tapestry. Likewise, the choices of millions ripple back toward the individual. The human brain cannot fathom the complex set of cause and effect factors within any chain of events. The examination of factors may be likened to tracing the branches of an immense tree. Our lives are defined by angular, intersecting branches of experience rather than a sequential set of exclusive decisions. To know "thyself" thereby requires a great deal of introspection and mindfulness. The pursuit of introspection and mindfulness is a difficult path, a continual challenge to the distractible human brain. Yet, it is well worth the effort. Every person can choose between uncountable life pathways. Each pathway leads to a different destination toward God or away from God. Only by knowing the complexities of self can the best individual pathways be ascertained. So, what are the pathways that lead toward God? What are the pathways that lead toward destruction? Although human pathways appear almost infinite, there are three broad, primary pathways chosen during human life. These paths include biology, ego, and divine mission.

Three Pathways in Time

Just about everyone can plead guilty for misspending time. Perhaps a measure of free time becomes healthy when it reduces stress. However, people who waste much of their time may jeopardize their spiritual mission. Time is wasted for a variety of reasons: apathy, disregard for authority, general irresponsible behavior, laziness. The aimless path mostly follows a course of human biological urges: eating, sleeping, intoxication, sex, violence, domination. In other words, the aimless person becomes driven to acquire and maintain a state of self-indulgence. Time has little relevance because immediate pleasures serve no lasting purpose. Furthermore, a person cannot sustain constant pleasures while being unproductive, so they either choose a parasitic or criminal life path. It is a path of entropy.

Entropy pervades the physical universe. The law states that everything in the universe will eventually break down and collapse without outside influence, either through revitalization or rebirth. Our sun, for instance, will eventually explode and create a new star. People's lives will likewise deteriorate if not revitalized by productivity. The aimless life is defined by perpetual self-gratification. Yet, continuous pleasurable fulfillment requires resources. Thus, this parasitic lifestyle becomes unsustainable for most people. Ironically, many people recognize that they can better sustain self-gratification by delaying gratification. This approach requires an individual to recognize the powerful parameters of time. It is the path of ego.

Serving the ego can best be maintained by postponing gratification. In other words, a person may increase gratification by sacrificing immediate pleasures. Imagine the path of a typical politician or business executive. They relentlessly study so that they can later bask in status, power, wealth, and earthly pleasures. Perhaps it is not fair to just pick on politicians or business executives. Many people are likewise motivated by ego, even an art professor such as Howard

Storm. During his life review, Storm witnessed himself erecting a monument of ego. He developed a new perspective about ego while visiting the spiritual realm:

> My life was devoted to building a monument to my ego... All my life, I'd fought a constant undertone of anxiety, fear, dread, and angst. If I could become famous, I could defeat powerlessness and beat death. If I didn't become famous, then I'd die and my whole life would be meaningless.[7]

Storm continued:

> It was horrifying to see how I had become so much like my father, putting status and success above everything else... Of course, one is never good enough because there is always a critic and another level of achievement to conquer.[7]

Howard Storm was motivated by the ego's need to author his own short eternity and defy death. But in the end, Storm was only stagnating. Status has no meaning. Material possessions are equally as empty. There is no mystery as to why Storm feared death. Death looms as a blasting siren of truth. Namely, death reveals the illusory nature of ego within the context of time. There is great wisdom in the old cliché, "You can't take it with you." Everything will be taken away, either gradually throughout life or immediately at death: power, money, material possessions, and health. Thus, the path of ego supersedes the aimless pathway only for the short run. During a moment of existential reflection, while feeling a little bit old, I wrote a poem called 'Sentience I Cling to Thee.' The poem was meant to capture the futility of ego and the law of entropy. I have included a section:

> Sentience I cling to thee
> Young in spirit I hope to be
> Living life under growing compromise
> Cuts my comforts to meager size
> New balances come in myriad form
> Duck I before the next rumbling storm
> Sentience I cling to thee
> Search I harder for my glee
> Life threads turn thinner
> Undo them not saint or sinner

Fewer threads turn brilliant gold
For those who grow hopeless old
Sentience I cling to thee
In my short eternity

Fear pervades the life of the ego-driven person. Whatever has been erected in the name of self may tumble down at any time. The crisis of ego often marches in step with age, especially for people who rely on fame, health, and money to elevate the self. Pick up any gossip magazine and you will likely read about the steady demise of actors and professional sports players, especially those who have worked past their prime. People driven by ego eventually realize, at some level, that their personal empire was built on a foundation of sand. How do people react when they discover everything they believed was just fiction? Some may turn to God. But most will desperately cling to any remaining life opportunities, even if they represent mere morsels of past glory. They will also desperately search for immediate gratification to prop up the self. The wealthy man may marry a young wife. The wealthy woman may spend a fortune on cosmetic surgery. The rich may tighten their control on others in order to maintain the illusion of relevance. Obviously, all efforts to prop up ego are futile in any short eternity. Physical death, the destroyer of earthly idols, looms ever closer as the years pass. This is the human condition. Philip Zimbardo writes about the power of death:

> If you imagine your life as infinite, you are unlikely to value time as more precious than gold and more likely to treat it as ordinary grains of sand on a beach. Ironically, denying death relieves anxiety and psychological stress, but it may also lead you to devalue life, so you may live less fully.[6]

Death motivates people into action in a similar way that a test motivates students to study. Finite time motivates productivity. But to what end? That question is the existential conundrum. People are propelled to succeed by earthly measure only to grow old and die. Without God, productivity becomes just a manmade invention created to fill time. Yet, there exists a third way. The third way values life and respects time. It is the way of divine mission.

Death motivates both the ego-and the mission-driven person into action. However, motivation between these two worldviews could not be more different. For the ego-minded person, death represents the finality of time. Consequently, death motivates people to engage in selfish and self-destructive behaviors out of fear. Instead of confronting these fears, the ego-minded person usually responds by making futile efforts to command time and ignore death. For the mission-minded person, death represents a portal to a greater existence. Life is not all about massing pleasures, but learning. In fact, a full life may even be a painful life. Accordingly, one NDEr wrote:

> Time is only a concept measured here. In the other realm it doesn't exist. So while we may experience pain and sorrow on earth, it is only a second in the grand scheme of things. We have an eternity to live and in reality, souls never really die. (NDERF #1634)

Death represents the closure of a mission phase, perhaps one of many faced throughout eternity. The mission-minded individual is motivated to accomplish various mission milestones before death. Mission milestones are usually expressed through acts of service toward family and community. Due to the vast needs of the world, mission-minded people feel the weight of time. They are motivated to help people beyond their allotted time on earth. For them, time is invaluable.

Although lofty goals may be admirable, the mission-minded person does not need to burden themselves with saving the world alone. We work collectively. Different missions may be individualized based on ability, need, and available time. There is no need to overburden ourselves and burn out. Unfortunately, too many people have the opposite problem. Ego-driven people waste precious time despite our planet crying out in need. As discussed in chapter nine, there are many distractions from our mission in the modern world, especially when diversions have replaced people. Prioritizing purposeful choices becomes more confusing in a modern, hedonistic culture. Similarly, Zimbardo writes, "Cell phones ring incessantly; e-mails pile up in our in-boxes; TV shows; movies; and books cry out for our attention. Many people in modern societies report feeling a time crunch, a sense of being continually hurried and pressed for time."[6]

Time vampires try to steal from us every day. Advertisers will steal your time and money. The 24-hour news media will hook-in your time with conflict and fear. Media entertainment seduces away your time by providing gratifications for a profit. Social networks lure your time away with hollow promises of connectedness. In a hedonistic society, where is the time to love one another as part of God's mission?

This artificial crunch of time only distracts people from what is truly important. At a fundamental level, the ego-minded person is always pressed for time. There is never enough time for them to self-promote because they can never reach their ultimate goal, to become omnipotent and eternal. The mission-minded person is also pressed for time. They want to accomplish their mission to its fullest. The former path creates fear and other emotional and cognitive correlates: anxiety, power, jealousies, anger, and division. The latter creates love and its emotional and cognitive correlates: growth, tolerance, respect, cooperation, and equality. It is up to each one of us to choose our own life pathway.

It should be noted that the three pathways described in this section are not mutually exclusive. People present with a varying mixture of ego, mission, and biology. Not even the most saintly person can completely replace ego with mission. Unfortunately, too many people choose a mixture of biology and ego as their primary pathway in life. They never fully consider the final destination of their path. This point has real world application. Our world, pulled apart by competing egos, does not appear to be heading in a very positive direction. The planet desperately needs a spiritual transformation based on a change in collective mission. Interestingly, spirituality around the world does appear to be changing. As we will see in the next chapter, these changes will continue to take course over the fullness of time.

CHAPTER SEVENTEEN

A CALL FOR SPIRITUAL TRANSFORMATION

People I meet tend to feel uneasy about this period of time in history. In fact, I sense an undercurrent of fear regarding world developments; economic worry, political infighting, environmental change. Some people are beginning to ask, "What is to become of us?" Perhaps a better question would be, "How can I help turn it around?" Many believe they can't make a difference, that they are just a pawn in a larger chess match. But even a pawn helps determine the outcome of the game. Events in the world are complicated, multi-dimensional, and interconnected. When we hate, we reverberate negativity across the tapestry of time and space. Likewise, we send positive influence across the tapestry when we love. Because everything is intricately interconnected, every individual influences the future in profound and mysterious ways. It is human hubris to think that we are aware of how people influence one another. Working as a psychologist, I have glimpsed these intangible causal threads. I am often amazed at the unintentional outcome of therapy sessions. Sometimes the most offhand, minor comments may have the most impact. Hopefully, clients respond by dealing with people in a more effective, loving way. If so, they will positively impact others in a cascade of cause and effect reactions. In this manner, many individuals could have been influenced by a single conversation.

One does not have to be a therapist to pull and push on the tapestry. World history has hinged on unseen dynamics; a snide comment here, a kind act there. We even nudge strangers who we will never meet. People remain largely unaware of the tapestry due to its inherent complexity. Acts of influence are often hidden because they become embedded, or blended, with the collective influence of various factors. Yet, even the most minimal, hidden causal factors can influence the future; everything we do matters more than we realize. Consequently, if we want to save the planet, each of us needs to send our love into the future, even if distantly. Individuals can even make large changes just through simple acts of caring. Sending out love does not have to follow a highly visible plan. Love can be as simple as helping a neighbor or volunteering towards a local cause.

I have observed that many people feel insignificant in the world. They can't fathom that God takes notice of them, much less utilizes their talents for good. Self-degradation puts limits on God. God does not differentiate the importance of the small from the large. God knows how small individuals significantly impact the tapestry. Conversely, God knows how each group impacts the tapestry, be it a tribe, race, nation, or species.

God could run the universe without assistance. However, God empowers trillions of sentient beings, scattered throughout the universe, the opportunity to co-create on the individual and group level. So far, we have explored how God co-creates with the individual to facilitate personal growth. In this chapter, we will examine how God co-creates with the individual to grow the human species. First, we will look at our individual responsibility to co-create with God. Next, we will discuss how the human species is falling short in their collective mission to serve God. Finally, we will examine the need for a wide-scale spiritual transformation.

Co-creation Responsibilities

People do not typically acknowledge the serious responsibilities that accompany the co-creation of reality. Such a lack of insight may be understandable due to our severed connection with God in the material realm. The vision of well-meaning people becomes myopic. They may think, "Why should I bother? The world will go on suffering with or without me." They fail to understand that human development is orchestrated by an all-powerful conductor. The conductor collects a wide variety of musicians, playing different instruments, to produce the complex tenor and cadences of a first-class symphony. Likewise, God utilizes the talents of every person to make positive global change. Unfortunately, many lack faith in themselves as agents of change because they minimize the power of God in their lives.

Most spiritual people, regardless of religious faith, intellectually accept the omnipotence of God. Such recognition may reflect only a fuzzy appreciation of God's true power. To be clear, God is the only source of power in the universe. The great Christian theologian, C.S. Lewis, uses a garden analogy to describe God's power and our complete dependency on divine dominion. He wrote:

> And when the garden is in its full glory the gardener's contributions to that glory will still have been in a sense paltry compared with those of nature. Without life springing from the earth, without rain, light and heat descending from the sky, he could do nothing. When he has done all, he has merely encouraged here and discouraged there, powers and beauties that have a different source.[1]

The power of nature comes solely from God. The laws of physics serve as the medium for our existence. By logical deduction, one must have a lawmaker to create and maintain a perfect set of exacting physical operations. Hugh Ross, an astronomer and Christian apologetic, notated twenty-five physical laws in the universe that are finely tuned to maintain life. He asserts that the universe maintains efficient order through molecules, ratio of elements, gravitational forces, electromagnetic forces, uniformity of radiation, and so forth. If one could change any of these laws, even by a small deviation, life could not exist.[2] In other words, every person, from the greatest to the smallest, could not exist without intelligent design. Human beings could not exist one moment without God. Consequently, we exist in a state of complete dependency.

Human helplessness demonstrates, in part, our dependent relationship with the Creator. God's perfect love is based upon giving whereas human love is based on need. C.S. Lewis, elaborated, "We begin at the real beginning, with love as the Divine energy. The primal love is Gift-love. In God there is no hunger that needs to be filled, only plenteousness that desires to give."[1] Lewis continues by using a rather earthy analogy to describe human dependency, "If

I may dare the biological image, God is a 'host' who deliberately creates His own parasites: causes us to be that we may exploit and 'take advantage of' Him. Herein is love."[1]

God delegates a degree of management of the universe in order to share creation with imperfect beings that are constantly in want. Herein is not just love, but unfathomable love. Related theological questions run deep. Foremost, why does God choose to co-create existence if God does not lack for anything? Part of the answer, as relayed by Howard Storm, involves God's desire to create. He writes, "They explained to me in a way that I could understand that God is like an artist who creates for the sheer pleasure of creating."[3] In addition to God's creative force, I personally believe that God desires to share love, as a natural extension of God-self, and furthermore be loved back by independently minded beings. Simply, God chooses not to exist alone. God desires our need-love, like a mother values the need-love from an infant who mainly wants to be fed, held, and changed. Yet, even need-love cannot be coerced. Just like a mature parent doesn't force love from children, God doesn't force us to love. C.S. Lewis continued:

> There is of course a sense in which no one can give to God anything which is not already His: and if it is already His, what have you given? But since it is only too obvious that we can withhold ourselves, our wills and hearts, from God, we can, in that sense, also give them. What is His by right and would not exist for a moment if it ceased to be His (as the song is the singer's), He has nevertheless made ours in such a way that we can freely offer it back to Him.[1]

Every person, great or small, lacks inherent value apart from God. At the same time, every person has great value because of God. People are gifted with value because God bestows it. Human beings certainly have not earned the right to co-create, or even to exist. Everything has been bestowed on us as a *gift of love*. We humans fail to fully appreciate the value and power of God's gifts because we only understand the miniscule and the mundane; we mostly focus on personal troubles and daily tribulations. Most people just try to get through the hectic day and forget about their responsibility to fulfill their role within the divine plan. Put more succinctly, humans lack perspective on what is truly important.

Despite the infinite vastness of the Creator, every individual shares an intimate relationship with God interconnected with the One. The

Creator's love is not dependent on the individual's size, power, or level of intelligence. God's love is a gift-love with no strings attached. Relatedly, the following NDEr wrote the following:

> The Light speaks to me, "Andy, do not be afraid. Andy, I love you. Andy, we love you." The Light - It actually knows me. The Light knows my name. The Light called me Andy. Surrounding the central Light form are millions and millions of other Lights welcoming me back home. I know them all and they know me, we are all pieces of the same Light. I hear myself say, "It's good to be back home." We are All home together again. (NDERF #687)

As described, the intimate, personal nature of God is not just a wish advocated by religious mystics. God intimately knows and loves every person, even though the individual is just one of a trillion sharing the universe. Complete intimacy is made possible because God can simultaneously interact with innumerable beings. This ability explains how God can hear billions of prayers and still organize and direct the universe.

Personally, I take special notice when someone bestows a gift on me, especially when that person expects nothing in return. I try to respond with gratitude, expressing my appreciation for even the smallest of gifts. How should I then respond to God for gifting me with my very existence? How should I respond to God gifting me with free will and co-creation? With every freedom comes responsibility and education. Inmates often fail to realize this truth. They want the freedom to do whatever they want whenever they want to do it. However, their selfish orientation toward independence has nothing to do with real freedom. Allow me to provide a personal example. I had the freedom to choose to become a psychologist. With that freedom came a great deal of responsibility. Namely, I had to relentlessly study for eight years, pass a licensing examination, and maintain the ethics of the profession throughout my career. When God gives us the freedom to co-create out of love, it is our individual and collective responsibility to meet the necessary requirements that come with that choice. If we exercise the freedom to choose God, we cannot choose and still pretend that we can act with full independence. Choosing a path of righteousness entails a variety of responsibilities under God's authority, including spiritual education and service to others. This is what is required for co-creating in a responsible manner. This is not the path of ego. Co-creating responsibilities should come naturally, however, for the humble. After all, the humble genuinely recognize God's authority and appreciate the gifts of existence, co-creation, and unconditional love.

On earth, we are called to love other people in accordance with our individually assigned mission. Doing anything less would amount to failure. What a waste it would have been if I paid large sums of money to study to be a psychologist in graduate school, but refused to study. Likewise, what a waste it would be to be gifted with life from God just to build illusionary monuments to ego. In any case, lapses in responsibility only indicate a misuse of freedom. If every person remotely respected the true power and scope of God's bestowed gifts, there would be collective change and a true transformation on earth. Unfortunately, the collective human response to God's gifts appears to be weak.

Falling Short in Mission

I am uncertain whether humanity has morally progressed, or digressed, based on my limited knowledge of world history. Regardless, God is fully aware of all human accomplishments and failings: past, present, and future. God is also aware of all group dynamics, ranging from racial relationships to international dialogue. NDErs report that the human species has been assigned a collective mission similar to the individual mission. Specifically, humanity has been tasked with elevating the world toward the good through collective acts of love. Because millions contribute to mission, accomplishments should be measured by trends and trajectories. If humanity orientates their path toward God, then our species will solve problems in the context of love. Consequently, humanity will enjoy the fruits of the spirit and facilitate a new era of harmony. Looking at the sordid history of humanity, the realist would scoff at this possibility, calling such a proposition "pie in the sky" wishful thinking. I concede to that sobering analysis, but only to a point. Although fallible human beings are incapable of creating any measure of utopia, we are capable of doing better than our current collective behavior would indicate.

One can point to bright spots in recent history, such as increased democratization and tolerance in parts of the world. A few famous people have recently modeled a brighter path for non-violent change, such as Mahatma Gandhi, Martin Luther King, and Nelson Mandela. Moreover, countless anonymous "saints" have also tirelessly labored for a better future. Will their work, and our work, be enough to significantly elevate the world? The benchmark of future success might be less racism, fewer wars, and less poverty. Cooperation between nations should help solve social, economic, and environmental problems. Conversely, if humanity orientates their path away from God, and embraces tribalism, then ego and hate will lead to a slow path of global decline. Divisiveness will generate disharmony. The benchmark of failure would be more individual conflicts, exploitation of the weak, environmental degradation, and war. To secure our own future, humanity will need to collectively sacrifice for the greater good. A number of NDErs indicate that humanity faces a critical period on earth. One NDEr reported the following:

> There are other planets and other beings out there, but for humans on the earth this is a very important time. We seem to be on a precipice and either total destruction or a better way seems to be on a razor edge. This love/Light is not going to do anything to us, or smite us. We do it all and we create it all. We choose by our love for others and helping - or selfishness. I was made aware of some things coming up that are very important but this again was blocked. It seemed as if two scenarios could play out on earth, one of them made me so sad but again I can't remember it, it's blocked. (NDERF #2366)

Apocalyptic themes are common throughout religious doctrine. Some people teach that God punishes sin through disease and catastrophe. Contrary to these religious themes, NDE warnings do not attribute catastrophic destruction to an angry God. Rather, NDErs understand that humanity should hold itself responsible for the outcomes of their collective choices. In this regard, one can connect clear cause and effect relationships between human greed and subsequent suffering. Most wars are caused by greed and hate. Economic collapse usually has roots in greed. Poverty may be caused by human exploitation and lack of educational opportunities. The list, of course, goes on.

The reader may ask, "If God loves people unconditionally, why doesn't God save us from ourselves?" The answer can be found in the last NDERF submission, "We do it all and we create it all." God not only preserves individual free will, but collective freedom. Humans are allowed great latitude of autonomy. God allows nations the freedom to make terrible blunders in order to teach human leaders responsibility. Does God ever intervene in national affairs? Surprisingly, the answer is affirmative when the collective mission becomes threatened. God does not want the human species to self-destruct. God does everything possible to nudge our species away from our own destructive nature while not violating human free will. Specifically, God nudges world leaders to act in the best interest of humanity. During an exchange with Jesus and spiritual beings during his NDE, Howard Storm was provided with some detail about how God influences human affairs:

> God allows war to happen when you are determined to be at war. God has influenced you in the course of your history to find more peaceful methods to resolve your differences. The vast majority of wars that you have desired have not taken place because God subtly influenced people to prevent war. There have been occasions when God has let you suffer the consequences of your desire for war. Every war is a lesson that war is undesirable, and that you need to learn better ways of achieving harmony with one another.[3]

God hates violence. Those who advocate peace are working in concert with divine will. Conversely, those who advocate violence in God's name are acting in sacrilege. Fortunately, God subtly influences national leaders, and others of influence, toward the good. With the help of spiritual beings, God influences leaders through the gentle nudge, as was discussed in chapter eleven. God also influences humanity by giving us direct warnings. In antiquity, prophets are said to have served that purpose. In the modern era, warnings have been issued through a direct conduit, namely the near-death experience. New warnings may be necessary because humanity has entered a new technologically advanced era; a dangerous time when irresponsible action can cause lasting, irreversible damage. Note that God revealed two possible scenarios in the last NDERF submission. Although the details were not revealed, a clear message was sent. Specifically, humankind must love each other or face a worsening, very trying future.

The reader may also wonder why God does not provide people with more detailed, clear warnings. Regarding the last submission, one may ask why God showed the NDEr two pathways instead of one. Doesn't God already know the future? God's knowledge about the future is not the issue. God knows time as a singular entity. Rather, God presents the future in a framework of choice to ensure human self-determination. In this manner, God issues warnings without telling people what they must do. The easy path of commanding does not teach us to love independently. Although God does not dictate human affairs,

God sometimes issues warnings about global dangers to nudge the world toward a better path. In the next submission, the NDEr shares a warning that echoes back to the recent real estate bubble. He reported the following:

> The economic turmoil we are now going through is one of those "world events" that was preset. People have a choice as to how to react to these events. From what I was shown, the spiritual way is to help each other and help those in need. This is the ultimate act of love. But there is also the choice of becoming more protective and self-centered; less sharing and keeping one's own possessions... So, what choices will the majority make? It is still to be seen. I was shown in 1981 that this time would come and that banks were paper empires, built on paper and nothing more. But, too, so are many other businesses, paper empires, built to collapse under pressure. How do people react to all of this? This is the key event and will test many. Will they reach out and take care of each other, or will they become more and more self-centered and protective of the material? There are always choices in this, just to determine which choices individuals will make. (NDERF #2932)

This submitted warning should not come as a surprise to anyone following recent world economic developments. According to the World Bank, international debt is approaching 57 trillion dollars at the time of this writing. Some countries have debts exceeding 1000% over their gross domestic product.[4] The fiscal problems keep worsening each year, without any clear resolution. The trend is not sustainable. Are there more economic bubbles ready to burst? If the last NDE submission is correct, then economic turmoil will indeed increase. How humanity will recover will be a matter of love. To minimize suffering, selfless giving will need to be a collective response. Otherwise, the gap between the rich and poor will further widen. Can humanity choose loving opportunities that naturally arise during periods of challenge and adversity? With eyes on God, anything is possible. The right decisions will be made only if humanity uses its God-given freedom to rule the world responsibly. The choice will be ours to make.

Other warnings are scattered throughout NDERF submissions. Some talk about potential pandemics and local wars. The next NDE submission discusses environmental change, perhaps a natural response to climate change. The author wrote:

The next vision was of floods, many of them spilling across the earth on different continents in different seasons. I am again walking among it, feeling the force and taking in the smell of death. Hundreds of lives and acres upon acres of crops were lost as well as hundreds of stock and wild animals floating away into the abyss. (NDERF # 737)

Global warming is a topic of controversy. It is not my intention to engage in a political debate; such controversy muddies the central message of this book. As a person maintaining a strong scientific leaning, I am personally concerned about the flow of scientific data supporting global warming. If the reader is open to consider the possibility of human-induced climate change, I recommend reading an eye-opening article, *Rising Seas*, in the September 2013 edition of National Geographic magazine.[5] Colorful graphs and maps present a not-so-appealing accumulation of scientific information about global warming, including estimates that ocean levels will rise over five feet by the year 2100. Such a rise in sea levels will have monumental impact, flooding many coastal cities from Shanghai to New York City. Whether global warming is real or not does not depend on any human belief system. It is an issue of atmospheric chemistry and physics, not politics. If global warming is real phenomenon, then flooding will not be humankind's only nemesis. Rather, temperature rises will also be associated with deadly storms, droughts, disease, migration, insurance collapse, and economic collapse.

Regardless of one's personal belief about global warming, there are countless opportunities for a caring, civically-oriented person to change the world for the better. People who are focused on divine mission should not be complacent in their mission. There is an increasing urgency for action. It is no accident that God is giving us warnings at this time in history. Healthier global trends need to be forged in order to prevent an unstoppable downward spiral on earth. Are there enough people heeding God's warning to counter those sacrificing others for their own ego? The answer depends on whether there are enough people listening to the call for spiritual transformation.

Spiritual Transformation

Christianity, in pure form, has waged a spiritual revolution for approximately two thousand years. The Christian call for spiritual transformation began with the teachings of Jesus. First millennium Jews were searching for a messiah to liberate them from Roman occupation. Clearly, Jesus did not fit their expectations. Jesus was a spiritual revolutionary; he facilitated transformation through the message of love, not violence. Political revolutions may include righteous anger, civil revolt, coup, violent uprising, or civil war. Spiritual revolution, conversely, requires that the long battles are waged between the soul and baser human drives. Spiritual battles involve revolts against hatred, coups by a loving heart, and a civil war between temptation and goodness. A genuine spiritual manifesto should list the many qualities of unconditional love: tolerance, greater equality, respect, sacrifice, mutual cooperation, humbleness, and forgiveness. The roots of revolution start with the individual but are quickly spread to the community by acts of love. Unlike political revolution, spiritual change must be voluntary and not forced through coercion. There can be no more inquisitions. Forced change will only lead to strife, violence, and suffering. Divisiveness will only sicken the world, not save it.

Spiritual revolution has been advocated by the near-death experience. A small number of NDErs learned about a global transformation though their interaction with spiritual beings. For instance, Jesus and other spiritual beings reportedly told Howard Storm, "The world is at the beginning of a major transformation. It will be a spiritual revolution that will affect every person in the world."[3] Storm further writes, "God is going to awaken every person to be the person he or she was created to be."[3] Imagine the world transformed by love. Living in relative harmony, nations would not have to invest in prisons, armies, lawyers, and police. With saved resources, think about the projects humanity could construct. Regrettably, there are worldwide elements moving in the opposite direction. In my line of correctional work, for instance, I can only be discouraged by the overflow of prisoners. Before a spiritual revolution can occur, a great deal of spiritual footwork will first need to be completed. Unfortunately, people will need to act quickly.

World events appear to be reaching a point of critical mass. Time, the relentless master of change, will force a response to pressing global challenges. Most global problems are insidious, not apocalyptic. Humanity may have decades, even a century, before life becomes irreversibly difficult. Yet, these challenges are just beginning to advance on daily life, at least in the United States. One can only hope that spiritual transformation will be stronger and sooner rather than weaker. Unfortunately, the latter appears to be our current course. Nations have not courageously tackled modern day problems because of the high cost of commitment. Why would political parties propose unpopular sacrifices when responsibility can be deferred to the next generation? Shortsightedness will fail to serve humanity as the enormity of earth's problems will only increase with time, as will the sacrifices needed to enact viable solutions. With current levels of complacency, the danger will be that humankind will not act in time.

Global problems require world cooperation. People from many walks in life must band together and work toward common solutions. There are many activists, religious or otherwise, who have already started this process. People who believe in the near-death experience can help vanguard cooperative efforts for global change as ambassadors from the spiritual realm. Specifically, they can convey God's messages of warning and suggest opportunities for change. Although a mass effort is required, change starts with the individual. The individual can create change through non-violent activist groups, receptive political parties, loving churches and other religious organizations. The individual can also express opinions by writing articles, publishing books, ministering to those in need, and engaging in one-to-one discussions. Even small efforts matter. Every constructive effort sends little shockwaves through the tapestry, like motions of an insect reverberating across a spider web.

People who share near-death experiences typically advocate for global change. After all, they are shown disturbing trends that most people do not see. Consequently, the NDE has the potential to be a force for positive change if others are willing to listen. Fortunately, the world is beginning to accept the message of the near-death experience. Thirty or forty years ago, NDErs were reticent to share their stories for fear of rejection and ridicule. Today, the near-death experience has been embraced by large segments of Western society. I was recently encouraged by reading *Love is the Link*,[6] by Dr. Pamela M. Kircher, M.D, who has long worked as a physician specializing in hospice care. Moreover, she has taught about the near-death experiences within various medical forums, primarily training medical caretakers to respect patients who report life after death. Dr. Kircher feared widespread rejection by her peers when she first began her work. Instead of rejection, students not only embraced the NDE, but some shared their own stories. Perhaps even more amazingly, she had the same experience speaking to a group of interfaith leaders. Her experience supports the notion that near-death experiences have already impacted Western culture.

Send Out Your Love

A spiritual transformation based on love sounds magnificent. To some, it may sound even quaint, like a feel-good Hollywood movie. But love is rarely simple or easy. A revolution based on love will require making courageous, difficult choices. Undoubtedly, there may be hard work involved and unexpected obstacles, especially when people risk retribution by dedicating their love for a new cause. The revolution of love may even lead to collective sacrifice for the greater good. People will need to be tolerant and cooperative at the local, national, and global level. In democratic nations, populations need to use their votes to hold governments accountable for engaging in self-serving practices. Sending love into the future means protecting the future. In this regard, heavy investment in science will be required to resolve serious medical and environmental threats. Spiritual transformation will also require people to turn off their electronics and become involved in the community; neighbor helping neighbor. And the list goes on. In sum, sending out love requires more than sending out well-wishes, smiles, and prayers. It will require a high level of personal responsibility and dedication.

Clearly, there is little that is revolutionary about any of these suggestions. There are various organizations working toward these very goals today. It has been my impression that most people desire peace and the creation of a better world. There is reason to be optimistic. Societies have risen to meet challenges in the past, such as the Great Depression in the 20th century. The two primary obstacles of change are lack of awareness and commitment to sacrifice for a common goal. Bottom line: more people need to learn how to love and more people need to teach love.

If the majority refuses to heed the call for spiritual transformation, it will probably never occur. After all, nations have rarely worked in tandem with God's will. Empires and nations have been built on competition and power. Based on world history, one may think it naïve to expect real change. Howard Storm thought the same, but was corrected during his near-death experience. He was shown a future where people lived in peaceful harmony after a period of increased struggle and strife.[3] How is that possible? Again, it can happen through spiritual revolution. There have been rare glimmers of hope in recent history. After World War II, the United States rebuilt Japan and Germany from the ashes under the Marshall Plan. The U.S. forgave its former enemies, despite the atrocities of war, and acted with benevolence. The Marshall Plan still bears good fruit as Germany and Japan remain two staunch allies for the United States. Can nations find that cooperative, loving spirit again?

Spiritual transformation will happen. It is just a matter of when. The question becomes, how many tough lessons we will choose to endure before we heed the call? Eben Alexander wrote hopefully, "Horrible and all-powerful as evil sometimes seemed to be in a world like ours, in the larger picture love was overwhelmingly dominant, and it would ultimately be triumphant."[7] All souls grow toward God in the fullness of time. Whatever blunders are made on earth, good will someday triumph over evil, even if it takes eons. We have God's promise on that. It is always important to remember that the eternal story far exceeds the human lifespan. Whatever turmoil may come, our individual pain is only temporary. Our main responsibility, for now and forever, is to send out our love to others. Part of realizing this primary responsibility requires people to appreciate the "big picture." I will use my own experience to illustrate this point.

Personal Reflections about the Big Picture

Like a protracted game of dominoes, my life has been playing out in small, steady increments. As I reflect back, I can visualize how the tiles in my life lay together in a long track. The little decisions made in my life amount to an overreaching gestalt. This means that the whole of my life is greater than the sum of its parts. The gestalt represents nothing less than a spiritual transformation. The gradual process of transformation started ever since a deceased inmate's sister challenged my faith thirteen years ago. In my life, gradual transformation has elevated me to a greater sense of purpose and peace. Although I remain frustratingly imperfect, I have never experienced as much spiritual connection as I do right now in my life. My spiritual path has slowly looped upwards, albeit with some fluctuation, to bring me to this new place in life.

I believe that learning about the near-death experience was the most powerful catalyst for personal change. By NDErs sharing their experiences, I have gained macroscopic perspective to the purpose of my life and the lives of others. In other words, NDErs have taught me about the "big picture." I have made every effort to share the "big picture" throughout this book: life after death, nature of eternal soul, mission, unconditional love, making God-consistent choices, diversity, time, the future of humanity, and spiritual transformation. As I reflect on what I have learned and written, I am duly impressed by the grandeur of reality. As the broader truth sinks in, I find myself moving away from the mundane. I do not want to waste precious time being entertained, seeking temporary power over others, or building transitory monuments to ego. I aim to think big instead of small. I aspire to see time holistically rather than as a linear flow of now. I seek to implement my personal mission given to me by God. Most importantly, I aspire to focus on what truly matters, to love others to the best of my human ability.

How could I ever wallow in despair? I have so much to look forward to in this life and in the next. I eagerly look forward to my going home to the spiritual realm. Although I do not seek death, I no longer fear death. By living a purposeful life on earth, I anticipate feeling gratitude by knowing that my mission on school earth has been well worth the effort. I also look forward to being bathed in the bliss of unconditional love, of being reunited with deceased loved ones, Jesus, and the Source of all existence. As a seeker of knowledge, I eagerly anticipate exploring the universe by tapping into the knowledge of everything. All the questions I now struggle with will finally be answered. Moreover, I anticipate being given a new work assignment as a spiritual being. As I move forward into eternity with new missions, I will be adding important threads to my ongoing spiritual transformation as well as the tapestry of the universe.

I hope that the present book has challenged you, the reader, to also think big. I wrote this book with a soul passion. I now understand, upon recent reflection, that my passion was based on my desire to inspire people to embrace love and their mission. Anyone can choose to embrace the divine. The wandering soul only needs to recognize its own eternal value. Radical spiritual transformation can occur when each individual knows that he or she is always loved by God, completely, without any strings attached. On a broader scale, I hope that this book inspires enough people to make a collective difference in the world. Probably the impact of any singular effort, such as this book, will be important but limited. But combined with other efforts, the power of God's people can nudge the world on the right side of the razor's edge.

Spiritual transformation can happen in the world. I know, because it happened to me. Some readers also know based on their own spiritual journey. This may be particularly true for those who have returned from the other side. Yet, there is hope for everyone, regardless of personal experience and history. For the struggling reader searching for spiritual direction, you too can forge a path toward the divine. There are many paths up the mountain. Some may walk a path of religious tradition. Others may transform a small part of the world. Still others may walk a path guided by the near-death experience. No matter the course of the journey, every legitimate path of love leads a person closer to God. So, whatever spiritual venue you choose, the most important thing to do is to send out your love in everything you do.

Some people will heed the call for spiritual transformation whereas others will choose a path of ego. Clearly, I wish that no one is left behind in realizing God's big picture. Such concern exemplifies my purpose in writing this book. The act of writing this book has certainly changed me in subtle and profound ways. To every reader, I sincerely hope that this book has served to advance your own spiritual journey.

REFERENCES

PROLOGUE

1. Long, J. (2010). *Evidence of the afterlife: The science of near-death experiences. History of religious ideas: From the stone age to the eleusinian mysteries*, volume 1. New York: Harper One: 2.

2. Kübler-Ross, E. (1992). *On life after death.* New York: Quality Paperback Book Club: 31.

1. THE REVOLUTION OF MEANING

1. Eliade, M. (1978). *A history of religious ideas.* Chicago: The University of Chicago Press: 11.

2. May, R. (1983). *The discovery of being.* New York: W. W. Norton & Company: 59.

3. Yalom, I. (1980). *Existential psychotherapy.* New York: Basic Books, Yalom Family Trust: 43, 479.

4. Becker, E. (1971). *The birth and death of meaning.* New York: Free Press: 112, 13, 139, 188, 197.

2. EMPIRICAL SUPPORT FOR THE NEAR-DEATH EXPERIENCE

1. Long, J. (2010). *Evidence of the afterlife: The science of near-death experiences*. New York: Harper One: 33, 151-155, 139, 4, 8.

2. Peart, N. (2011). *Far and away: A prize every time*. Toronto: ECW Press: 283.

3. van Lommel, P., van Wees, R., Meyers, V., Elfferich, I. (2001). Near-death experience in survivors of cardiac arrest: A prospective study in the Netherlands. *The Lancet*, 358, 2039-2042.

4. van Lommel. P. (2004). *A Reply to Shermer: Medical Evidence for NDE's*. Retrieved from http://dailygrail.com/Essays/2004/12/Shermer-

5. Johnson, M.K., Foley, M.A., Suengas, A.G., & Raye, C.L. (1988). Phenomenal characteristics of memories for perceived and imagined autobiographical events. *Journal of Experimental Psychology: General*, 177 (4), 371–376. doi:10.1037/0096-3445.117.4.371

6. Thonnard, M., Charland-Verville, V., Bredard, S., Dehon, H., Ledoux, D., Laureys, S., & Vanhaudenhuyse, A. (2013). Characteristics of near-death experience memories as compared to real and imagined event memories. *PLoS ONE 8*(3): e57620. doi:10.1371/journal.pone.0057620

7. Kübler-Ross, E. (1992). *On life after death*. New York: Quality Paperback Book Club: 9.

8. Moody, R. (2000). *Life after life*. New York: Harper One.

9. Beauregard, M., & O'Leary, D. (2008). *The spiritual brain: A neuroscientist's case for the existence of soul*. New York: Harper Collins: 294.

10. May, R. (1983). *The discovery of being*. New York, W. W. Norton & Company: 94.

11. Kuhn, T. (1970). *The structure of scientific revolutions*. Chicago: The University of Chicago Press: 66, 111.

3. WE ARE NOT ONLY HUMAN

1. (1973) In *Merriam-Webster's New Collegiate Dictionary*. Springfield, MA: Merriam-Webster, Inc.

2. *Carl Jung biography*. (2014). Retrieved from http://www.carl-jung.net/biography.html

3. Jung, C. (1969). *The collected works of C.G. Jung* (Vol 11 *Psychology and religion: West and east)*. New Jersey: Princeton University Press: CW11 par 154, CW11 par 153, CW 9/2 par 257, CW 9/2 par 264, CW11 par 427, CW11 par 398.

4. Alexander, E. (2012). *Proof of heaven: A neurosurgeon's journey into the afterlife*. New York: Simon and Shuster Paperbacks: 81, 155, 161.

5. Moorjani, A. (2012). *Dying to be me: My journey from cancer, to near death, to true healing*. New York: Hay House Inc: 151, 144, 71-72.

6. van Lommel. P. (2004). *A Reply to Shermer: Medical Evidence for NDE's*. Retrieved from http://dailygrail.com/Essays/2004/12/Shermer-

7. Bandura, A. (1986). *Social foundations of thought and action: A social cognitive theory*. New Jersey: Prentice Hall, Inc., Englewood Cliffs: 116, 125, 125.

8. Skinner, B. F. (1953). *Science and human behavior*. New York: MacMillan.

9. Storm, H. (2005). *My descent into death: A second chance at life*. New York: Doubleday, a division of Random House Inc: 56, 48.

10. May, R. (1983). *The discovery of being*. New York: W. W. Norton & Company: 147.

11. Dietz, L. (2012). *Wise Mind*. Retrieved from http://dbtselfhelp.com/html/wise_mind.html

12. Seligman, M. (2002). *Authentic happiness: Using the new positive psychology to realize your potential for lasting fulfillment*. New York: The Free Press: 109.

13. O'Brien, B. (2013, March 20). *Right mindfulness: A foundation of Buddhist practice*. Retrieved from http://buddhism.about.com/od/theeightfoldpath/a/right-mindfulness.htm

14. Kübler-Ross, E. (1992). *On life after death*. New York: Quality Paperback Book Club: 37.

Near-Death Experience Research Foundation. *Current NDERF: Individual NDE experiences*. Retrieved from http://www.nderf.org/NDERF/NDE_Archives/NDERF_NDEs.htm

4. THE SPLENDID SOUL

1. Carman, E., & Carman, N. J. (2003). *Plato's myrth of er: A near-death experience?* Retrieved from http://www.cosmiccradle.com/plato.html

2. Moody, R. (1975). *Life after life.* Atlanta: Mockingbird Books.

3. Parnia, S. (2013). *Erasing death: The science that is rewriting the boundaries between life and death.* New York: Harper One: 9-10, 23.

4. Brown, S. K., & Bean, F. D. (2006, October). *Assimilation models, old and new: Explaining a long-term process.* Retrieved from www.migrationinformation.org/USfocus/display.cfm?ID=

5. Moorjani, A. (2012). *Dying to be me: My journey from cancer, to near death, to true healing.* New York: Hay House Inc: 73, 62.

6. Williams R.W., & Herrup, K. (1988). The control of neuron number. *Annual Review of Neuroscience,* 11, 423–453.

7. Beck, A., Rush, J., Shaw, B., & Emery, G. (1979). *Cognitive therapy of depression.* New York: The Guilford Press.

8. Alexander, E. (2012). *Proof of heaven: A neurosurgeon's journey into the afterlife.* New York: Simon and Shuster Paperbacks: 82-83, 102-103.

9. Funder, D.C. (2010). *The personality puzzle.* New York: W.W. Norton & Company, Inc.

10. Schachter, S. & Singer, J. E. (1962). Cognitive, social, and physiological determinants of emotional state. *Psychological Review,* 69(5), 379-399.

Near-Death Experience Research Foundation. *Current NDERF: Individual NDE experiences.* Retrieved from http://www.nderf.org/NDERF/NDE_Archives/NDERF_NDEs.htm

5. GOD'S OWN OPEN ROAD

1. Moorjani, A. (2012). *Dying to be me: My journey from cancer, to near death, to true healing.* New York: Hay House Inc: 65.

2. Alexander, E. (2012). *Proof of heaven: A neurosurgeon's journey into the afterlife.* New York: Simon and Shuster Paperbacks: 46, 150, 151, 45, 83.

3. Hawking, S. (1996). *A brief history of time.* New York: Bantam Books: 68.

4. Chaisson, E., & McMillan, C. (2011). *Astronomy today.* San Francisco: Pearson: 232.

5. Carter, C. (2010). *Science and the near-death experience: How consciousness survives death.* Rochester: Inner Traditions: 38-41, 59.

6. Anderson, M. (2009, February). Entangled life. *Discover Magazine,* 61.

7. Cohen S., Porac C., & Ward L. (1984). *Sensation and perception.* (2nd ed.). London: Academic Press: 52, 91.

8. Cytowic, R., Eagleman, D. (2011). *Wednesday is indigo blue: Discovering the brain of synesthesia.* Cambridge: MIT Press: 232, 227, 24, 28.

9. Bandura, A. (1986). *Social foundations of thought and action: A social cognitive theory.* New Jersey: Prentice Hall, Inc., Englewood Cliffs: 441.

10. Goffman, E. (1959). *The presentation of self in everyday life.* New York: Doubleday a Division of Random House Inc.

11. Izard, C., Kagan, J., & Zjonc, R. (1984). *Emotions, cognition, and behavior.* Cambridge: Cambridge University Press: 114.

12. Ritchie, G. (1978). *Return from tomorrow.* Grand Rapids MI: Fleming H. Revel: 70-71.

Near-Death Experience Research Foundation. *Current NDERF: Individual NDE experiences.* Retrieved from http://www.nderf.org/NDERF/ NDE_Archives/NDERF_NDEs.htm

6. THE MISSION

1. Clark Sharp, K. (2003). *After the light: What I discovered on the other side of life that can change your world.* Lincoln: Authors Choice Press: 26.

2. Long, J. (2003). *Life review, changed beliefs, universal order and purpose, and the near-death experience.* Retrieved from http://www.nderf. org/beingsstudy.htm

3. Greyson, B., Flynn, C. (1984). The Near-Death Experience Scale. Scale retrieved from *The Near-Death Experience, Problems, Prospects, Perspectives.* Springfield, IL: Charles C. Thomas.

4. Ritchie, G. (1978). *Return from tomorrow.* Grand Rapids MI: Fleming H. Revel: 51, 52-53.

5. Storm, H. (2005). *My descent into death: A second chance at life.* New York: Doubleday, a division of Random House Inc.: 30.

6. Hovland, C. I., & Sherif, M. (1980). *Social judgment: Assimilation and contrast effects in communication and attitude change.* Westport: Greenwood.

7. Price, M. (2009, June). Revenge and the people who seek it. *Monitor on Psychology, 40*(6). Retrieved from http://www.apa.org/monitor/2009/06/revenge.aspx

8. Long, J. (2010). *Soul to soulmate.* Copyright, Jody Long: 75.

9. Gollwitzer, P.M. (1990). *Handbook of motivation and cognition* (2nd ed.). E.T. Higgins & R.M. Sorrentino, (Eds.) New York: Guildford Press.

10. Kübler-Ross, E. (1992). *On life after death.* New York: Quality Paperback Book Club: 27.

Near-Death Experience Research Foundation. *Current NDERF: Individual NDE experiences.* Retrieved from http://www.nderf.org/NDERF/NDE_Archives/NDERF_NDEs.htm

7. LOVE

1. Lewis, C.S. (1960). *The four loves: An exploration of the nature of love.* Boston and New York: Mariner Books.

2. Buss, D. (2006). *The evolution of love.* In Sternbert, R.J., & Weis K., (Eds.). *The New Psychology of Love.* New Haven: Yale University: 70.

3. Yalom, I. (1980). *Existential psychotherapy.* New York: Basic Books, Yalom Family Trust: 371.

4. Fromm, E. (1956). *The art of loving.* New York: Bantam Books: 34.

5. Peart, N. (2011). *A prize every time. Far and away: A prize every time.* Toronto: ECW Press: 294.

6. Rogers, C. (1951). *Client-centered therapy.* Boston: Houghton Mifflin Company: 20.

7. Bell, R. (2012). *Love wins: A book about heaven, hell, and the fate of every person who ever lived.* New York, Harper One: 103-104.

8. Seligman, M. (2002). *Authentic happiness: Using the new positive psychology to realize your potential for lasting fulfillment.* New York: The Free Press: 77.

9. Baumeister, R.F., Exline J.J., & Sommer, K.L. (1998). *The victim role, grudge theory, and two dimensions of forgiveness.* In E. L. Worthington Jr. (ed.), *Dimensions of forgiveness: Psychological research and theological perspectives* (pp.79-104). Philadelphia: Templeton Foundation Press.

10. Moorjani, A. (2012). *Dying to be me: My journey from cancer, to near death, to true healing.* New York: Hay House Inc: 171.

11. Worthington, E. (2001). *Forgiving and reconciling: Bridges to wholeness and hope.* Madison: InterVarsity Press: 113-131.

12. Hamilton, W.D. (1964). The genetical evolution of social behaviour, I. *Journal of Theoretical Biology*, 7(1), 1–16.

13. Radice, B. (Ed.). (1962). *Bhagavad Gita.* Middlesex England: Penguin Classics: v.4:32.

14. Alexander, E. (2012). *Proof of heaven: A neurosurgeon's journey into the afterlife.* New York: Simon and Shuster Paperbacks: 84.

15. Storm, H. (2005). *My descent into death:* A second chance at life. New York: Doubleday, a division of Random House Inc.: 21, 61, 80.

16. Chiles, J., & Strosahl K. (1995). *The suicidal patient: Principles of assessment, treatment and case management.* Washington, DC: American Psychiatric Press.Near-Death Experience Research Foundation.

Near-Death Experience Research Foundation. *Current NDERF: Individual NDE experiences.* Retrieved from http://www.nderf.org/NDERF/NDE_Archives/NDERF_NDEs.htm

9. THE END OF ISOLATION

1. Yalom, I. (1980). *Existential psychotherapy.* New York: Basic Books, Yalom Family Trust: 355, 353.

2. Clark Sharp, K. (2003). *After the light: What I discovered on the other side of life that can change your world.* Lincoln: Authors Choice Press: 113.

3. Putnam, R. (2000). *Bowling alone: The collapse and revival of American community.* New York:Simon and Schuster Paperbacks: 45, 72, 67, 67, 100, 222, 224, 231.

4. Kubey, R., & Csikszentmihalyi, M. (2002, February). Television addiction is no mere metaphor. *Scientific American.*

5. Television Bureau of Advertising (2014). *Average Internet use of Americans in 2010* [Data file].Retrieved from http://www.statista.com/statistics/191552/average-daily-internet-use-of-us-americans-in-2010-by-age-group

6. Turkle, S. (2011). *Alone together: Why we expect more from technology and less from each other.* New York: Basic Books: 295, 155, 179.

7. Seligman, M. (2002). *Authentic happiness: Using the new positive psychology to realize your potential for lasting fulfillment.* New York: The Free Press: 103, 105.

8. Csikszentmihalyi, M. (1991). *Flow.* New York: Harper Perennial Modern Classics.

9. Storm, H. (2005). *My descent into death: A second chance at life.* New York: Doubleday, a division of Random House Inc.: 77.

Near-Death Experience Research Foundation. *Current NDERF: Individual NDE experiences.* Retrieved from http://www.nderf.org/NDERF/NDE_Archives/NDERF_NDEs.htm

10. SPIRITUAL BEINGS

1. *Navajo-religion and expressive culture.* (2014). Retrieved from http://www.everyculture.com/North-America/Navajo-Religion-and-Expressive-Culture.html

2. Long, J. (2002). *Another look at beings encountered during the near-death experience.* Retrieved from http://www.nderf.org/beingsstudy.htm

3. Storm, H. (2005). *My descent into death: A second chance at life.* New York: Doubleday, a division of Random House Inc.: 140, 70.

4. Kelley, H.H., Berscheid, E., Christensen, A., Harvey, J. H., Huston, T. L., Levinger, G, Peterson, D. R. (1983). *Close relationships.* San Francisco: W.H. Freeman and Company: 423.

5. Harvey, J., Paulwels, B., & Zickmund, S. (2002). Relationship connection: The role of minding in the enhancement of closeness. In Snyder, C.R., & Lopez, S.J., (Eds.). *Handbook of Positive Psychology.* Oxford, United Kingdom: Oxford University Press. pp. 423-445.

6. Moorjani, A. (2012). *Dying to be me: My journey from cancer, to near death, to true healing.* New York: Hay House Inc: 73, 168, 108.

7. Kübler-Ross, E. (1969). *On death and dying.* New York: Quality Paper Book Club: 142.

8. Long, J. (2010). *Evidence of the afterlife: The science of near-death experiences.* New York: Harper One: 192.

9. Alexander, E. (2012). *Proof of heaven: A neurosurgeon's journey into the afterlife.* New York:Simon and Shuster Paperbacks: 41, 40, 40, 39.

Near-Death Experience Research Foundation. *Current NDERF: Individual NDE experiences.* Retrieved from http://www.nderf.org/NDERF/NDE_Archives/NDERF_NDEs.htm

11. THE BETTER ANGELS OF OUR NATURE

1. Gallup Poll. *More than 9 in 10 Americans Continue to Believe in God* (May 2011). Retrieved from http://www.gallup.com/poll/147887/Americans-Continue-Believe-God.aspx

2. Hobbes, T. (2010). *Leviathan.* (Revised Ed.). Martinich, A.P., & Battiste, B. (Eds.). Toronto: Broadview Press.

3. Storm, H. (2005). *My descent into death: A second chance at life.* New York: Doubleday, a division of Random House Inc: 155, 139, 56, 140, 28, 139, 70, 40, 139.

4. Chaisson, E., & McMillan, S. (2011). *Astronomy Today.* San Francisco: Pearson: 418.

5. Royal Astronomical Society (RAS). (2013, April 3). Astronomers anticipate 100 billion Earth-like planets. *ScienceDaily.* Retrieved October 24, 2013, from http://www.sciencedaily.com /releases/2013/04/130403131315.htm

6. Long, J. (2010). *Soul to soulmate.* Copyright, Jody Long: 118-119.

7. Bandura, A. (1986). *Social foundations of thought and action.* New Jersey: Prentice Hall, Inc., Englewood Cliffs: 225.

8. Kübler-Ross, E. (1969). *On death and dying.* New York: Quality Paper Book Club: 142.

After Death Communication Research Foundation: *ADC stories.* (2013, July 1-August 1). Retrieved from http://www.adcrf.org/ADC%20Stories.htm

Near-Death Experience Research Foundation. *Current NDERF: Individual NDE experiences.* Retrieved from http://www.nderf.org/NDERF/NDE_Archives/NDERF_NDEs.htm

14. LOST SOULS

1. Baylor Religion Survey. (2007). *Belief in hell* [Data set]. In The Association Association of Religion Data Archives. Retrieved from http://thearda.com/QuickStats/QS_72.asp

2. Turner, A.K. (1993). *The history of hell.* San Diego: Harcourt, a division of Harvest Books: 18, 4.

3. Bell, R. (2012). *Love wins: A book about heaven, hell, and the fate of every person who ever lived.* New York, Harper One: 108.

4. Ritchie, G. (1978). *Return from tomorrow.* Grand Rapids MI: Fleming H. Revel: 65, 64.

5. Storm, H. (2005). *My descent into death: A second chance at life.* New York: Doubleday, a division of Random House Inc.: 63-64, 65.

6. Moorjani, A. (2012). *Dying to be me: My journey from cancer, to near death, to true healing.* New York: Hay House Inc.: 170.

7. Radice, B. (Ed.). (1962). *Bhagavad Gita.* Middlesex England: Penguin Classics: v.16:9-11, v.16:16.

8. Samenow, S. (2004). *Inside the criminal mind.* (Revised and updated Ed.). New York: Crown Publishers: 11.

9. Meloy, J. R. (1988). *The psychopathic mind: Origins, dynamics, and treatment.* Northvale New Jersey: Jason Aronson Inc.: 331, 68, 91.

10. Walters, G. D. (1990). *The criminal lifestyle: Patterns of serious criminal conduct.* Newbury Park: Sage Publications.

11. Alexander, E. (2012). *Proof of heaven: A neurosurgeon's journey into the afterlife.* New York: Simon and Shuster Paperbacks: 83.

Near-Death Experience Research Foundation. *Current NDERF: Individual NDE experiences.* (2013, January 01-October 22). Retrieved from http://www.nderf.org/NDERF/NDE_Archives/NDERF_NDEs.htm

15. GUIDED BY GOD'S DIVERSITY

1. Storm, H. (2005). *My descent into death: A second chance at life.* New York: Doubleday, a division of Random House Inc.: 62, 73, 73.

2. Moorjani, A. (2012). *Dying to be me: My journey from cancer, to near death, to true healing.* New York: Hay House Inc.: 155.

3. Ng, P. C., Levy, S., Huang, J., Stockwell, T. B., Walenz, B. P., Li, K. ...Venter, J. C. (2008). 4. Genetic variation in an individual human exome. In Schork, Nicholas J. *PLoS Genetics, 4*(8). e1000160. doi:10.1371/journal.pgen.1000160.

Near-Death Experience Research Foundation. *Current NDERF: Individual NDE experiences.* Retrieved from http://www.nderf.org/NDERF/NDE_Archives/NDERF_NDEs.htm

16. TIME

1. Hawking, S. (1996). *A brief history of time.* New York: Bantam Books: 147.

2. Greene, B. (2005). *The fabric of the cosmos: Space, time, and the texture of reality.* New York: Vintage Books, A Division of Random House: 141.

3. Quotes.net (13 Oct. 2013) *Albert Einstein Quotes.* Retrieved from http://www.quotes.net/quote/9385

4. Alexander, E. (2012). *Proof of heaven: A neurosurgeon's journey into the afterlife.* New York: Simon and Shuster Paperbacks: 48.

5. Moorjani, A. (2012). *Dying to be me: My journey from cancer, to near death, to true healing.* New York: Hay House Inc: 67.

6. Zimbardo, P. (2008). *The time paradox: The new psychology of time that will change your life.* New York: Free Press: 9, 316, 21, 45.

7. Storm, H. (2005). *My descent into death: A second chance at life.* New York: Doubleday, a division of Random House Inc.: 21, 35.

Near-Death Experience Research Foundation. *Current NDERF: Individual NDE experiences.* Retrieved from http://www.nderf.org/NDERF/ NDE_Archives/NDERF_NDEs.htm

17. A CALL FOR SPIRITUAL TRANSFORMATION

1. Lewis, C.S. (1960). *The four loves: An exploration of the nature of love.* Boston and New York: Mariner Books: 117, 126, 127,128-129.

2. Ross, H. (1993). *Creator and the cosmos: How the latest scientific discoveries of the century reveal god.* Colorado Springs: NAVPRESS Books: 111-114.

3. Storm, H. (2005). *My descent into death: A second chance at life.* New York: Doubleday, a division of Random House Inc: 68, 39-40, 44, 47, 45.

4. World Bank (2013, October 15). *World Bank Data by Countries.* Retrieved from http://data.worldbank.org/country.htm5. Folger, T. (2013, September). Rising Seas. *National Geographic* (Vol. 224, No. 3), 39-57.

6. Kircher, P.M. (2013). *Love is the link: A hospice doctor shares her experience of near-death and dying.* Pagosa Springs: Awakening Press.

7. Alexander, E. (2012). *Proof of heaven: A neurosurgeon's journey into the afterlife.* New York: Simon and Shuster Paperbacks: 48.

Near-Death Experience Research Foundation. *Current NDERF: Individual NDE experiences.* Retrieved from http://www.nderf.org/NDERF/ NDE_Archives/NDERF_NDEs.htm

Paperbacks also available from
White Crow Books

Elsa Barker—*Letters from
a Living Dead Man*
ISBN 978-1-907355-83-7

Elsa Barker—*War Letters from
the Living Dead Man*
ISBN 978-1-907355-85-1

Elsa Barker—*Last Letters from
the Living Dead Man*
ISBN 978-1-907355-87-5

Richard Maurice Bucke—
Cosmic Consciousness
ISBN 978-1-907355-10-3

Arthur Conan Doyle—
The Edge of the Unknown
ISBN 978-1-907355-14-1

Arthur Conan Doyle—
The New Revelation
ISBN 978-1-907355-12-7

Arthur Conan Doyle—
The Vital Message
ISBN 978-1-907355-13-4

Arthur Conan Doyle with
Simon Parke—*Conversations
with Arthur Conan Doyle*
ISBN 978-1-907355-80-6

Meister Eckhart with Simon Parke—
Conversations with Meister Eckhart
ISBN 978-1-907355-18-9

D. D. Home—*Incidents in my Life Part 1*
ISBN 978-1-907355-15-8

Mme. Dunglas Home; edited,
with an Introduction, by Sir
Arthur Conan Doyle—*D. D.
Home: His Life and Mission*
ISBN 978-1-907355-16-5

Edward C. Randall—
Frontiers of the Afterlife
ISBN 978-1-907355-30-1

Rebecca Ruter Springer—
Intra Muros: My Dream of Heaven
ISBN 978-1-907355-11-0

Leo Tolstoy, edited by Simon
Parke—*Forbidden Words*
ISBN 978-1-907355-00-4

Leo Tolstoy—*A Confession*
ISBN 978-1-907355-24-0

Leo Tolstoy—*The Gospel in Brief*
ISBN 978-1-907355-22-6

Leo Tolstoy—*The Kingdom
of God is Within You*
ISBN 978-1-907355-27-1

Leo Tolstoy—*My Religion:
What I Believe*
ISBN 978-1-907355-23-3

Leo Tolstoy—*On Life*
ISBN 978-1-907355-91-2

Leo Tolstoy—*Twenty-three Tales*
ISBN 978-1-907355-29-5

Leo Tolstoy—*What is Religion
and other writings*
ISBN 978-1-907355-28-8

Leo Tolstoy—*Work While
Ye Have the Light*
ISBN 978-1-907355-26-4

Leo Tolstoy—*The Death of Ivan Ilyich*
ISBN 978-1-907661-10-5

Leo Tolstoy—*Resurrection*
ISBN 978-1-907661-09-9

Leo Tolstoy with Simon Parke—
Conversations with Tolstoy
ISBN 978-1-907355-25-7

Howard Williams with an Introduction
by Leo Tolstoy—*The Ethics of Diet:
An Anthology of Vegetarian Thought*
ISBN 978-1-907355-21-9

Vincent Van Gogh with Simon Parke—
Conversations with Van Gogh
ISBN 978-1-907355-95-0

Wolfgang Amadeus Mozart with Simon
Parke—*Conversations with Mozart*
ISBN 978-1-907661-38-9

Jesus of Nazareth with Simon Parke—
Conversations with Jesus of Nazareth
ISBN 978-1-907661-41-9

Thomas à Kempis with Simon
Parke—*The Imitation of Christ*
ISBN 978-1-907661-58-7

Julian of Norwich with Simon
Parke—*Revelations of Divine Love*
ISBN 978-1-907661-88-4

Allan Kardec—*The Spirits Book*
ISBN 978-1-907355-98-1

Allan Kardec—*The Book on Mediums*
ISBN 978-1-907661-75-4

Emanuel Swedenborg—*Heaven and Hell*
ISBN 978-1-907661-55-6

P.D. Ouspensky—*Tertium Organum:
The Third Canon of Thought*
ISBN 978-1-907661-47-1

Dwight Goddard—*A Buddhist Bible*
ISBN 978-1-907661-44-0

Michael Tymn—*The Afterlife Revealed*
ISBN 978-1-970661-90-7

Michael Tymn—*Transcending the
Titanic: Beyond Death's Door*
ISBN 978-1-908733-02-3

Guy L. Playfair—*If This Be Magic*
ISBN 978-1-907661-84-6

Guy L. Playfair—*The Flying Cow*
ISBN 978-1-907661-94-5

Guy L. Playfair —*This House is Haunted*
ISBN 978-1-907661-78-5

Carl Wickland, M.D.—
Thirty Years Among the Dead
ISBN 978-1-907661-72-3

John E. Mack—*Passport to the Cosmos*
ISBN 978-1-907661-81-5

Peter & Elizabeth Fenwick—
The Truth in the Light
ISBN 978-1-908733-08-5

Erlendur Haraldsson—
Modern Miracles
ISBN 978-1-908733-25-2

Erlendur Haraldsson—
At the Hour of Death
ISBN 978-1-908733-27-6

Erlendur Haraldsson—
The Departed Among the Living
ISBN 978-1-908733-29-0

Brian Inglis—*Science and Parascience*
ISBN 978-1-908733-18-4

Brian Inglis—*Natural and Supernatural:
A History of the Paranormal*
ISBN 978-1-908733-20-7

Ernest Holmes—*The Science of Mind*
ISBN 978-1-908733-10-8

Victor & Wendy Zammit —*A Lawyer
Presents the Evidence For the Afterlife*
ISBN 978-1-908733-22-1

Casper S. Yost—*Patience
Worth: A Psychic Mystery*
ISBN 978-1-908733-06-1

William Usborne Moore—
Glimpses of the Next State
ISBN 978-1-907661-01-3

William Usborne Moore—
The Voices
ISBN 978-1-908733-04-7

John W. White—
The Highest State of Consciousness
ISBN 978-1-908733-31-3

Stafford Betty—
The Imprisoned Splendor
ISBN 978-1-907661-98-3

Paul Pearsall, Ph.D. —
Super Joy
ISBN 978-1-908733-16-0

**All titles available as eBooks, and selected titles available in Hardback and
Audiobook formats from www.whitecrowbooks.com**

CPSIA information can be obtained
at www.ICGtesting.com
Printed in the USA
FSOW01n1925110516
20234FS

9 781910 121429